Trading Culture

Montage of a Dream Deferred: Harlem

What happens to a dream deferred?

Does it dry up
like a raisin in the sun?
Or fester like a sore –
And then run?
Does it stink like rotten meat?
Or crust and sugar over –
like a syrupy sweet?

Maybe it just sags
like a heavy load.

Or does it explode?

Langston Hughes

Trading Culture

Global Traffic and Local Cultures in Film and Television

Edited by Sylvia Harvey
University of Lincoln, UK

British Library Cataloguing in Publication Data

Trading Culture: Global Traffic and Local Cultures in Film and Television

A catalogue entry for this book is available from the British Library

ISBN: 0 86196 669 4 (Paperback)

Cover image from *The Terrorist* (Santosh Sivan, India 1998).
[British Film Institute and Tartan Video.]

Published by
John Libbey Publishing, Box 276, Eastleigh SO50 5YS, UK
e-mail: libbeyj@asianet.co.th; web site: www.johnlibbey.com

Orders: **Book Representation & Distribution Ltd**. info@bookreps.com

Distributed in North America by **Indiana University Press**, 601 North Morton St, Bloomington, IN 47404, USA. www.iupress.indiana.edu

Distributed in Australasia by **Elsevier Australia**, 30–52 Smidmore Street, Marrickville NSW 2204, Australia. www.elsevier.com.au

Distributed in Japan by **United Publishers Services Ltd**, 1-32-5 Higashi-shinagawa, Shinagawa-ku, Tokyo 140-0002, Japan. info@ups.co.jp

© 2006 Copyright John Libbey Publishing. All rights reserved.
Unauthorised duplication contravenes applicable laws.

Printed in Malaysia by Vivar Printing Sdn. Bhd., 48000 Rawang, Selangor Darul Ehsan.

Contents

	Acknowledgements	vii
	Notes on Contributors	ix
	Trading culture in the era of the cultural industries: An introduction *Sylvia Harvey*	11
Section One:	**RE-THINKING THE TRADE IN CULTURE**	
	Introduction	1
Chapter 1	Trade wars, culture wars *Geoffrey Nowell-Smith*	13
Chapter 2	Media policy-making in the free trade era: the impact of the GATS negotiations on audiovisual industries *Des Freedman*	21
Chapter 3	The 'wrong type' of television: New Labour, British broadcasting and the rise and fall of an exports 'problem' *Simon Blanchard*	33
Chapter 4	Indigenous culture and the politics of place: regulation for regionalism in British broadcasting *Sylvia Harvey*	47
Section Two:	**NATIONAL INDUSTRIES, GLOBAL CURRENTS**	
	Introduction	59
Chapter 5	Ahead of the bandwagon: Lebanon's free media market *Dima Dabbous-Sensenig*	61
Chapter 6	Trading genie out of the bottle: global currents in India's film and television industries *Manjunath Pendakur*	77
Chapter 7	Going global: the Brazilian scripted film *Lúcia Nagib*	95
Chapter 8	Copycat TV and new trade routes in Asia and the Pacific *Albert Moran and Michael Keane*	105

TRADING CULTURE

Chapter 9	From Latin Americans to Latinos: Spanish-language television and its audiences in the United States *John Sinclair*	119
Chapter 10	National cinema as cultural exchange: the international circuit of Scottish films *Duncan Petrie*	133

Section Three: NATIONAL CULTURES IN A TRANSATLANTIC CONTEXT

	Introduction	145
Chapter 11	Special relationships: Anglo-American screen romance and nationality *Sarah Street*	147
Chapter 12	American production in Britain during the 1950s: culture, economics and geography *Tom Ryall*	161
Chapter 13	Adventure, exchange and identity: British, American, and Un-American involvement in costume adventure TV series and films in the postwar era *Steve Neale*	175
Chapter 14	Brigitte Bardot and Hollywood's takeover of the US art film market in the 1960s *Tino Balio*	191
Chapter 15	Crossing over: exporting indigenous heritage to the USA *Andrew Higson*	203

AFTERWORD

Chapter 16	Trading cultural commodities or promoting cultural diversity? UNESCO's new convention *Sylvia Harvey and Carole Tongue*	221
	Index	231

Acknowledgements

The editor would like to thank the Arts and Humanities Research Council for their financial support for this project, the members of the AHRB Centre for British Film and Television Studies (2000–2005) for their support for the *Trading Culture* Conference where most of the chapters in this volume were first presented as papers, Sheffield Hallam University and the University of Lincoln who have also supported the work, the BBC and the Canadian High Commission who sponsored the Conference and the Director and staff of the Showroom Cinema, Sheffield, who provided a convivial location for the event in July 2002.

Thanks are also due to the contributors to this book for their carefully crafted and up-dated chapters and for their patience during the lengthy process of locating the right publisher, to Dave Morley for his help and to Manuel Alvarado and John Libbey for finding a public platform for the project.

The cover image from the film *The Terrorist* (Santosh Sivan, India, 1998) is reproduced by kind permission of Tartan Video and the British Film Institute. The poem 'Montage of a Dream Deferred: Harlem' was published by Pluto Press in *Langston Hughes. Selected Poetry*, London, 1986, p. 268; this collection was first published by Alfred A. Knopf Inc. in New York in 1959. The poem is reproduced here by kind permission of Serpent's Tail, London. Stills from Lynne Ramsay's *Gasman* and from Peter Mullan's *Fridge* are reproduced by kind permission of Scottish Screen and BBC Scotland. Stills from *Into Shangri-la* are reproduced by kind permission of Chen Qiang, Weihan Cultural Production Company. Images from *Sábado Gigante* and *El Show de Cristina* are reproduced by kind permission of Univision. The image from *Cara o Cruz* and the channel logo are reproduced by kind permission of Telemundo.

Finally, special thanks are due to the librarians at the University of Lincoln and at Sheffield Hallam University who assisted in tracking down some elusive documents, to Erin Bell who prepared the images and captions, to my colleague Ann Gray and to my sisters Fiona and Sarah Harvey.

All other acknowledgements are given by the authors at the end of each chapter.

Notes on Contributors

Tino Balio is Emeritus Professor of Communication Arts at the University of Wisconsin-Madison. A specialist in the history of the American film industry, Balio is the author or editor of six books, including a two-volume history of United Artists, *The American Film Industry*, *Hollywood in the Age of Television*, and *Grand Design: Hollywood as a Modern Business Enterprise, 1930–1939*. The 2001 recipient of the inaugural Academy Film Scholar Grant from the Academy of Motion Picture Arts and Sciences, Balio is currently working on a book tentatively entitled, 'A Radically Different Cinema: Foreign Films in America, 1948 to the Present'.

Simon Blanchard is a Senior Research Fellow at the University of Lincoln. He has written extensively on broadcasting and media politics in the UK since the 1980s. Recent publications include *A Third Tier of Television* (2001), and *Community Media: Access, Skills and Social Enterprise* (2002). He is currently preparing (with Andrew Hill) an edited collection on National and Regional Screen Cultures across the UK.

Dima Dabbous-Sensenig is an assistant professor of communication and Director of the Institute of Women's Studies in the Arab World at the Lebanese American University, Beirut. She has published several scholarly articles on broadcast regulation in the Arab World, with particular emphasis on public service, cultural diversity, and cultural production and exchange. She is currently doing research on gender in Lebanese reality TV programming and the gendered portrayal of violence on Arab satellite television. She was expert trainer and consultant on a European Union project titled : 'Media Literacy, Decoding the Stereotyping of Arabs and Muslims in the Media Targeting Children and Youth'.

Des Freedman is the head of undergraduate theory in the Department of Media and Communications at Goldsmiths College, University of London. He is reviews editor of *Global Media and Communication* and the UK representative on the management committee of the COST research network examining 'the impact of the internet on the mass media in Europe'. Recent publications include *The Television Policies of the Labour Party, 1951–2001* (Frank Cass) and *War and the Media: Reporting Conflict 24/7* (Sage) (co-editor).

Sylvia Harvey is Professor of Broadcasting Policy and Co-Director of the Centre for Media Policy, Regulation and Ethics at the University of Lincoln, UK. Her recent publications are on film and broadcasting policy in the journals *Screen* and *Political Quarterly* and she has written about issues in broadcasting history and regulation in the edited collections: *A Companion to Television* (Wasko, 2005), *The Television History Book* (Hilmes, 2003) and *Toward a Political Economy of Culture* (Calabrese and Sparks, 2004). She was Principal Associate Director of the AHRB Centre for British Film and Television Studies; her current research interests are in broadcasting regulation and regionalism.

Andrew Higson is Professor of Film Studies and Head of the School of Film and Television

Studies at the University of East Anglia in the UK. He has written extensively on British cinema and on questions of national cinema, and is the editor of four books and the author of two more, his most recent publication being *English Heritage, English Cinema: Costume Drama since 1980* (Oxford University Press, 2003). He is the Director of the British Cinema History Project, based at the University of East Anglia.

Michael Keane is an Australian Research Council Post-doctoral fellow at the Queensland University of Technology. Interests are Asian media systems and television programme formats. Recent publications include *Media in China: Consumption, Content and Crisis* (RoutledgeCurzon 2002); *Television Across Asia: Television Industries, Programme Formats and Globalisation* (with Albert Moran 2004); and *New Television Formats and the East Asian Cultural Imagination* (Hong Kong University Press 2006) (with Fung and Moran). He is also the moderator of Creative Industries Research East Asia. http://cirac.qut.edu.au/asia/ and the Created in China web forum. http://createdinchina.org

Albert Moran is a Senior Lecturer in the School of Arts, Media and Culture at Griffith University. He has written extensively on film and television in Australia and in other parts of the world. His interest in TV programme formats stems from research that led to *Copycat TV: Globalisation, Program Formats and Cultural Identity* (University of Luton Press 1998). More recently, he has co-edited *Television across Asia: Television Industries, Formats and Flows* (RoutledgeCurzon 2003). Current related research includes writing a handbook that deals with business, devising and legal aspects of formats and a study of how formats might be given legal protection.

Lúcia Nagib is Professor of World Cinemas at the University of Leeds. Her major research subjects are cinematic realism, the New Waves of the 1960s and contemporary New Cinemas of the world. She has published several books on Brazilian, Japanese and German cinemas, among them: *Born of the Ashes – The Auteur and the Individual in Oshima's Films* (São Paulo: Edusp), *Werner Herzog – Film as Reality* (São Paulo: Estação Liberdade) and *The New Brazilian Cinema* (editor, London/New York: I.B. Tauris). Her book *Brazil on Screen – Cinema Novo, New Cinema and Utopia* is coming out in 2006 with I.B. Tauris (London/New York). She is currently developing a project on corporeal realism with reference to Japanese and East-Asian Cinemas.

Steve Neale is Chair of Film Studies in the School of English at the University of Exeter. He has contributed to *Screen*, *The Velvet Light Trap*, *The Historical Journal of Radio, Film and Television*. He is the author of *Genre and Hollywood*, co-author of *Popular Film and Television*, editor of *Genre and Contemporary Hollywood*, and a contributor to *The Cinema Book* and to *Television Genres*. He is currently working on the Hollywood blacklistees and television, and on a history of epics, spectacles and blockbusters in Hollywood from the teens to the present day.

Geoffrey Nowell-Smith is Senior Research Fellow in the Department of History at Queen Mary, University of London, where he directs a research project on the history of the British Film Institute. He is editor of *The Oxford History of World Cinema* (Oxford University Press, 1996) and co-editor (with Steven Ricci) of *Hollywood and Europe* (British Film Institute, 1998) and has written numerous articles on cultural theory and on Italian, French and British cinema.

Manjunath Pendakur is Professor in the Department of Radio-TV and also the Dean of the College of Mass Communication and Media Arts at Southern Illinois University Carbondale, USA. His research interests are in the political economy of communication, ethnography, critical cultural theory, and Third World cinema. He has done fieldwork in various parts of the world including Africa and India. His current work focuses on globalization of India's industries and public policy issues.

Notes on Contributors

Duncan Petrie is Professor of Film and Head of the Department of Film, Television and Media Studies at the University of Auckland. He is the author of *Contemporary Scottish Fictions* (Edinburgh University Press, 2004), *Screening Scotland* (BFI, 2000), *The British Cinematographer* (BFI, 1996) and *Creativity and Constraint in the British Film Industry* (Macmillan, 1991) and has edited or co-edited a further nine books. Duncan was a member of the Scottish Screen Lottery Panel from 2001 to 2003.

Tom Ryall is Professor of Film History at Sheffield Hallam University. He has written on various aspects of British and American cinema and his books include *Anthony Asquith* (2005), *Britain and the American Cinema* (2001), and *Alfred Hitchcock and the British Cinema* (1996). He has also contributed to collections such as *The British Cinema Book* (2001) and *The Cinema of Britain and Ireland* (2005), and to film journals such as *Screen*, the *Journal of Popular British Cinema* and *Sight and Sound*.

John Sinclair is Australian Research Council Professorial Fellow in the Australian Centre at the University of Melbourne for 2005–10. His published work covers various aspects of the globalization of the media and communication industries, with a special emphasis on Latin America and also India. He is author of *Images Incorporated: Advertising as Industry and Ideology (1987)*, and *Latin American Television: A Global View (1999)* ; co-editor/author of *New Patterns in Global Television: Peripheral Vision (1996)*, and *Floating Lives: The Media of Asian Diasporas (2001)*; and editor of *Contemporary World Television (2004)*. He has one book in Spanish, *Televisión: Comunicación Global y Regionalización* (2000).

Sarah Street is Professor of Film at the University of Bristol. She has published extensively in the area of British cinema. Her latest books are *Transatlantic Crossings: British Feature Films in the USA* (2002); *The Titanic in Myth and Memory (*co-edited with Tim Bergfelder, 2004) and *Black Narcissus* (2005). She is currently working on set design in European cinema in the 1930s.

Carole Tongue is a former Member of the European Parliament where she represented her East London constituents for fifteen years. During this time she authored the 'Tongue Report' on the *Future of Public Service Broadcasting in the Digital Age,* contributed to the drafting of the clause on public service broadcasting in the *Treaty of Amsterdam* and played a leading role in the development of audio-visual policy. She currently works in the fields of public policy and cultural consultancy in London, is a Visiting Professor at the London University of the Arts, holds an Honorary Doctorate of the University of Lincoln and is the Chair of the UK Independent Film Parliament.

Introduction

Trading culture in the era of the cultural industries

Sylvia Harvey

Can culture be traded? Insofar as the word 'culture' refers to the whole way of life and experience of a people this is clearly not something amenable to market-based exchange. As the Senegalese film-maker Osmane Sembene has noted:

> In the four African languages I speak there is no word for culture because culture consists of a succession of situations ... Words are loaded with potential for violence but also with potential for poetic gentleness. It depends on how we use them (Sembene, 1993: 75).

This commentator notes that 'culture' consists of meaningful gestures and actions as well as words; and that, in addition, an appreciation of the context and *use* of forms of human expression is vital for understanding the meaning that has been generated and communicated. As the history of social semiotics has taught us the production and circulation of meaning is both socially situated and variable. But the term 'culture' has also come to designate artefacts and services – in music, in story-telling, in visual design – that can be bought and sold, and not only by the sort of elite patrons who commissioned the work of an ancient Chinese ceramicist or a European Renaissance painter.

As new technologies from cinematography to broadcasting and from digitised sound to internet downloading have made possible the relatively cheap and widespread dissemination of cultural products, so the issue of culture considered as a globally tradable commodity has come to the fore. And the battle for market share has become especially intense in the richer countries of the world where the majority of the population has been able to increase the proportion of household income devoted to leisure spending. In the poorer parts of the world where significant sections of the population may not have access to clean water, electricity or universal secondary education, and may lack the kind of predictable income that allows parents to feed their families, spending money on leisure goods and services may seem a relatively low priority. Although the popularity of television and radio services in shanty towns and in poor desert communities as well as the remarkable growth of mobile phone use in Africa, for example, serve as a reminder that human communities are drawn towards innovative forms of communication, attractive entertainment and new sources of knowledge and understanding (Standage, 2005: 123).

The issue of audio-visual trade is becoming increasingly important for countries both inside and outside the magic circle of the rich nations of the 'G8'. And this is not entirely a new issue, since cultural commodities that are rich and strange, exotic, beautiful and newly familiar have been moved across the trade routes of the world for centuries. But in the early twentieth century some European countries were among the first to protest about the perceived negative consequences of the dominance of films imported from the United States. Thus in 1927 one commentator spoke with alarm and puzzlement of the ways in which British audiences seemed, in the act of movie-going, to become 'temporary American citizens', in a year when some 80 per cent of films in circulation were imported from the US. Subsequent analysis has suggested that it was the energetic and apparently classless tone of these American movies that made them attractive to working class audiences trapped in the rigid hierarchies of inter-war Britain (Maltby and Vasey, 1999: 34; Thompson, 1999: 64).

The popularity of certain images and sounds has its own story to tell and one that is not always audible to cultural nationalists. Although the analysis of popularity can also be conducted from an opposite direction, and may conclude that profitability in trade is frequently linked to the erasure of difficulties and differences in public story-telling. So it may be argued that even countries with large and successful national film and television industries fail, on both large and small screens, to reflect the diversity of the lives of their own people and their place in a wider world. For a country in this position the result may be that – as Peter Wollen suggests – it becomes imprisoned in the reproduction of 'powerful yet provincial cinematic myths about itself' (Wollen, 1998: 134).

Following the launch of various objections to foreign cultural invasion in inter-war Europe, other and different criticisms were to emerge. In the second half of the twentieth century the voices of anti-colonial struggle were to protest against the kind of foreign cultural domination that was associated with the process of militarised imperial conquest, the deliberate construction of a sense of inferiority among the colonised, and the complete absence of citizenship status (Nehru, 1941; Fanon, 1967). As the Martiniquan poet and politician Aimé Césaire observed of the effects of European colonization: 'It has undermined civilizations, destroyed countries, ruined nationalities, extirpated "the root of diversity"' (Césaire, 1972: 59).

It is worth noting at this point that the concept of 'foreign' cultural commodities has changed in the post-colonial period. For in response to the development of trade barriers or of local subsidies to cultural producers – designed by national governments to enhance their domestic cultural industries – powerful foreign investors have entered into either international co-productions or other forms of local investment, and this has masked the location from which control of content may come. This development is clearly outlined in an interview with a US trade representative conducted in 1994:

> US companies must make films that will count as European films. We need to identify how US-owned firms can get access to European subsidy programs, even though we

regard all regulation as censorship. The cooperation between industries will eventually make regulation obsolete because it's going to be impossible to tell a US and a European firm apart. (Venturelli, 1998: 217)

In one of the familiar tropes of contemporary capitalist practice it becomes clear that whilst individual human beings are required to carry national citizenship identity and to respect the existence of national borders, the same rule is not applied to money or – where the rules of free trade apply – to firms. Thus in the case of making a film, for example, the locations, the actors and the creative personnel may bear a particular national affiliation but capital itself does not, and the source of control of content is sometimes obscured as a result. The sources of control may become apparent if we are able to 'follow the money' and to identify where profits are returned. On occasion these processes are made transparent as, for example, in the order issued by Paul Bremer, American head of the occupying Coalition Provisional Authority following the war in Iraq in 2003. In respect of a variety of business activities there must be, he noted, 'full ownership rights by foreign firms of Iraqi businesses' and 'full repatriation of foreign profits' (Harvey, 2005: 6).

The pressures exerted to control content are alluded to by scholars working within the political economy tradition of research, but these seldom take the form of a specific analysis of the ways in which final versions of stories or scripts are approved. Ethnographic accounts of this process of regulation or censorship are almost impossible to find. Moreover, since the textual analysis tradition within film and media studies finds it logically necessary to focus upon present not absent signifiers, much published work will find itself unable to recognise the cultural significance of what is absent, of what Césaire referred to as 'extraordinary *possibilities* wiped out' (Césaire, 1972: 21). This is an under-developed and almost forbidden territory of analysis.

One final comment about the theoretical difficulties entailed in speaking of either 'foreign' or 'indigenous' cultural production may be in order here. In a world of increased migration and of cross-border flows of news and of entertainment there has emerged a common way of speaking about lived cultures as hybrid, plural, varied, and of the great cities of the world as polyglot and multi-cultural. Political geographers, social scientists and political economists alike have reflected upon the 'de-nationalization' of national territories, on the loss of sovereignty and the submission of local political representatives and parliaments to the superior force of multi-national companies and of international trade agreements (Sassen, 1996; Castells, 1998; Jawara and Kwa, 2004). And yet, within political and academic circles, and in organisations like the United Nations and its educational, scientific and cultural wing (UNESCO), there remains a strong body of thought favouring a positive role for the nation state – considered as the only currently available vehicle for democratic governance. In addition, the debate about freedom of expression and cultural diversity has increasingly and interestingly been linked to an emerging international 'human rights' paradigm as well as to the view that 'cultural diversity is as necessary for humankind as biodiversity is for nature' (UNESCO, 2001: Article 1).

These views have encouraged support for the continuing role of the nation state and this has been accompanied by advocacy of the need to protect and develop forms of cultural expression specific to particular groups and language communities – often existing at either sub-national or transnational level – and by the view that state intervention may be required to enhance cultural diversity, establishing forms of regulation and support that cannot be dismissed as 'censorship'. Thus, for example, governments may establish screen quotas in order to favour local production and may provide support for public service broadcasting and grants or subsidies for film-making.

The debate about the 'trade in culture', about the international market for cultural commodities, finds itself caught up with some of these larger questions about human rights and cultural diversity. And the debate is pulled between two distinct political philosophies. The first of these sees the free or unregulated market as the guarantor of consumer freedom and therefore of individual freedom and even of democracy itself, while the second sees the role of elected political representatives – and therefore of national parliaments and their legislative actions – as an important counter-weight to exclusively market-based decision-making.

The international lawyer Philippe Sands has described the establishment of a new *international* legal order arising, he suggests, from the Atlantic Charter of 1941, a document agreed upon by the President of the United States and the Prime Minister of Britain at the height of the Second World War and intended to facilitate, in the longer term, 'abandonment of the use of force', an end to the 'crushing burden of armaments' and the creation of a 'wider and more permanent system of general security' (Sands, 2005: 240–241). It was this Charter that led, among other things, to the creation of the United Nations and the establishment of a new set of economic institutions and practices designed to provide a period of stability and growth following the war. Developments in the subsequent half century have, of course, demonstrated that not all countries have benefited from this plan to create a politically and economically stable world, even though certain minimum standards regarding human rights and the use of force have become more widely recognised if not implemented.

What Sands goes on to identify is a more recent breakdown in the consensual order proposed by the Atlantic Charter and a process whereby powerful states have pursued their own perceived sovereign interests at the expense of previously agreed global rules, whether these have involved agreements about national territorial integrity, environmental degradation, the upholding of human rights, the treatment of prisoners or the use of torture. In Sands' view there continues to be a compelling case in favour of international regulations if created for the benefit of all. But how might this play out in relationship to the rules of trade that govern the import and export of cultural commodities?

The last two decades of the twentieth century saw strong attempts being made by a variety of powerful audio-visual businesses to boost global trade in this sector. And international negotiations – conducted within the framework of the older General Agreement on Tariffs and Trade or GATT – were the chosen instrument for this advance. The GATT arrangements were initially adopted in 1948 by 23 countries (Grantham, 2000: 91). These negotiations, led by the richer and more powerful nations as part of the post-1945 settlement, were designed to liberalise trade by preventing nation states from intervening to protect or subsidise their local industries. The objective was to remove the trade-inhibiting effects that stemmed from discrimination against imported goods, even where increased imports created local job losses. And the corresponding principle of open borders for the sale of goods and services was regarded as paramount, and seen as part of the regulatory toolkit for preventing the sort of chronic economic instability that had characterised the 1930s.

In the cultural sector, particularly during the Cold War period, it was often convenient to present this approach as also a free speech measure – designed to improve the circulation of ideas and information – at least as much as a measure designed to increase trade, improve profitability and boost foreign sales. In this regard the interlinked values of free speech, free markets and free societies emerged as a powerful and persuasive ideological triumvirate. And as the cultural industries, from magazine design to movie-making, grew in economic significance in the second half of the twentieth century so also the issue of how to manage and how to develop world trade in the audio-visual sector came to the fore.

However, it was soon apparent that the open borders and anti-tariff approach was regarded by many nation states as inadequate in respect of the perceived social significance of film and television. For in so far as the products of the audio-visual sector generated meanings and values that expressed and shaped national, cultural and sub-cultural identities they could not be relegated to the sole status of commodities operating within a market. Moreover, even where it was regarded as desirable to protect the economic value of intellectual property, there were voices also raised in favour of nurturing the cultural commons. Herein lies the conundrum of cultural production in the twenty-first century, namely that it both *is* and *is not* a market-based form of activity.

Even the most vigilant apostle of free trade in the audio-visual sector, the Motion Picture Association of America, has now recognised the force of the cultural diversity argument, while seeking to limit some of the potentially negative economic consequences for its members. Bonnie Richardson, Vice President of the MPAA, noted early in 2005:

> Films, like other types of cultural goods and services, reflect the culture of the creators and societies that produce them. They express the history, aspirations, language and values of their creators. The world is a richer place because small art films and big budget blockbusters, films from China, France, Brazil, Korea, Nigeria, India, Iran, join American films in delighting or challenging worldwide audiences. (Richardson, 2005).

How did the free trade arguments that the most cost-effective producers must be enabled to sell successfully in all world markets and that efficient production should wipe out inefficient production (among the 'global rules' indicated by Sands), come to be modified or partially recast in this way? A brief inspection of developments indicates that the interests of big businesses in the audio-visual sector have been both advanced and challenged over the last half century.

Economic interests have been advanced through the strong organisation and lobbying of trade bodies such as the MPAA, and as a consequence of the nature of the product itself. The high 'first copy' costs of films and television programmes and the low or marginal costs of multiple copies (especially when circulated by means of broadcast transmission) have given considerable strength and bargaining power to companies enjoying a large home market, where most or even all costs can be recovered prior to the start of foreign sales. The Canadian lawyer Peter Grant has provided some illuminating data in this regard. Based on a variety of trade sources he gives examples of what he calls 'price discrimination' in the global TV market. Thus a one-hour American TV drama, costing $2m to make in 2003, was sold to broadcasters in the US, the UK, Canada, Poland and Hungary at respectively: $1.4m, $75,000, $50,000, $25,000 and $10,000 (Grant and Wood, 2004: 129–130). Thus prices are differentially set at attractive levels in various markets and extensive foreign sales facilitate continuing investment while ensuring that high levels of profitability are maintained.

From the point of view of audiences and cultural producers in the importing countries, the relatively high costs of 'first copy' production make local or indigenous production increasingly uncompetitive when faced with the relatively low costs of imported programmes. Grant points to the example of a locally successful Canadian teen drama of the 1980s, *Degrassi Junior High*. This programme cost the local producer approximately $750,000 per hour to make and the rights were then sold to a Canadian broadcaster for $252,000. The same broadcaster could buy an hour of imported US drama for $50,000 per hour (Grant and Wood, 2004: 18). From a market point of view, there is clearly no rational justification for purchasing the more expensive and indigenously produced work – even if increased audience size and appreciation indices are taken into account. In this case, the Canadian station only purchased the programme because of conditions attached to its broadcasting licence – conditions specified by elected political representatives in Canada.

Grant's general comment on the economic rationale of this situation is that big businesses operating under the 'ubiquitous calculus of maximum return' will therefore 'quite rationally seek to eliminate all but the most highly profitable of creative expressions from circulation' (Grant and Wood, 2004: 18). But this rational market activity does not always take place within a fully competitive environment; and Jeanette Steemers, for example, refers to 'price-fixing and the co-ordination of overseas sales' by American companies acting in concert to ensure maximum returns, and arguably permitted by their own government to operate in violation of the anti-trust or competition requirements that would govern domestic activity (Steemers, 2004: 2).

However, the *Degrassi* example may be taken to indicate both a problem and a solution, but a solution that relies upon public intervention within the market. There are a number of examples of global rules that have – as a result of hard fought campaigns by particular nation states – permitted such intervention. Thus the initial 1948 GATT agreement allowed – in its famous Article 4 – for the retention of national quotas for film screenings (Grantham, 2000: 92). And this has been followed more recently by the cliff-hanging outcome of the GATT negotiations of 1993 when a major package of new trading agreements was nearly destroyed by last-minute bargaining around the rules to be established for the audio-visual sector. In that case the conflict between the US and the European Union was resolved if only temporarily in favour of the latter, with the exclusion or 'exemption' of the audio-visual sector from the final agreement (Grantham, 2000: 129; Palmer, 1996). The same exemption of films and television programmes from otherwise liberalised

Introduction • Trading culture in the era of the cultural industries

rules of trade may be found in the 1994 North American Free Trade Agreement, and this gives continuing opportunities for Canada and Mexico to take steps to develop their indigenous industries, if only in this sector (Grant and Wood, 2004: 362).

It is clear that the particular economic characteristics of film and television production, combined with historical control of distribution, have assisted global businesses in protecting and advancing their interests. However, these interests have also been questioned and challenged. A conference held in Stockholm in 1998, hosted by UNESCO and held to mark the end of the 'World Decade for Cultural Development', noted that intensification of the global trade in cultural products and services 'may also be detrimental to our creative diversity and to cultural pluralism'. And in 2000 a group of cultural practitioners from 21 countries – the International Network on Cultural Diversity (INCD) – declared itself dedicated to 'countering the homogenizing effects of globalization on culture' (Grant and Wood, 2004: 382, 387).

The theme of global security – focus of the 1941 Atlantic Charter – also emerged. Both before and after the attack on the World Trade Center in New York in September 2001 the issue of cultural diversity, and its role in the promotion of a more peaceful world, emerged in the statements of a number of organisations. The Stockholm conference had already proposed the 'dialogue between cultures' as 'an essential condition of peaceful co-existence' (Grant and Wood, 2004: 382). And UNESCO's *Universal Declaration on Cultural Diversity* – adopted unanimously in November 2001, just after the events of '9/11' – carried an ambitious preface with the assertion that promotion of cultural diversity was necessary to 'prevent segregation and fundamentalism'. The main text declared that cultural goods and services 'must not be treated as mere commodities or consumer goods'. And cultural pluralism was said to be: 'essential to ensure harmonious interaction among people and groups with plural, varied and dynamic cultural identities' and to be 'conducive to cultural exchange and to the flourishing of creative capacities that sustain public life' (UNESCO, 2001: Preamble, Articles 8 and 2).

The 2001 Declaration also included an action plan, and high on the agenda was the creation of a new international legal instrument. This 'instrument' was intended to provide a legal framework for supporting public intervention in support of indigenous cultural production and designed to place some limits on the pressure to further liberalise audio-visual trade. In particular it was thought that such an agreement could be used – perhaps especially by poorer and politically weaker countries – in negotiating their way through the opportunities and dangers represented by the World Trade Organisation.

A number of nation states had been considering their needs in this respect and Canada had been involved in a complex and on-going trade dispute with its US neighbour concerning the control and cultural content of magazines. It was therefore the Canadian Minister of Heritage, Sheila Copps, who took the initiative of convening an international group of Ministers, in 1998. By 2002 this group – the International Network on Cultural Policy or INCP – consisted of ministerial level representatives from over twenty countries including Canada, Mexico, Brazil, France, Russia and China. In 2004 its 'special guests' included India and Iran (INCP,

2004); it had received observers from the UK and the European Union and its events tended to be accompanied by parallel meetings of the cultural practitioners group – the INCD (Grant and Wood, 2004: 383–388).

The 2001 meeting of the INCP Ministers' group had asserted the 'legitimate role of government to preserve and promote cultural diversity through the development and implementation of cultural policies at all levels'. And by the following year the group was ready to designate UNESCO as the appropriate institution to 'house and implement an International Instrument on Cultural Diversity', designed to specify exactly what measures nation states could and could not take to protect their local cultural industries without violating other international trade agreements (Grant and Wood, 2004: 388, 397). It took another three years for this instrument to be drafted and agreed. In November 2005, and re-named as the *Convention on the Protection and Promotion of the Diversity of Cultural Expressions*, the document was accepted by the General Council of UNESCO; 148 countries voted in support, four abstained (Australia, Honduras, Nicaragua and Liberia) and two opposed (the United States and Israel) (UNESCO, 2005; MPAA, 2005). Further details of the Convention are given in the Afterword to this volume.

At the time of writing, 30 countries will be required to ratify the Convention before it can become operational. Nonetheless, with its acceptance by the UNESCO General Council, a broad alliance of very different countries has succeeded in framing a set of international rules-in-waiting, designed to foster the cultural sector. Something new has been created and, as the Indian film-maker Santosh Sivan appears to suggest in his film *The Terrorist* (1998), and as the philosopher Hannah Arendt noted half a century ago, this newness seems to offer a promise of hope for the future:

> With word and deed we insert ourselves into the human world, and this insertion is like a second birth. (Arendt, 1958: 176–177)

The issues raised by the cultural diversity debate and by the actions of large corporations active in the cultural field have, of course, been commented upon by many scholars over the last two decades. Some have concentrated on the commercial interests at stake and on the detail of economic activity (Wildman and Siwek, 1988; Noam and Millonzi, 1993; Miller et al., 2001; Steemers, 2004); some have offered a critical analysis of the concept of imperialism (Tomlinson, 1991) or examined the significance of particular trade agreements (Van Hemel et al., 1996). Others have offered useful 'overview' documentation and focused on the concept of globalization and the role of the state (Balnaves et al., 2001; Morris and Waisbord, 2001; Iosifidis et al., 2004, Grant and Wood, 2004; Chalaby, 2005), or have explored the cultural politics of globalization with reference to the consequences for particular territories (Sinclair et al., 1996; Nowell-Smith and Ricci, 1998; Grantham, 2000). And many have considered the broader cultural and political implications of the trade in culture (Golding and Harris, 1997, Thussu, 1998).

The present volume makes a contribution to this literature with material offered in three sections. The Introduction and Section One raise some broader historical and contextual issues, considering some of the key concepts involved in the debate about the trade in culture and looking at examples of actions taken by individual nation states and by international organisations. Section Two offers brief case studies of developments in six countries or regions (Lebanon, India, Brazil, Asia and the Pacific, the United States and Scotland). The last section considers both recent and historical examples of the complex trans-Atlantic relationships of the film and television industries of the United States, France and the United Kingdom.

The issues at stake were identified – more than half a century ago – by the lawyer and political leader, Mahatma Gandhi. He wrote of the complex interplay between independence and inter-dependence in cultural matters:

> I do not want my house to be walled on all sides and my windows to be stuffed. I want the culture of all lands to be blown about my house as freely as possible but I refuse to be blown off my feet by any one of them. (Gandhi, 2006)

The trade winds of culture will not cease to blow, some will appear to be local or indigenous though their origins may be obscure. But these are the 'winds' that are generated by human beings, not by nature, and it is their purposes and effects that are important. Propelled forwards at hurricane strength they may provide popular and profitable entertainment while drowning out the voices of a multiplicity of cultures. But there is another story that could be told – one where nation states, international agreements and new technologies combine to secure a future for more localised forms of cultural expression. In this other story might and money are not the only keys unlocking the door to new ways of seeing.

References

Arendt, H. (1958) *The Human Condition*. Chicago: University of Chicago Press.

Balnaves, M., Donald, J. and Hemelryk Donald, S. (2001) *The Global Media Atlas*. London: British Film Institute.

Castells, M. (1998) *End of Millenium*. Vol. III of *The Information Age: Economy, Society and Culture*. Oxford: Blackwell Publishers.

Césaire, A. (1950/1972) *Discourse on Colonialism*. New York and London: Monthly Review Press.

Chalaby, J. (ed) *Transnational Television Worldwide. Towards a New Media Order*. London and New York: I. B. Tauris.

Fanon, F. (1967) *Black Skin. White Masks*. New York: Grove Press.

Gandhi, M. (2006) 'Worlds of Difference' at URL: http://www.mkgandhi.org/momgandhi/chap90.htm or at URL: http://homelands.org/worlds/quotes/html (accessed on 30 January, 2006).

Golding, P. and Harris, P. (1997) *Beyond Cultural Imperialism. Globalization, Communication and the New International Order*. London: Sage.

Grant, P. and Wood, C. (2004) *Blockbusters and Trade Wars. Popular Culture in a Globalized World*. Vancouver: Douglas and McIntyre.

Grantham, B. (2000) *'Some Big Bourgeois Brothel'. Contexts for France's Culture Wars with Hollywood*. Luton: University of Luton Press/John Libbey Publishing.

Harvey, D. (2005) *A Brief History of Neoliberalism*. Oxford: Oxford University Press.

INCP (2004) 'Shanghai Statement' at URL: http://incp-ripc.org/meetings/2004/statement_e.shtml (accessed on 6 June, 2005).

Iosifidis, P., Steemers, J., and Wheeler, M. (2005) *European Television Industries*. London: British Film Institute.

Jäckel, A. (2003) *European Film Industries*. London: British Film Institute.

Jawara, F. and Kwa, A. (2004) *Behind the Scenes at the WTO: the Real World of International Trade Negotiations*. Updated edition. London and New York: Zed Books.

Maltby, R. and Vasey, R. (1999) '"Temporary American Citizens": Cultural Anxieties and Industrial Strategies in the Americanisation of European Cinema' in A. Higson and R. Maltby (eds) *"Film

Europe" and "Film America". Cinema, Commerce and Cultural Exchange. Exeter: University of Exeter Press, pp. 32–55.

Miller, T., Govil, N., McMurria, J. and Maxwell, R. (2001) *Global Hollywood*. London: British Film Institute.

Morris, N. and Waisbord, S. (eds) (2001) *Media and Globalization. Why the State Matters*. Lanham: Rowman and Littlefield.

MPAA (2005) 'Glickman expresses disappointment at outcome of cultural diversity discussions' at URL: http://www.mpaa.org/press_releases/2005_10_21.pdf (accessed on 16 December 2005).

Nehru, J. (1941) *The Unity of India. Collected Writings 1937–40*. London: Lindsay Drummond.

Noam, E. and Millonzi, J. (eds) (1993) *The International Market in Film and Television Programs*. Norwood, New Jersey: Ablex Publishing Corporation.

Nowell-Smith, G. and Ricci, S. (eds) *Hollywood and Europe. Economics, Culture, National Identity: 1945–95*. London: British Film Institute in association with the UCLA Film and Television Archive.

Palmer, M. (1996) 'GATT and culture: a view from France' in A. Van Hemel, H. Mommas and C. Smithuijsen (eds) *Trading Culture. GATT, European cultural policies and the transatlantic market*. Amsterdam: the Boekman Foundation.

Richardson, B. (2005) 'Globalization and Diversity, UNESCO and Cultural Policy Making: Imperatives for US Arts and Culture Practitioners and Organisations', seminar at the Smithsonian Institution at URL: http://www.folklife.si.edu/center/cultural_policy/unesco.html (accessed on 6 June 2005).

Sands, P. (2005) *Lawless World. America and the Making and Breaking of International Rules*. London: Allen Lane, Penguin Books.

Sassen, S. (1996) *Losing Control? Sovereignty in an Age of Globalization*. New York: Columbia University Press.

Sembene, O. (1993) 'Discussion among the Writers' in S. Gadjigo, R. H. Faulkingham, T. Cassirer and R. Sander (eds) *Ousmane Sembène. Dialogues with Critics and Writers*. Amherst, Mass.: University of Massachussetts Press.

Sinclair, J., Jacka, E., Cuningham, S. (eds) *New Patterns in Global Television. Peripheral Vision*. Oxford and New York: Oxford University Press.

Standage, T. (2005) 'Connecting the next billion: mobile telephony's new mass market', in *The World in 2006*. London: The Economist, p. 123.

Steemers, J. (2004) *Selling Television. British Television in the Global Marketplace*. London: British Film Institute.

Thompson, K. (1999) 'The Rise and Fall of Film Europe' in A. Higson and R. Maltby (eds) *"Film Europe" and "Film America". Cinema, Commerce and Cultural Exchange*. Exeter: University of Exeter Press, pp. 56–81.

Thussu, D. (ed) (1998) *Electronic Empires. Global Media and Local Resistance*. London: Edward Arnold.

Tomlinson, J. (1991) *Cultural Imperialism*. London: Pinter Publishers.

UNESCO (2001) *Universal Declaration on Cultural Diversity* at URL: http://portal.unesco/culture/en/ev.php (accessed on 6 June 2005).

UNESCO (2005) *Convention on the Protection and Promotion of the Diversity of Cultural Expressions* at URL: http//portal.unesco.org/culture/en/ev.php-URL_ID=11281&URL_DO=DO_PRINTP... (accessed on 16 December, 2005).

Van Hemel, A., Mommaas, H. and Smithuijsen, C. (eds)(1996) *Trading Culture. GATT, European cultural policies and the transatlantic market*. Amsterdam: the Boekman Foundation.

Venturelli, S. (1998) *Liberalizing the European Media. Politics, Regulation and the Public Sphere*. Oxford: Clarendon Press.

Wildman, S. and Siwek, S. (1988) *International Trade in Films and Television Programs*. Cambridge, Mass.: American Enterprise Institute/Ballinger Publication.

Wollen, P. (1998) 'Tinsel and realism' in G. Nowell-Smith and S. Ricci (eds) *Hollywood and Europe. Economics, Culture, National Identity: 1945–95*. London: British Film Institute in association with the UCLA Film and Television Archive.

SECTION I:
Rethinking the Trade in Culture

Introduction

The four chapters in Section One address historical and definitional issues with a focus on the role of intervention by nation states or by transnational bodies such as the World Trade Organisation (WTO). Geoffrey Nowell-Smith challenges the concept of a trade in culture by making a distinction between forms of *cultural exchange* that involve 'the activity of exposing one people to another people's culture' and what might more properly be called a trade in *cultural commodities*, where goods are exchanged for other goods or for money. He also offers a brief historical overview of the transition from a trade in physical goods of a cultural kind – such as cans of celluloid or long-playing records – to a trade in the 'immaterials' of intellectual property. In this latter phase, characteristic of digital media and of the internet downloads of the twenty-first century, the trade in property rights supersedes the trade in physical goods. And this transition is itself seen as part of the 'long process of commodification of cultural signifiers' stretching from the take-up of local stories by multi-national companies (for example, the appropriation of the Chinese story of Mulan by Disney, or the acquisition of exclusive brand rights in Winnie the Pooh) to the mixing and matching of iconographies that removes all images from their original context and belonging.

Des Freedman examines the shift in international trade negotiations from a focus on goods to a focus on services, tracing the attempts made by a variety of countries to resist pressure from the United States designed to further liberalise trade in the audio-visual sector. This resistance was particularly marked in the last stages of the 1993 'Uruguay' round of negotiations for the General Agreement on Tariffs and Trade (GATT), and resulted in the establishment of a temporary 'cultural exemption' in these trade talks. Following the 1993 debacle that saw American and European interests sharply pitted against each other, a new wave of negotiations for trade liberalisation has developed over the last decade. However, progress in these 'multi-lateral' talks has been slow, partly as a consequence of the public protests against the work and values of the WTO and partly because, in the audio-visual sector, many countries have been far from ready to demolish trade barriers, wishing instead to protect their indigenous film and television industries with quotas and subsidies

The theme of national interventions is explored further in chapters by Simon Blanchard and Sylvia Harvey. Blanchard examines the configurations of 'New Labour' policies in the United Kingdom, tracing what he calls the 'rise and fall' of an exports problem. The Labour governments of 1997 and 2001 had shown themselves to be sympathetic to the principles of trade liberalisation and had sought to encourage a significant increase in UK television exports. However, as the chapter sets out to demonstrate, the government gradually became aware not only of the relative success of this industry in exporting to overseas markets but also of the dangers of departing from patterns of production designed first and foremost to satisfy home audiences. Thus, while the competitiveness agenda remained a key one for government, the supposed problem of TV exports faded away as policy-makers became aware of the significant surpluses generated by the creative industries when considered as a whole.

Harvey examines the longer history of state intervention in British broadcasting, taking the development of regional broadcasting as a case study. This chapter notes that broadcasting in one relatively rich country has used the tools of public policy to enable 'geographically specific modes of representation' ensuring – in the early history of the BBC and subsequently in the era of commercial broadcasting – that radio and television programmes are made for and from the four nations of England, Northern Ireland, Scotland and Wales. The use of public policy instruments to underwrite the growth of a significant indigenous production industry in broadcasting is contrasted with the situation in the British cinema industry where the majority of films screened have – since the 1920s – been imported from the United States. However, the renewed emphasis on market liberalism is seen to have affected and diminished the commitment to regional representation in the British commercial television sector in the twenty-first century.

Chapter 1

Trade wars, culture wars

Geoffrey Nowell-Smith

I shall start this chapter with what in the context of this book is probably a subversive remark. Cultures are not traded. Trade, by definition, is an exchange of goods – of goods for other goods, or of goods for money. A trade in cultures would therefore have to be a trade in a particular kind of goods, which I have elsewhere (Nowell-Smith, 1998) called culture-goods. You can have some sort of cultural exchange which is not an exchange of goods. A programme which sends students abroad to spend a year in a foreign country as part of their studies might be called a cultural exchange in this sense. Or a visit by a choir from Soweto to Britain, or a British orchestra to Soweto, where the money that changes hands to make the visit possible is less important than the activity of exposing one people to another people's culture. But far more often, when we look at exchanges between cultures in the modern world what we see is a trade flow, the exchange of commodities of a particular type, in which some economies have surpluses and others have deficits. We therefore come to think of cultures as somehow embodied in these exchangeable commodities and the trade in CDs, films, videos, TV programmes, computer games, etc. as a way in which cultures themselves get exchanged across the globe.

I want to cast doubt on the widely-held notion that a trade in culture-goods – that is to say, goods which embody cultural values, as films, TV programmes, CDs, etc. undoubtedly do – is tantamount to a trade in culture itself. There certainly is a relationship between the trade in those goods which embody cultural values and an actual cultural exchange, but it is a complex and mediated one, as the history of the film industry shows. (Indeed the very term film industry is a symptom of the ambivalence inherent in the subject, as are terms like cultural industry, creative industry, and so on.)

As is well known, the American film industry, popularly known as Hollywood, has dominated the movie trade throughout the western world since the 1920s. American-made films have provided the major part of viewing for people in western Europe, Canada and Australia since the end of the First World War, capturing between 50 per cent and 80 per cent or even 90 per cent of the market in those countries and periods where films were freely traded. Not only have the films been American, but the companies distributing the films and sometimes the companies owning the cinemas where they were shown have been offshoots of the same

American companies. American companies have also often acted as worldwide distributors for films made in other countries. The movie trade has been very much a one-way business, since there is not much trade going westwards across the Atlantic bringing European films to market in the USA (Balio, 1998a, 1998b). This basically one-way trade has contributed enormously to the much deplored 'Americanisation' of culture in Europe, but it remains the case that it is *goods* which have been traded, not cultures *per se*.

The trade in culture-goods – physical goods embodying cultural values – is very much a 20th century phenomenon. It starts with the phonograph and the cinematograph and the mass press at the end of the 19th century and coincides with the emergence of the United States as a world power. What Europeans think of as American culture is very often things instantiated in market products such as CDs and movies. Conversely, what Americans think of as European culture is often stuff that doesn't move but has to be visited, like art treasures in a museum. Culture-goods are very 20th century, capitalistic obviously, and more visibly the product of American culture than any other.

But as we enter the 21st century the scene is changing. Increasingly the trade is not in physical goods – long-playing records, cans of celluloid – but in immaterials. A film can now be distributed over the Internet without a single physical copy of it actually travelling anywhere. This de-materialisation of the trade in culture-goods has focused attention on the fact that it is actually, and to a great extent always has been, a trade in property rights, in what is now called intellectual property or IP. All trade contains this aspect of intellectual property. Whether you buy a drug from another country or manufacture it yourself under licence or manufacture it without a licence is a matter of intellectual property rights. But it is trade in culture-goods which is most acutely a question of intellectual property rights rather than a simple trade in manufactured goods.

Once this fact comes to light the whole question of cultural trade acquires a new aspect. In modern capitalism, anything is tradeable. Anything can belong to somebody or some entity and be traded between that somebody or entity and another body or entity and conversely other bodies or entities can be denied access to it because they haven't got the money or aren't members of the right trading club. And it doesn't matter what the thing is – a pile of bricks, a film, a painting or a patent. More and more things are traded, and the terms of trade are terms of power.

As is well known, the Uruguay Round of the General Agreement on Tariffs and Trades (GATT) ended in 1993 without a definitive resolution of the question of whether or not the countries of the European Union could maintain quotas discriminating against non-EU culture-goods such as movies and TV programmes. (Non-EU in this case is shorthand for American since there was never much chance of our airwaves being suddenly overtaken with Japanese animé or telenovelas from Argentina, nor, sadly, music from Mali or Senegal.) In the negotiations the Americans had a strong hand, which they did not play particularly well, leaving the Europeans, led by the French and with pretty lukewarm support from Britain and the Nordic countries, able to maintain the notion of the *exception culturelle* – that is to say the idea that culture-goods, simply by virtue of being cultural, could be exempted from agreements governing trade in goods of every other kind. The weakness of the European position lay not in the principle of exceptionality, which has a lot to recommend it, but in its application to an entity called Europe.

The original discriminatory GATT agreement, negotiated in the case of France in 1946 and enshrined in law in 1948, and in Italy at about the same time, was designed in the first instance to defend indigenous film industries against foreign imports of whatever origin (though, obviously, mostly American) and, in a way that was both subsidiary and yet central, to defend national cultures against Americanisation. By protecting the film industry, the negotiators and their supporters also hoped to create space for nationally-oriented films, whether neo-realist as in Italy or 'qualité française' as in France. This made sense so long as the films made by the protected industry were in some way (however defined) expressive of a recognisable national culture. By the time of the Uruguay Round (1986–93), however, it was no longer possible to defend national industries, let alone cultures, in this way. European law made it illegal for any EU country to discriminate economically against films or TV programmes from other EU partners, with two consequences.

The first consequence was that the discrimination now became overtly what it had always been covertly: discrimination against goods produced in one country in particular, viz the United States. The second and more problematic one lay in the fact that the cultural pretext for this discrimination could no longer be grounded on the defence of single national cultures but had to be cast in terms of European cultures collectively, or even of European culture *tout court*. This European culture, moreover, was identified with Western Europe (excluding Switzerland), which had identity as a trading bloc but not necessarily as a cultural entity. Since France could no longer discriminate against Germany, Denmark or Portugal (say) in order to defend the exceptionality of its national culture, it could be forced into arguing that European cultures, or culture, needed collective defence against American culture which was somehow different and not European. Given that the roots of so much of American culture lie in Europe, this is transparent balderdash.

The original American negotiating team, set up under the administration of George Bush Sr. and led by Carla Hills, was aware of the contradictions in the European position and saw there a possible trump card. But when the crunch came in 1993, the new Clinton administration team under Jack Valenti decided not to use it (Grantham, 2000: 111). Why they didn't use it is not entirely clear, but it is probably the case that the US Administration simply didn't want to prolong the argument. Valenti, on behalf of the Hollywood industry, was keen to get the most favourable deal possible, even if it meant going up to the wire to secure it. But the Administration was more concerned with getting an across-the-board agreement on all the issues, and if this meant sacrificing film and television, then so be it. It was also prepared to recognise, as was Valenti, that there was no longer that much for them to gain, or for the Europeans to lose, over quotas. The United States already had almost all the access it needed to the European market and the screen time reserved for European films and programmes under the European Directive would probably be taken up by European product anyway, even if there was no quota. Besides, they had bigger fish to fry, and a big new pan in which to fry them.

What did they want to do next? They wanted to move on to a new phase, a new *conquista*, in which the prize at stake was not tradeable goods in the traditional sense but rights in immaterials. It had been clear for some time that the Bugs Bunny 'concept' – the notion of a wisecracking rabbit with large bendy ears and a white flash down his front – was worth more than any actual Bugs Bunny cartoon, because once you had rights to the concept you could materialise it any way you liked: as a toy, on a tee shirt, or on the Internet. There was also an upcoming battle to be fought about the patenting of nature – about whether if you had specialised knowledge of a naturally existing thing you could claim a patent on the thing itself. This was probably a bridge too far, since up to now it has been easier to asserts rights to a fictional creation or an invention than to something that already exists in reality. That is, you can register Jurassic Park but not Hyde Park or Jurassic limestone, King Solomon's Mines but not Marton colliery. It therefore seems unlikely that at the end of the day the would-be patenters of gene sequences will get all they want. But in the 1990s a new frontier was definitely opening up. There was a new Gold Rush where gold was to be found in the patenting, copyrighting, registering and trade-marking of concepts first and their material embodiments second. Under the circumstances, leaving behind the odd unconquered pocket of resistance called *exception culturelle* was merely intelligent tactics. You could leave your opponents to fight a war in which nothing much was at stake any longer while you went on to fight a new one whose importance the opposition had not yet recognised.

Where does this leave the notion of trading cultures? What is clear is that so much that in the old days was either common property or individual or family property is now owned and traded by capitalist corporations, and that so much that used to have a natural belonging, associated with communities or places or customs that had roots in those communities or places, is now tradeable and indeed traded. So one has increasingly to ask the question: what becomes of a culture if more and more of the things that go to make it up have become commodities, bought and sold by corporate entities which have no living connection to the culture but see in these components an opportunity to increase shareholder value?

The answer is very clear in general, if only because we see the evidence of it all about us. There is a clear loss of specificity, a blurring of identities, which affects material and cultural life in much the same way. There is an increasingly global cuisine mixing ingredients associated with different localities, and an increasingly global pop culture. In each case the machinery operating the globalisation is capitalist. Global products come from global or at any rate multi-national suppliers. But the demand for these products can also come from consumers. We may be dupes if we think that a 'chicken tikka baguette' contains either French bread or Punjabi chicken. But we are willing dupes to the extent that we prefer both the taste and the cultural associations of a chicken tikka baguette to those of a sandwich made from sliced bread and 'cheddar' cheese. Fusion culture is not just a capitalist plot.

If we turn from generic observation of what seems to be going on in the cultural world at large to matters more specific to cinema we can note some curious developments. Chief of these is an apparent limitation on the extent to which American (or solely American) companies, by controlling the market, also promoted the worldwide consumption of American culture-goods. What we are witnessing is a globalisation of the cultural industry in which the United States is the strongest but not the only player. We can note in this connection the takeover of American film studios by international rather than purely American capital: of Columbia and now MGM by Sony, of Universal for a while by Vivendi, of Fox by News Corporation. This has not led to Columbia mass-producing Japanese movies, or Universal French movies, or Fox a peculiar amalgam of Anglo-American-Australian movies appropriate to ownership by Rupert Murdoch. On the contrary, these companies produce for the international market as they always did. They also rely – as again they always did – on the unstated assumption that American cultural references are the *koiné*, the common idiom, of worldwide popular culture.

So in a sense no change here. But in a contradictory development the European art film is being drained of its specificity as a kind of cinema associated with particular parts of Europe to become an insipid mishmash of notionally 'European' signifiers. The word 'Europudding' was coined in the 1980s (originally, I think, by Jeremy Isaacs) to describe the effects of European Union policies aimed at promoting generically European and altogether denationalised films and TV programmes. In fact, however, as far as the cinema is concerned, the EU is not the major culprit. It is the global film industry itself which is promoting this development. 'Art cinema' has become a recognisable and quite profitable market niche. Miramax was probably the first company to exploit this in a systematic way. Whereas previously American companies invested in European films in the hope they could make them mainstream, Miramax in the 1980s and 1990s deliberately developed borderline product which could in some cases make its way into the mainstream but could also do nicely-thank-you in an arthouse niche provided it was not too challenging in either form or content (unless the content was sexual).* In this it was followed by the major companies such as Warner Bros., and also by Disney which, rather than set up its own arthouse outfit, simply bought Miramax. The Miramax formula was to invest in films which offered middle-class American audiences a little taste of Europe but a bland and palatable one. The American audience was only a small part of the audience the film was intended to reach – it would have one in its home country as well, and internationally – but it was the one out of which Miramax itself would make most of its profit, so that was why the company invested in it. The result is apparent in a film like *Chocolat* (2000, directed by Lasse Hallström from the novel by Joanne Harris) with its international cast (Johnny Depp, American; Juliette Binoche, French; Leslie Caron, Franco-American; Alfred Molina, British; etc.) acting out a folkloric Frenchness. But it is no less real, though less apparent, in the films that Miramax chose not to support because they did not fit the formula. How many of these there are nobody knows. I shall cite just one anecdote, which I take to be true and can also be taken as typical, to the effect that Miramax rejected a script set in Portugal in the 1920s, requesting instead that it be set in Spain in the 1930s, which more people knew about. Needless to say, the script (by Ann Lamche and Eduardo Guedes) never made it onto celluloid.

It is not only Europe that is being affected. The entry of China into the world market has created opportunities both for American companies to distribute in China and for Chinese film-makers to produce for a wider market than either the arthouse one

---

* In the 1960s and 1970s the majors did invest in quite a lot of modestly budgeted 'art' or 'auteur' films in order to obtain American or worldwide distribution rights, but this was never a concerted strategy and did not give the company rights to control the content.

to which the 'Fifth Generation' films of Chen Kaige and Zhang Yimou were directed or the niche market for martial arts traditionally supplied by Hong Kong. The result is twofold. On the one hand Zhang is now making *chinoisieries* such as *The House of Flying Daggers* (*Shi mian mai fu*, 2004), which many people in China regard as less authentically Chinese than an ordinary Hong Kong martial arts movie. And on the other hand Disney has appropriated the classics of Chinese culture in the same way as it previously appropriated European ones in order to refashion the world after its own middle-American image. Disney's *Mulan* (1998) turns a Confucian tale of filial piety into a westernised love story. Very progressive, no doubt, in its insipid sub-feminist way, but not very Chinese.

What we are seeing, in my opinion, is a new phase in a long process of commodification of cultural signifiers. There are three aspects to this. First there is globalisation. To take the example of *Mulan* again. Here we have a story which originally belonged to China. Every Chinese school child knew the original poem, but outside China few people had even heard of it. Now it is available to all, in edulcorated form, courtesy of the Disney Corporation. But here the second aspect comes in, which is privatisation. *Mulan* has joined a long list of cultural entities over which a capitalist concern asserts as many property rights as it can get away with. In the case of *Mulan* these are relatively limited, but in the case of Winnie the Pooh, Disney now owns exclusive rights in every manifestation of this amiable creature and his friends except the original books and drawings. Winnie has escaped the confines of the English middle-class and gone global, but only as private property. Belonging has been replaced by ownership.* It may seem democratic that Winnie the Pooh no longer belongs exclusively to the English middle class; it is less democratic that his availability to a wider world is mediated through corporate monopoly

Thirdly, cultural signifiers have become almost infinitely permutable. Anything can be mixed with anything else (subject to the rights of private property), but the permutability of signifiers devalues the signs that they carry since it deprives them of the context which they need if they are to carry their full range of meanings.

This is not the apocalypse. The changes taking place in the cultural marketplace can be deplored *ad infinitum*, whether from a conservative or a radical point of view, but that is not the point. They are in any case far from absolute. They represent a tendency, not an inescapable reality. Plenty of films still get made and distributed which resist the trend. Developments in computer software and Internet technology are undermining the ability of the major companies to enforce control of the market, both legally and illegally. And, as I said at the beginning, culture is not identical with the products which carry cultural signifiers. We are not what we consume.

---

* The word 'ownership' is not without its own ambiguities, since it can now mean 'have managerial responsibilities for' without necessarily according any property rights. This is weasel-speak, since it serves to cover up the underlying reality. Needless to say, I use the word here in its traditional and to my mind proper sense. See Nowell-Smith (2002).

References

Balio, T. (1998a) 'The Art Film Market in the New Hollywood', in G. Nowell-Smith and S. Ricci (eds), *Hollywood and Europe: Economics, Culture, National Identity, 1945–1995*. London: British Film Institute: 63–73.

Balio, T. (1998b) '"A Major Presence in All the World Markets": The Globalization of Hollywood in the 1990s', in S. Neale and M. Smith (eds) *Contemporary Hollywood Cinema*. London: Routledge: 58–73.

Grantham, B. (2000) *Some Big Bourgeois Brothel: Contexts for France's culture wars with Hollywood*. Luton: University of Luton Press.

Nowell-Smith, G. (1998) 'Introduction', in G. Nowell-Smith and .S. Ricci (eds) *Hollywood and Europe: Economics, Culture, National Identity, 1945–1995*. London: British Film Institute: 3–13.

Nowell-Smith, G. (2002) 'Own your own target ... now!', *Critical Quarterly*, 44 (4), Winter: 11–16.

Chapter 2

Media policy-making in the free trade era: the impact of the GATS negotiations on audiovisual industries

Des Freedman

Introduction

One of George Bush's favourite visions (at least measured by the number of times he refers to it in speeches) is of a 'world that trades in freedom'. He uses it to justify his pursuit of trade liberalization where open markets and the free movement of capital are, in his opinion, good not only for business but for the human spirit. Drawing directly on Bush's words, the US trade representative Robert Zoellick argues that this is a 'vision of a world in which free trade opens minds as it opens markets, encouraging democracy and greater tolerance' (USTR, 2004: 8). It is hardly surprising then that television programmes, movies and music – with their cultural as well as economic significance – should increasingly feature in world trade talks that are designed to bring about a less regulated and a more marketized and competitive trading environment.

One of the central mechanisms through which this is to be achieved is the General Agreement on Trade in Services (GATS), administered under the auspices of the World Trade Organization (WTO). The objective of the GATS is to ensure that markets for services, which now account for the majority of world trade, are progressively liberalized and privatized. Trade disciplines that have traditionally been applied to goods – measures that made it harder to justify domestic subsidies and tariffs – are now to be applied to industries including water, health, education and audiovisual media. This chapter will explore the background to the GATS, assess the dynamics of the negotiations, evaluate the likely impact of the GATS on the audio-visual industries and, finally, reflect on the reasons why, as the negotiations draw to a close, little progress has been made in the sphere of audiovisual as compared to other areas.

Trade agreements and the culture industries

In December 1993, the entire Uruguay Round of GATT negotiations was very nearly derailed by French determination to maintain its right to use quotas and subsidies to protect its audiovisual industries. In the end, a compromise was reached between the desire of the US to see full liberalization of the sector and the wish expressed by Canada, France and some other EU states to see the sector exempted from free trade rules. Member states were allowed to make no commitments regarding liberalization of their audiovisual industries so that, in reality, the whole sector was excluded from the disciplines of the new trade agreement. Audiovisual industries have also been largely exempted from many subsequent trade agreements, for example the North American Free Trade Agreement (NAFTA) and the MERCOSUR agreement involving Brazil, Argentina, Uruguay and Paraguay. Hernan Galperin (1999) is correct to conclude that:

> No other industry [than audiovisual] has been the subject of more exceptions and qualifications to free-trade principles, despite the present unchallenged reign of the neoliberal dogma among policymakers of most quarters. Annexes and side-agreements abound in references to communications industries, limiting trade liberalization and investment across borders.

On the other hand, the audiovisual sector *has* been subject to trade disciplines in a number of important ways. Copyright protection was strengthened with the signing of the TRIPS agreement on intellectual property rights. Although there was already an agreed international framework for copyright (enforced by the World Intellectual Property Organisation), TRIPS ensured that any deviations would be resolved through the particularly harsh disputes procedure of the WTO and has provided an effective means for the world's largest rights holders to pursue disciplinary action against smaller states (O Siochru and Girard, 2002: 91–93). With the entry into WTO membership of China, the use of TRIPS to deal with copyright infringements of audio-visual material is likely to be accelerated.

Secondly, in February 1997, the WTO concluded an extremely important agreement on telecommunications that brought an increasingly vital sphere of international communications under the aegis of free trade rules. Some 69 countries representing the vast majority of global telephone traffic and revenue agreed to liberalize their telecoms markets and open up domestic markets to foreign competition. Although the broadcasting of radio and television programmes was explicitly omitted from the agreement, the phenomenon of convergence around digital platforms will complicate the ability to distinguish between telecommunications and broadcasting and therefore undermine the ability to exclude the latter from WTO rules. Thirdly, audiovisual issues have been raised in relation to accession to WTO membership. The US, for example, objected to the applications of both Latvia and Croatia to join the WTO because they had adopted what the US view as the protectionist audiovisual policies of the EU (see Wright, 2000: 8).

Finally, trade officials are increasingly willing to apply WTO rules to cultural goods. For example, the WTO ruled in favour of the US in 1997 and against Canada's attempt to protect its domestic magazine industry by severely taxing advertising in so-called 'split-run' magazines (i.e. Canadian editions of US magazines). The Canadians tried unsuccessfully to argue that this was a tax on a service and not a good and were eventually forced (after the threat of $4 billion in sanctions) not only to allow US 'split-runs' to solicit Canadian advertising but also to remove foreign ownership restrictions on magazine publishing (see *Financial Times*, 1999: 4).

The background to audiovisual negotiations in the GATS

The GATS (WTO, 1994) is the first multilateral trade agreement dedicated to the provision of services. It was agreed as part of the Uruguay Round of GATT negotiations and included a specific reference to 'communication services'. The GATS imposed some crucial general obligations on member states, notably, the requirement not to discriminate against foreign suppliers (Articles II, XVI and XVII), to minimize domestic regulation (Article VI) and to avoid the 'trade-distortive' effects of subsidies (Article XV). With the launch of GATS negotiations in January 2000, it was expected that the audiovisual sector would be dealt with and the logjam from the Uruguay Round finally confronted.

The negotiations immediately ran into opposition from anti-corporate activists who argued that the GATS raised the prospect of further privatization, deregulation and liberalization of services that ought not to be at the mercy of the market. Groups like the World Development Movement (WDM) and Public Citizen warned that the aim of GATS was to extend market principles into areas where they have no right to be: education, health, the environment as well as audiovisual. According to the WDM (2000a: 3), the 'significance of these new negotiations cannot be overestimated …Governments are under pressure to drastically reorganise the ownership and delivery of services within their countries, and subject them to even tighter "free trade" rules'. The WDM identify three areas of particular concern: the handing-over of basic services to private companies; the weakening of government's ability to regulate provision of these services and the consequences for democracy; and the irreversibility of commitments made under GATS. It is, they argue, an agreement specifically sought by the corporate lobby in the US services sector and, above all, an 'agreement by, and for, multinationals' (WDM, 2000b).

Stung by this criticism and concerned by the growing international movement against agreements like the GATS, the WTO issued a response, *GATS: Fact and Fiction* (WTO 2001a), introduced by a quote from Nelson Mandela about the value of trade agreements, and placed very visibly on the homepage of the Trade in Services division. It extols the value of services in the world today and argues that the 'production and distribution of services, like any other *economic* activity, is ultimately destined to satisfy individual demand and social needs' (ibid.: 3 – emphasis added). By conceptualizing services as an economic phenomenon, the WTO does little to address the criticisms that it seeks to commodify all areas of activity under its aegis. It does, however, take great pains to reject the idea that all forms of domestic regulation and democratic accountability would effectively come to an end under the GATS. Firstly, the GATS (unlike the GATT) relies on a 'bottom-up' approach where member states are free to choose which commitments they wish to make under the two liberalizing clauses concerning market access and national treatment. Secondly, the WTO insists that member states may continue with their sovereign right to regulate service provision, but that these forms of regulation must be applied equally and fairly to all service providers, both domestic and foreign. Thirdly, the WTO points out that as the GATS excludes those services provided by government alone (i.e. not in competition with any other suppliers), some of the most crucial services lie outside of the scope of the Agreement.

How true are these claims that the GATS offers no threat to the regulatory sovereignty of member states? It is certainly true that the GATS contains opt-out clauses, or more particularly, opt-in clauses that provide member states with some flexibility. The initiative, however, lies clearly with the liberalizers. Firstly, the US is attempting to include all service sectors in the GATS negotiations, making it harder for poorer countries to ask for exemptions and refuse commitments across the board in case they are held responsible for damaging the talks. The likelihood is that developing countries will be forced to trade off some sectors against others. Next, the idea that the GATS presents no threat to domestic regulatory regimes flies in the face of its general attitude towards regulation as a trade impediment and its commitment to make regulations 'not more burdensome than necessary to ensure the quality of the service' (WTO, 1994: Article VI, clause 4b). Finally, the WTO is disingenuous about its claim that some of the most important public services are likely to be excluded from the GATS as they are not provided in competition with private suppliers. In many countries, health, education and, of course, broadcasting are core public services with ever-increasing modes of private delivery and are thus eligible for negotiations under the GATS.

The negotiations were launched on the basis of a background note on audiovisual services produced by the WTO secretariat in June 1998 (WTO 1998). It is largely a descriptive document, containing quantitative statistics on the scale of the sector and details of state support mechanisms for audiovisual industries. However, it does cover two other areas, the classification of the audiovisual sector and the need for regulating its industries, both of which have generated further debate and require some comment here.

The background note confirms audiovisual services as a sub-sector of communication services (along with postal, courier and telecommunication services) which is then divided into a further six categories: motion picture and videotape production and distribution services; motion picture projection services; radio and television services; radio and television transmission services; sound recording; other audiovisual services (ibid.: col. II.3). The note acknowledges that technological convergence is making it increasingly difficult to distinguish between telecommunications and audiovisual classifications, particularly in the case of broadcasting transmission services. In general, however, it resolves to classify issues concerning programming content under audiovisual while those involving the transmission of information are classified under telecommunications, a distinction that is increasingly problematic in a digital environment. The potential overlap between telecommunications and audiovisual reflects a larger problem within WTO rules as to the difference between goods and services, defined by one British negotiator as that of 'visible/invisible, physical/intangible' (DTI, 2001). The problem is that all physical goods have to be distributed in a context where distribution has been defined by the WTO as a service while many intangible services assume physical form (videos, film prints, CDs). Such confusion is bound to produce serious controversies in future negotiations over both 'goods' and 'services'.

The background paper also acknowledges the cultural and political importance of the audiovisual industries and the consequential need for regulatory regimes and support mechanisms. However, it leans very heavily on arguments proposed by the pro-liberalization Organisation for Economic Co-Operation and Development (OECD) that take regulatory reform for granted. The WTO concludes that to 'accommodate rapid technological change and the new multimedia services, governments will, according to the OECD, need to modify their regulatory structures (WTO, 1998: para. 2). The OECD's arguments are themselves heavily swayed by technological determinism and a neo-liberal commitment to free markets. For example, the OECD argues that 'rapid technical innovation and globalisation in the market' is undermining cross-media ownership restrictions and boldly states that 'the necessity for reviewing current regulations to determine whether they may continue as best practices to meet policy goals is arising from the viewpoint of stimulating further competition and developing new services and applications (OECD, 1999: 114). Ownership restrictions are seen here as impediments to business expansion and corporate profitability, no longer as necessary mechanisms to prevent concentration and conglomeration and extend cultural diversity. While the background paper does not take an explicit position on regulation, both the general obligation in the GATS to minimize regulation and the specific assumption that regulatory regimes in the audiovisual sector will impede technological development seem to reinforce the notion that audiovisual negotiations will focus on deregulation as much as liberalization.

The WTO secretariat's paper was followed by the tabling of three negotiating papers on audiovisual issues: two liberalizing ones (from the USA and Brazil) and one more 'defensive' one from Switzerland calling for a 'cultural diversity safeguard'. The US paper is, not surprisingly, the most forceful in arguing for specific commitments to be made in the sphere of audiovisual, although its tone is rather different to earlier approaches. It condemns an 'all or nothing' approach to audiovisual negotiations in which '[s]ome argue as if the only available options were to exclude culture from the WTO or to liberalize completely' (WTO, 2000: para. 5). This is a particularly ironic statement given that the USA played a major part in establishing an 'all or nothing' position in the Uruguay Round with its attempt to secure full liberalization of the audiovisual sector. However it now recognises the 'special cultural characteristics' of audiovisual media, acknowledges the validity of subsidies in promoting cultural diversity and simply requests more transparent rules for such subsidies.

The US paper argues that the best way to protect cultural diversity is precisely through further liberalization. This reflects the more general argument made by pro-market supporters that free trade agreements contribute not simply to economic growth but to various social and political objectives: maintaining world peace, increasing personal choice, stimulating 'good government' (see the WTO's *10 Benefits of the WTO's Trading System* for such an analysis [WTO. 1999]). So the US paper claims that 'in today's digital environment, it is quite possible to enhance one's cultural identity and to make trade in audiovisual service more transparent, predictable, and open. Indeed ... the two objectives may reinforce each other' (WTO, 2000:

3). The preservation of cultural diversity is directly connected, in the eyes of US negotiators, to the extent to which trade barriers are dissolved and free trade flows accelerated.

The communication from Brazil (WTO, 2001c) supports the call for liberalization in the US paper but reflects on its own distinctive economic interests. Noting that Article IV of the GATS specifically seeks the increasing participation of developing countries and the market liberalization of sectors that would be to their benefit, the paper asks a pertinent question. How can we 'promote the progressive liberalisation of the sector in a way that creates opportunities of effective market access for exports of developing countries ... without affecting the margin of flexibility of governments to achieve their cultural policy objectives as they find appropriate' (ibid.: 3)? In other words, how can developing countries liberalize areas of audiovisual in which they have a comparative advantage while maintaining import restrictions on areas in which they are more vulnerable? The fact that Brazil is asking this question supports the comments of theorists like Straubhaar (1997) and Sinclair et al. (1996) that there is a new, more multi-dimensional structure to international media flows, characterized by emerging regional centres of production in Latin America, the Middle East and South-East Asia.

On the other hand, Brazil is not a typical 'developing' country but one that has especially strong audiovisual export interests that it is attempting to expand through instruments that may arise out of the GATS. While it positions itself as the voice of the developing world, Brazil seems to be more determined to further its own interests at the expense of the USA, than to democratize the patterns of audiovisual flow in the international market. Brazil's paper therefore calls for member states to make firm commitments in areas like television services (in which Brazil has an interest through its export of *telenovelas*) but maintain trade defence mechanisms in areas in which they are weaker (in particular film production and distribution). It proposes an 'anti-dumping' discipline, presumably aimed at the USA, to prevent the offloading of audiovisual goods at prices that will undermine domestic and regional production. The problem for those who wish to see an end to the domination of audiovisual exports by the USA is that they are likely to receive little sympathy inside the WTO. According to a WTO counsellor, what Brazil calls dumping 'does not correspond to the traditional [economic] definition of dumping. Simply because US movies and series are already amortised, the costs are already recouped on the US market so they can sell them cheaply abroad. But this is not the definition of dumping where you purposely sell abroad cheaper than you sell in your own market' (WTO, 2001b). It appears that any attempts to secure *new* trade restrictive practices will be met, not surprisingly given its brief, with hostility inside the GATS framework.

Negotiations at snail's pace

Negotiations formally started in January 2000 with a timetable agreed at the Doha ministerial meeting in November 2001. Member states would make initial requests for commitments on market access by 30 June 2002 with initial offers, i.e. the response to the requests, tabled by the end of March 2003. Months of hard bargaining and trade-offs would follow with the talks, it was hoped, concluded by

Chapter 2 • Media policy-making in the free trade era

January 2005. In reality, progress in the audiovisual sphere has been excruciatingly slow. Only two countries out of the 147 WTO member states made preliminary *commitments* in all sub-categories of the audiovisual sector: the USA and the Central African Republic. Details of *requests* made by member states were not publicized although very few requests involved the audiovisual sector. According to the World Development Movement (WDM 2003a), the European Union, for example, tabled requests to 109 countries in the areas of telecommunications, water, business and financial services, and transport. It did not, however, make any requests in the sphere of audiovisual in line with EU audiovisual policy 'for the room for manoeuvre negotiated in the Uruguay round to be maintained, both for existing measures and for future developments' (EC, 1999: 22).

The USA, on the other hand, was more vigorous in its requests for liberalization. It is reported to have requested of the EU 'binding commitments to liberalization...in areas such as motion picture and home video entertainment, production and distribution services, radio and television production services and sound recording services' (WDM 2003b). When EC trade commissioner Pascal Lamy refused to budge on not making any commitments in the audiovisual sector, the assistant US trade representative replied that another audiovisual exemption for the EU is 'not something that we could agree to' (quoted in ibid.).

Details of the *offers* made by member states are slightly more accessible but, for pro-liberalization interests, worryingly few in number. By the end of 2004, some 21 months after the deadline, only 47 offers had been made with another 45 still outstanding. Officials at the British DTI admit to being disappointed by the low numbers of offers on the table and describe many of those as being 'thin – in the sense of not offering any new commitments' (DTI, 2004). Many of the offers make no reference to the audiovisual sector, the exceptions being:

- Liechtenstein, Norway and Canada whose offers merely reiterate their support for the idea of a cultural exemption;
- New Zealand where liberalization commitments are made in the production, distribution, exhibition and broadcasting of audiovisual works
- Japan where commitments are made in many areas of film and in sound recording services but not broadcasting
- The USA whose offer allows 'foreign ownership of cable television networks and allows non-US satellite companies to broadcast directly to American viewers' (USTR, 2003).

Because of the very slow tabling of offers, the January 2005 deadline has now been set aside for an indefinite end date. British trade officials express the hope that 'it will still be concluded within a reasonable time scale – many of us think that 2006 is achievable and desirable for beneficiary countries both developed and developing' (DTI, 2004).

One major reason for the slow pace of the negotiations is that, apart from the USA, few countries are willing to seek commitments on audiovisual liberalization if this requires them to open up their own markets and put further pressure on domestic regulatory regimes. Given the domination of US rights holders in the international audiovisual market, the likelihood is that there would only be one winner (in economic terms). This is what lies behind the WTO advisor's statement that 'relatively few delegations speak on audiovisual as opposed to other sectors [because] the sector is not one where many delegations have offensive interests' (WTO, 2001b). The distinction between 'offensive' (i.e. liberalizing) and 'defensive' (i.e. protectionist) interests is one that permeates discussion of trade negotiations in the audiovisual sector. Most developing countries have little to offer in terms of selling broadcasting and film products on the international market. While this is starting to change with the emergence of developing countries like Brazil, Mexico, Egypt and India as significant regional exports of film, music and television, audiovisual is still unlikely to be a major priority for many states in the context of US hegemony of exports.

Another reason why audiovisual issues do not sit that comfortably in trade talks concerns the issue of 'cultural distance', defined by Galperin (1999) as referring to the 'barriers in language, viewing habits, and genre preferences that hamper cultural products' flow between two given nations'. For example, it is true that the USA dominates the international television programme trade, but it is also true that, where they have the choice, most people prefer domestic to imported programmes: *Mexican* telenovelas, *British* soap operas, *Egyptian* serials. Despite the arguments of liberalization proponents, it is not simply trade restrictions but also cultural barriers that impede the free flow of audiovisual materials. Given this preference for cultural specificity and given the collective and symbolic importance of the audiovisual sector, defensive interests appear to be better organised than offensive ones in almost all countries (even those with export industries) when it comes to multilateral trade negotiations. This stand-off is likely to be reinforced by the international movement against organizations like the WTO and the IMF as citizens start to become aware that free-market policies do not offer them more choice in crucial services but facilitate the transfer of public resources into private hands. The GATS, therefore, may be too blunt an instrument for 'freeing up' audiovisual trade given the growing determination of citizens to resist further encroachments of capital into important areas of their social and economic lives.

Negotiators on all sides are becoming increasingly aware of this problem. The Cancun WTO ministerial meeting in September 2003 – where key decisions about GATS were to be adopted – was severely affected by the refusal of developing countries to accept an agenda which they viewed as reflecting the Western bias of trade talks. The US trade negotiator Robert Zoellick suggested that this represented the 'transformation of the WTO into a forum for the politics of protest' and warned that '[a]s WTO members ponder the future, the US will not wait: we will move towards free trade with can-do countries' (Zoellick, 2003).

The consequence of this threat has since become clear. The US has now concluded (or is in the process of concluding) bilateral free trade agreements (FTAs) with 24 countries including Australia, Chile, Morocco and Singapore, all of which include liberalizing clauses that refer specifically to audiovisual industries. The US/Australia FTA, for example, allows Australia to maintain existing quotas for terrestrial television, pay-TV and commercial radio but prevents it from raising them. Australia will no longer have the ability to introduce screen quotas and its scope to determine the level of local content in new media services is even more limited. According to the executive director of Australia's film and television producers' association, 'US interests are now allowed to sit at our table before an Australian government can implement any increase in drama content regulations on Pay TV. We have to argue the merits of our case up against the interests of the US industry' (quoted in CCD, 2004). It appears that the US is willing to sanction the survival of existing subsidies and quotas (as long as they are not increased) but is ensuring that new media markets – particularly in terms of digital delivery and broadband networks – are kept free of such 'barriers'. According to one experienced commentator on audiovisual trade policy, the US has adopted a new approach to audiovisual trade negotiations that explains its apparent softening towards subsidies and quotas:

> The new strategy of the United States in the cultural sector rests quite clearly on the view that while measures that do not confirm to national treatment, most-favored-nation treatment and free market access can be tolerated as they presently exist in the traditional audiovisual sector because they are bound one way or another to disappear with time, no such tolerance must be accepted for digitally delivered content which are at the heart of the new communication economy and should therefore remain free of cultural protectionism (Bernier, 2004: 19/20).

The US is, therefore, busily negotiating FTAs which leave co-signees with a limited amount of control over their audiovisual industries while reducing their responsibility over new media industries and which, most importantly, signal the end of 'cultural exemptions' – the US' ultimate objective.

Frustration with the slow pace of GATS negotiations and the awareness that trade deals are being struck in bilateral contexts has surfaced in the talks themselves. At a meeting at the end of 2004, the representative from Norway argued that

> the complexity of the services negotiations, including the bilateral request-offer process, would make it difficult if not impossible to reach an agreement quickly…[If] members could not achieve the desired level of trade liberalization in the WTO, they would seek to secure their trade interests through bilateral and regional trade agreements. The number of free trade agreements [is] rapidly increasing, which diminished the significance of the multilateral trading system (WTO, 2005).

It is clear from the minutes that other delegates shared this perspective and that the desire to secure bilateral trade deals is not confined to the US alone.

The final reason for the slow pace of audiovisual negotiations in the GATS concerns the ongoing discussions under the auspices of UNESCO for an international convention on cultural diversity (UNESCO, 2005). This is designed to be a legal instrument that would safeguard the rights of individual states to take necessary steps to support their cultural industries and to protect diversity of cultural expression, including those mechanisms most likely to be threatened by trade deals. Negotiations started in September 2004 and were completed in October 2005 and many participants in the GATS process are waiting to see what kind of instrument emerges before making particular commitments in the area of audiovisual trade. It is clear that some countries – notably France and Canada – were eager to secure a framework that could be counter-posed to the deregulatory principles of GATS while others – the US and Japan – were happy to agree to the convention as long as it could not be used to undermine trade disciplines.

The key debate during the negotiations concerned what finally emerged as Article 19, the relationship of the convention to 'other instruments', most obviously the

GATS. Two options were proposed. Option A would allow signatories the ability to derogate from another agreement 'where the exercise of those rights and obligations would cause serious damage or threat to the diversity of cultural expressions' while Option B simply stated that '[N]othing in this Convention shall affect the rights and obligations of the States Parties under any other existing international instruments' (UNESCO, 2004: 10). Option B was the one accepted in the final version.

There are two major problems for those who hope that what comes out of UNESCO will make a successful resolution of the GATS more difficult. Firstly, the language of the convention is very vague – necessarily so in order to secure a consensus. For example, how would it be possible to prove 'serious damage' as opposed to mere 'damage' to cultural diversity? The EU's compromise solution, to seek a 'third way' where signatories shall 'respect, in interpreting and applying international instruments, the provisions of this Convention' and shall 'foster mutual supportiveness between this Convention and other international instruments' (CCD, 2005) does little to resolve this problem. Secondly, the fact that the US decisively backed Option B and would most likely have refused to sign up to a convention that would in any way compromise its perception of the legitimacy and supremacy of trade rules, means that the UNESCO convention risks being a sideshow to the various locations in which audiovisual trade deals are currently being conducted.

Conclusion

It remains a fact that, as of now, the worst fears of the anti-liberalization movement have not been realized, at least not in the sphere of audiovisual negotiations under the GATS. This is not to argue that the GATS is not having a serious impact on other service areas, in particular health, education and public utilities where its provisions are likely to have significant consequences on citizens' access to basic services However, it is possible that audiovisual issues, which have so far been marginal to this GATS round – partly because of the EU's 'defensive' position and partly because most developing countries with limited audiovisual industries have little to gain by offering commitments in this area – will start to surface as talks draw to a close. One British negotiator describes the audiovisual sector as 'more of an end-game' and 'not as something to sell an offer' (DTI, 2004). It may well be therefore that areas like broadcasting, film and music are reserved as bargaining tools for trade officials when attempting to make deals in other areas like environmental, business and financial services. It could also be that we see a repeat of the arguments between the US and at least some EU member states over an audiovisual exemption that we saw some ten years ago during the Uruguay Round.

The lack of movement thus far in the GATS talks does not mean that trade talks are of no consequence to the audiovisual sector. Firstly, as Graham Murdock and Peter Golding put it, '[w]hether or not all the proposals currently on the table are incorporated into the revised version of the GATS, the marketised world view that underpins them is already firmly entrenched' (Murdock and Golding 2001: 116). We can see this in recent national policy developments in the US and UK where the 2003 Review of Broadcast Ownership Rules and the 2003 Communications Act respectively are the latest examples of pro-liberalization initiatives in the sphere of media and communications. Secondly, while multilateral talks are a slow and tortuous process, bilateral talks present fewer problems. The numerous free trade agreements (FTAs)concluded by the US in recent years include commitments on the audiovisual and entertainment sectors and, in particular, measures to pre-empt regulation of the digital environment and to tackle copyright infringements of US intellectual property. While these FTAs do not completely remove the ability of individual states to protect their audiovisual industries, they certainly do undermine the possibility of securing a 'cultural exemption' in broader trade agreements. So while we should watch the conclusion of the GATS talks with interest, we should not turn our attention away from the domestic and bilateral contexts where audiovisual liberalization and neo-liberal globalization are very much on the agenda. The 'everyday' market manoeuvres of domestic corporations and pro-market policies of national states should remind us that the struggle for public control over the audiovisual industries will continue to take place very close to home.

References

Bernier, I. (2004) 'The recent free trade agreements of the United States as illustration of their new strategy regarding the audiovisual sector', *Media Trade Monitor*, available at http://www.mediatrademonitor.org/node/view/146

CCD (Coalitions for Cultural Diversity) (2004), *Coalition Currents*, Vol. 2(2), March, available at http://www.cdc-ccd.org/coalition_currents/Mars04/coalition_currents_en.html

CCD (2005), *Coalition Currents*, Vol. 3(1), January, available at http://www.cdc-ccd.org/coalition_currents/Janv05/coalition_currents_en_janv05.html

DTI (Department of Trade and Industry) (2001) Interview with head and deputy head of the trade in services unit of the DTI, London, 13 December.

DTI (2004) Interview with officials from the Trade in Services Unit of the DTI, London, 9 September.

EC (European Commission) (1999), *Principles and Guidelines for the Community's Audiovisual Policy in the Digital Age*. Brussels, COM (1999) 657 final.

Financial Times (1999), 'Canada and US agree magazine deal', 27 May.

Galperin, H. (1999), 'Cultural Industries in the Age of Free-Trade Agreements', *Canadian Journal of Communications*, Vol. 24, Number 1, available at
lang1033 http://www.wlu.ca/~wwwpress/jrls/cjc/BackIssues/24.1/galperin.pap.html

Murdock, G. and Golding, P. (2001), 'Digital Possibilities, Market Realities: The Contradictions of Communications Convergence' in L. Panitch and C. Leys (eds), *A World of Contradictions: Socialist Register 200*. London: Merlin Press, 111–129.

O Siochru, S. and Girard, B. (2002), *Global Media Governance: A Beginner's Guide*. Lanham, MA: Rowman and Littlefield.

OECD (Organisation for Economic Co-Operation and Development) (1999), *Communications Outlook 1999*. Brussels: OECD.

Sinclair, J., Jacka, E. and Cunningham, S. (eds) (1996) *New Patterns in Global Television*. Oxford: Oxford University Press.

Straubhaar, J. (1997) 'Distinguishing the global, regional and national levels of world television' in A. Sreberny-Mohammadi, D. Winseck, J. McKenna and O. Boyd-Barrett (eds) *Media in Global Context: A Reader*. London: Arnold, 284–298.

UNESCO (2004). *Preliminary draft on a convention of the protection of the diversity of cultural contents and artistic expressions*, Paris, available at
http://portal.unesco.org/culture/en/file_download.php/382d532908a5a5258ffe1465d5a15c2aEng-PreliminaryDraftConv-conf201-2.pdf

UNESCO (2005), *Convention on the Protection and Promotion of the Diversity of Cultural Expressions*, Paris, available at http://unesdoc.unesco.org/images/0014/001429/142919e.pdf

USTR (United States Trade Representative) (2003) 'Free Trade in Services: Opening Dynamic New Markets, Supporting Good Jobs, 31 March, available at cf10 http://www.ustr.gov/assets/Document_Library/Fact_Sheets/2003/asset_upload_file40_4138.pdf.

USTR (2004), *The President's Trade Policy Agenda*, March, available at http://www.ustr.gov/Document_Library/Reports_Publications/2004/2004_Trade_Policy_Agenda/Section_Index.html

WDM (World Development Movement) (2000a) 'Stop the GATSastrophe: Campaign briefing', November.

WDM (2000b) 'General Agreement in Trade in Services: In whose service?', available at lang1033 http://www.wdm.org.uk/cambriefs/WTO/Inwhoseservice.htm.

WDM (2003a) 'Whose Development Agenda? A preliminary analysis of the 109 EU GATS requests', 25 February, available at cf10 http://www.wdm.org.uk/cambriefs/Whose per cent20development per cent20agenda per cent20v-4.pdf

WDM (2003b) 'GATS: From Doha to Cancun', 25 August, available at cf10 http://www.wdm.org.uk/cambriefs/gats/gatscancunupdate1.htm

WTO (World Trade Organisation) (1994) *General Agreement on Trade in Services*. Geneva: WTO.

WTO (1998) Background note by the secretariat on audiovisual services, S/C/W/40.

WTO (1999) *10 Benefits of the WTO's Trading System*, available at lang1033 http://www.wto.org/english/thewto_e/whatis_e/10ben_e/10b00_e.htm

WTO (2000) Communication from the United States on audiovisual and related services, S/CSS/W/21.

WTO (2001a) *GATS – Fact and Fiction*, available at
lang1033 http://www.wto.org/english/tratop_e/serv_e/gatsfacts0109_e.pdf

WTO (2001b) Interview with counsellor, trade in services division of the WTO, Geneva, 17 December.

WTO (2001c) Communication from Brazil on audiovisual services, S/CSS/W/99.

WTO (2005) Report of the meeting held on 29 November and 3 December 2004, Council for Trade in Services Special Session, TN/S/M/13, 28 January.

Wright, R. (2000) 'Croatia's new government looks to EU accession', *Financial Times*, 7 January.

Zoellick, R. (2003) 'American will not wait for the won't-do countries', *Financial Times*, 22 September.

Chapter 3

The 'wrong type' of television: New Labour, British broadcasting and the rise and fall of an exports 'problem'

Simon Blanchard

Introduction

In 1999 the UK Government's Department for Culture, Media and Sport (DCMS) published two reports on the export performance of British television in overseas markets. This concern with TV exports was part of a wider pattern of engagement with what the DCMS termed the 'creative industries', and with their 'hidden potential' in export markets (DCMS, 1998, 1999a, 1999b, 1999c).

This paper offers a brief reading of the policy 'moment' surrounding these two reports, and proposes a sceptical assessment of the way the issues were framed and – in due course – resolved.

The paper is in four Sections. Section One sketches out the immediate context of the 'creative industries' agenda, and its place in the policy platform of the 'New Labour' government elected in May 1997. Section Two summarises how this agenda then shaped the operations and policy goals of New Labour during its first term, and how the TV export 'problem' emerged. Section Three offers a reading of how the ensuing debate was framed and – in due course – resolved. Finally, Section Four draws conclusions about this policy 'moment' and what it tells us about the broader significance of the 'creative industries' platform.

Section One: Task forces, mapping and exports

The 'creative industries' agenda pursued by New Labour was not unexpected. The broad outlines of their thinking on this topic had been emerging for some time (Mulgan and Worpole, 1986; Fisher and Owen, 1991; Mandelson and Liddle, 1996) and were set out very clearly in the Party's March 1997 policy document *'Create the future – a strategy for cultural policy, the arts and the creative economy'* (Labour Party, 1997).

After the May 1997 Election victory the Blair government moved rapidly to pursue

TRADING CULTURE

Left: Building a Global Audience, *April 1999;*
Right: The TV Exports Inquiry Report, *November 1999.*

the 'creative industries' project. Under the aegis of a new DCMS (formerly the Department for National Heritage) the government set up an inter-departmental Creative Industries Task Force (CITF) in June 1997. Its remit was:

> ... to provide a forum in which Government Ministers could come together with a few senior industry figures to assess the value of the creative industries, analyse their needs in terms of Government policies and identify ways of maximising their economic impact. (DCMS, 1999c).

The CITF met formally for the first time in October 1997, and set in train a fresh audit of the scale and scope of the UK's creative industries economy. The results of this audit were published by the DCMS in November 1998 as the '*Creative Industries Mapping Document*' (DCMS, 1998). The Report estimated that:

> ...The creative industries in the UK generate revenues approaching £60bn and employ more than 1.4 million people.. For those industries for which material is available (ie excluding software) the aggregate value of exports is estimated at £7.5bn. (DCMS, 1998: 008).

It also announced that a Creative Industries Export Promotion Advisory Group (CIEPAG) had been formed, and that it would be '..considering strategies for export promotion across the creative sector..' (DCMS, 1998: 009). Reinforcing this orientation, the Report's overview finished with a checklist of topics headed 'Growing the Creative Industries – Issues for Consideration'. This stressed the importance of:

> ... focussing increasingly on global opportunities, with government playing its role in promoting creative industry exports, removing obstacles to free trade or opposing the

Chapter 3 • The 'wrong type' of television

introduction of measures which would harm the international competitiveness of UK companies and promoting an image of Britain as the creative and innovative hub of the world…(DCMS, 1998: 010).

The publication of the *Mapping Document* provided a symbolic turning point. Its findings were not novel, its themes had been widely anticipated. Nonetheless, they were now 'official' – visibly part of the mainstream Whitehall agenda. Attention was now beginning to turn to the details – to the opportunities and constraints within the various industry sectors which made up this complex arena.

The Trade Balance in Television

In examining the 'state of play' in the television sector, the *Mapping Document* provided a summary of the recent tends in the sector's balance of payments (BOP) position. As was well known in industry circles, the BOP position had changed since the mid-1980s.

In 1985 the industry ran a modest BOP surplus of £24m. By 1996, this had become a deficit of £282m. The trends underlying this movement were apparent from the data.

Exports had more than doubled (from £110m to £234m), but imports had grown even faster – increasing sixfold (from £86m to £516m). On the import side, the forces driving this rapid growth were also obvious. As the *Mapping Document* put it, the trend was '..largely attributable to the growth in multi-channel cable and satellite television..' (DCMS, 1998: 103). In the mid-1980s cable and satellite had been in their infancy in the UK. A decade later they were an established part of the media landscape, with about 10 per cent of total viewing. Whilst these new arrivals made varying degrees of investment in original programming, the bulk of their schedules were made up from imports, particularly from the USA. As this sector grew in scale and scope, so did the volume of imports.

Table 1. UK television trade balance

Year	Exports	Imports	Surplus/deficit
1985	£110m	£86m	+£24m
1987	£117m	£130	–£13m
1990	£128m	£207m	–£79m
1993	£181m	£268m	–£87m
1994	£255m	£317m	–£62m
1995	£245m	£400m	–£155m
1996	£234m	£516m	–£282m
1997	£313m	£606m	–£293m
1998	£444m	£692m	–£248m
1999	£440m	£843m	–£403m

Source: ONS/British Television Distributors Association, reported in DCMS, *Creative Industries Mapping Document*, 1998, 2001.

Having reviewed these trends, the *Mapping Document* went on to note that '... the broadcasting industry is expected to experience strong growth over the next decade. In seeking to take the opportunity to reap the economic benefit in the UK, a number of issues will need to be considered ...'. (DCMS, 1998: 107). These included:

- How to develop regulation to continue to protect the public interest while ensuring that it does not create unnecessary obstacles to the development of the industry
- How to improve the export performance of the television sector
- How to ensure that the expansion of broadcast outlets does not simply lead to higher imports and a further widening of the trade gap (p. 107).

For our purposes, what is of note here is that this agenda was carefully balanced, and studiously neutral – recognising that the television BOP position was the product of two trendlines – exports *and* imports – and that a robust policy framework would be one which paid attention to both.

Section Two: The emergence of a television exports agenda

In the event, the *Mapping Document*'s suggestion that Government and industry would need to look at both halves of this BOP equation was ignored. There are at least four inter-related reasons why this happened.

The first was that it did not fit with the Government's 'export drive' and 'competitiveness' agenda.* In this model, imports were de facto politically 'off-limits' to policy-makers. Moreover, attempts by Government even to *examine* this side of the BOP agenda in any detail would have been seen as a serious deviation from 'free market' conventions.

Both trade policy and corporate regulation in general now take place in an intensely 'mediated' environment (Davis, 2000; Kelsey, 1995, McArthur, 2000; Teivainen, 2002) – one in which government policies are continuously 'vetted' by media commentators and elite opinion for any departures from the prevailing orthodoxy (Chomsky, 1989). When it comes to issues touching the corporate prerogatives of transnational media companies this scrutiny is especially intensive (McChesney, 2001).

Any attempts to develop an agenda for TV imports would therefore be seen as an assault on the 'principles' of 'free trade' and likely to produce sermons on the 'evils' of 'protectionism', the 'failure' of 'import controls', references to the Soviet era, North Korea, and so forth.

Secondly, there was what might be called the Rupert Murdoch factor. New Labour had judged it essential to cultivate the support of the Murdoch media empire as part of their election campaign strategy, and both Murdoch and his advisers enjoyed privileged access to New Labour once they were in office (Chenoweth, 2001; Palast, 2001). Given that Murdoch's BSkyB was the key player in the satellite and cable channel market, any agenda to reduce import dependency would of necessity impinge on this terrain. For a New Labour team whose declared game plan was to

---

* For a rich comparative history of the 'competitiveness' agenda, see Miyajima, Kikkawa and Hikino, 1999. For a recent dissection of the agenda's problems as a policy framework (by a former Director General of the Confederation of British Industry) see Turner, 2001.

win at least two terms in office this meant that the 'risk-reward ratio' in tackling TV imports was highly unfavourable.

Thirdly, there was another counter-argument embedded in the 'competitiveness' agenda which worked against policy-making on this front. As we might expect from a profoundly neo-liberal current of thinking, the competitiveness framework was one which had been carefully crafted to present imports as essentially and invariably *positive* – an index of national open-ness and dynamism, and a source of additional rivalry and innovation incentives for domestic producers (Porter, 1990). In this paradigm there was no viable space for public policy on imports – any shifts in the trade balance would have to work themselves out in the marketplace.

Finally – and probably most decisively – the tenor of discussion within the TV industry itself was already firmly focused on the export performance agenda. Moreover, this focus had been emerging for some time – starting during the latter part of John Major's Conservative government.

Under Major, the Department of National Heritage (DNH) had already made an exports mandate a key aspect of its policy for the BBC (Department for National Heritage, 1994). The DNH continued the Thatcher strategy of holding down the BBC's licence fee, and –in effect – requiring them to increase export income as a source of programme revenue. Following on from this, the DNH commissioned consultants to look at the wider dynamics of the TV production sector (Goodall and Graham, 1997).

As this work was being completed, the DNH and the Department for Trade and Industry (DTI) began discussions with industry representatives about a further study of UK television performance in export markets (Barrett, 1997). These discussions continued after the change of government in May 1997, and work finally started on the study in October 1997. The study was carried out by the research consultants David Graham Associates (DGA), and funded by a consortium of companies active in the TV export market with match funding from the DTI.

This was the policy context in which the *Mapping Document*'s findings appeared. The *Document* served to highlight an issue which the industry and government were already engaged in exploring, and one which had been shaped to favour an 'exports' agenda. Press commentary after the *Mapping Document*'s launch continued to highlight the trade gap issue (Anon., 1998, Anon., 1998a) and the preferred 'exports' solution. Nonetheless – given that the DGA study was still in progress – further action would have to wait on its completion, and the response to its findings.

Section Three: The 'wrong type' of television

In the event, DGA finished their work in January 1999. The study's detailed findings remained confidential to its industry sponsors, but a summary of its main arguments and policy proposals were then published by the DCMS in April 1999 – in a Report entitled *'Building a Global Audience: British Television In Overseas Markets'* (DCMS, 1999a) (hereafter BAGA).

In line with early press reports of the study's agenda and findings (Barrett, 1997; Clarke, 1998; Anon., 1998a) the conclusions of the BAGA study offered a resolutely negative assessment of the TV industry's export performance. A lengthy rehearsal of the study's arguments is beyond the scope of this paper, but its both its overarching diagnosis and the proposed remedy were quite unambiguous, and can be summarised in outline. The BAGA study started by defining what it saw as its agenda:

> ... the relevant questions are whether we are falling short of our potential, andwhether there are steps that would enable us to do better... (p. 08).

What followed was a portrait of the TV industry which left the reader in no doubt about the BAGA study's view: the industry *was* under-performing and would have to change its ways. The report's executive summary argued that:

> ... UK distributors are regarded as efficient and competitive. The main problem is a lack of suitable programmes to sell (p. 08).

The study went on to argue that the problem of under-supply was most notable in two genres: drama and comedy. According to BAGA, international buyers found British TV drama unappealing. As the study put it:

> ...Time and again, we are told that our drama is too dark, too slow; unattractive; too gritty or socio-political ... the 'image' of Britain portrayed overseas by our television drama is not an attractive one (p. 24).

Comments from overseas buyers about British TV comedy were reported to be equally negative:

> ... Our mainstream comedy production has begun to dry up...we are told that the comedies being produced in the UK have lost their appeal (p. 27).

In both genres, the BAGA study also argued that these reported problems were made worse by failure to produce programmes in the right numbers or right lengths, and by a perceived lack of interest in co-production with overseas partners. As result of all these declared failures, the BAGA study summed up its case as follows:

> ... Whatever its historic achievements and present virtues, viewed as an industry, television is now looking out of date (p. 41).

If BAGA's diagnosis was emphatic, so was its solution. The report noted that the British TV industry had developed within a regulatory and industrial culture which was firmly focused on the domestic audience. In a concluding section – under a heading entitled 'The Wrong Model' – the BAGA study argued that British TV was, in effect, making the 'wrong type' of television.

In the study's view, this in turn was because the industry producing the TV was the 'wrong type' of industry. If the aim was to increase exports, British TV would have to adopt the 'right' model, and that was to be found in the USA, where Hollywood provided '... a model of a creative industry at full stretch..' (p. 33). Moreover, it argued, this US model was now also becoming more influential in Europe, where the TV industry was '... adopting many features of US practice ...' (p. 32).

The BAGA study was also quite clear that adopting the US model would require a sea-change in the regulatory framework for UK TV. As BAGA put it:

> ... UK regulation was designed to ensure high standards for British viewers, not to facilitate exports. But, for companies that sell our product overseas, excessive regulation can leave catalogues of material that are incompatible with overseas audiences (p. 32).

The implication was clear. Regulation was a fetter on export performance, and the

Chapter 3 • The 'wrong type' of television

solution was to remove these '... restrictive regulations that disable ... broadcasters from commissioning genuinely commercial programmes.' (p. 32). With its shackles struck off, the TV industry would finally be free to model itself along US lines, and make the '... positive, glossy, mainstream drama series that would command interest overseas.' (DCMS, 1999a: 26).

The Task Force on TV Exports – rejecting the 'wrong model' argument

Predictably enough, the BAGA study's arguments were taken up and amplified with evident glee by both tabloid and broadsheet commentators – the study was described as 'scathing' in *The Guardian* (Barrie, 1999) and reported by the *Evening Standard* under the headline 'Britain's TV shows "too dull to sell abroad"' (Shannon, 1999). Nonetheless, given the bluntly commercial tenor of its arguments and its antipathy to domestic regulation, the report required careful handling – not least because its thesis soon attracted notes of dissent from established industry sources (see Willis, 1999).

As a result, the DCMS decided to set up a fresh review, this time under the auspices of the Creative Industries Task Force. The CITF's Inquiry into UK TV Exports first met in May 1999, and finished its deliberations at the end of September 1999. Their Report, *'Creative industries: UK television exports inquiry'* (DCMS, 1999b) was then published by the DCMS in November.

The Inquiry had been organised as three working groups, each handling a distinct part of the overall agenda: market intelligence (data collection, industry promotion & trade lobbies, etc.), investment (fiscal incentives, merchandising, etc.) and a third group on 'The Right Product' (hereafter RPG). As discussion progressed, it was this third group – chaired by the BBC's Rupert Gavin – which was to produce a review of the issues which (without being openly declared as such) amounted to a comprehensive rebuttal of the core premises of the BAGA study. We outline the main points made by the Gavin group below. However, before looking at them we need to revisit briefly the broad trends in performance which provided the foundation for the 'Right Product' group's conclusions.

UK TV Export Performance since the mid-1980s

As the Gavin group were aware, the fundamental problem with the BAGA study was that it drew a picture of export 'failure' which was not sustained by the available data.

As Table 1 indicates, by 1996 the industry's export earnings had broadly doubled from their levels in the mid-1980s, and were now comfortably in excess of £200m a year. Trend data for the second half of the 1990s show that – by the time the BAGA report appeared – the earnings levels had almost doubled again, to well over £400m a year.

In other words, the official statistics showed an industry which – since the mid-1980s – had doubled its overseas earnings in ten years, and then nearly doubled them again in a further two years (between 1996 and 1998). On any balanced assessment of the evidence, these long-run trends were *not* indicative of an industry indifferent to overseas sales, nor one whose product portfolio was failing in overseas markets.

39

Indeed, what this data showed was *not* failure but its reverse: considerable success in export performance, and a pattern of accelerating earnings growth over the second half of the 1990s.*

The Right Product Group rebuttal

The RPG's analysis began with a brief overview by Rupert Gavin, who was quick to begin by stressing that the industry's overall performance was *not* one of failure or under-performance: 'First, I think it is worth emphasising that at present the UK has a healthy export position ...' (DCMS, 1999b: 37).

In the analysis which followed, Gavin and his colleagues proceeded to refute the core assertions of the BAGA study. They started by re-examining the data for the UK's share of the world TV export market:

> BAGA noted that the UK accounts for 9 per cent (by volume) of the international television export market... Although we are a distant second to the US (68 per cent of the market), our share is three times that of our next closest rivals, France and Australia. This indicates a strong international position ... The UK claims a 13 per cent share of primetime, which can be assumed to be the highest value daypart. This is more than six times the primetime share of our nearest competitor ... (p. 39).

In addition, they noted that other relevant benchmarks reinforced this picture of considerable success, most obviously the strong growth in export earnings:

> With 9 per cent of the market the television industry is outperforming our global GDP position (we have 4.7 per cent of global GDP) ... The official trade statistics for the years 1991 to 1997 indicate that UK television exports grew at an average compound rate of 30 per cent. During the same period, world trade in television services grew by an average compound rate of 10 per cent ... (p. 40).

Having refuted the BAGA study's core diagnosis (industry under-performance) the RPG went on to also reject its proposed remedy (adoption of the 'US model').

The RPG noted firstly that the style of UK television was driven by the tastes of its domestic audiences, and that attention to the home market was not evidently incompatible with export success:

> UK audiences are inclined to watch UK programmes, with their particular 'gritty' or 'realistic' characteristics. What is more, when our programmes are of the highest quality, international buyers appear to be less pre-occupied with their grittiness. Neither *Cracker* nor *Prime Suspect* – both successful international sellers – can be described as light-hearted escapism (pp. 46–47)

It then went on to re-assert the over-riding centrality of the domestic programming agenda:

> Developing the international business is important for the industry, but serving the UK audience is essential. Dramatic modification to the style of UK programming is not, therefore, a realistic aim (p. 47)

Having rejected the BAGA arguments, the Gavin group went on to look at the scope for further incremental improvements in export performance, and made a series of

---

* The figures are not adjusted for inflation. Re-stating them using a suitable deflator for the broadcasting sector would make the trendline less emphatic, but would not alter the overall dynamics or trajectory. In any case, the debate as conducted used these numbers as their statistical ground.

suggestions for additional information, training and industry coordination. Nonetheless, their central findings amounted to a conclusive demolition of the BAGA prognosis. The hypothesis of 'failure' had been shown to be emphatically untrue, and – as a direct corollary – the suggested remedies emerged as both un-necessary and inappropriate.

Section Four: Conclusions

With the publication of the CITF Inquiry Report, this current of debate about the TV industry's supposed export 'failure' ran aground. In its place, industry and government concentrated on a more low-key, pragmatic agenda of piecemeal enhancements to the export promotion machinery and ritual exhortations to 'do better' in overseas markets. Subsequent discussions would still contain echoes of the BAGA thesis (Graham, 2000; Phillips, 2000), but the drastic remedies it had scouted were no longer under consideration. The CITF emphasis on the primacy of the domestic audience had been reasserted as the linchpin of policy – as was evident in the Government's formal response to the CITF Report, which commented that:

> The healthy export position reported by the Inquiry is gladly noted. Government and industry will work together to improve on this – although this must not be at the expense of the home broadcasting market ... (DCMS, 2000: 4).

How then should we assess this export debate ? Viewed in a broader context it offers insights into the still evolving politics of the two core constituencies involved: namely the TV industry and the New Labour government. We can consider these in turn.

TV exports: banging on an open door

As I have indicated, the exports agenda for UK TV began to come to the fore under the Major government. As I have argued elsewhere (Blanchard, 1989) the broadcasting policy agenda pursued by the Conservatives from the mid-1980s onwards was clearly destined to reconfigure the UK TV industry along more commercial and deregulated lines. A drive to increase earnings in overseas markets thus became both a commercial imperative and a political mandate.

As a result, when we look at the data trends we find an industry whose degree of export orientation was expanding steadily in the first half of the 1990s, and then gaining further momentum from 1996 onwards. By the time New Labour came to power this export dynamic was fully formed and gathering speed. In that respect, the New Right's commercialising agenda had proved very successful.

Given this pattern, how do we account for the export 'failure' debate under New Labour? What purpose did it serve? Here the answer seems clear enough. The trends of the early mid-1990s had produced not just a new managerial awareness about TV exports but a distinct business sub-sector – a constituency whose defining focus was on overseas markets. This was the social and corporate base behind the BAGA study.

As regards the study itself, given its sponsors, its outlook was inevitably geared towards encouraging the industry to see exports as a primary objective rather than a welcome but secondary consideration. In this context, the rhetorical strategy of the BAGA report was scarcely surprising. An acknowledgement of the industry's comparative success and dynamism in exports was not politically or conceptually an option. What was required was the construction of an apparent 'failure' which could serve as the rationale for a more fundamental restructuring of the industry towards exports. Without a drastic 'problem' there would be no meaningful case for drastic 'solutions'.

As we have seen, this rhetorical gambit failed, and its policy agenda was visibly rebuffed. However, we need also to recognise the degree to which this 'defeat' was largely symbolic and tactical. If we examine the broader picture since the mid-1980s the balance sheet is one in which the 'competitiveness and exports' agenda has continued to *gain* ground, not lose it – as a can be seen in New Labour's Communications White Paper (DTI/DCMS, 2000; Blanchard, 2001). In that respect, the 'failure' rhetoric has proved effective – shaping the debate and sustaining the one-sided emphasis on exports. Equally, whilst the CITF Inquiry effectively sidelined the proposed wholesale adoption of the US model, the overall 'logic of process' in the UK TV industry is one which continues to migrate in the direction of US precedents and models. This can be seen in the plans for an OFCOM along FCC lines, the emergence of a common regulatory ethos, the growth of trans-Atlantic TV formats sales, and the ongoing commercialisation of both ITV and BBC schedules (Adamson, 2000; Barnett and Seymour, 1999; Bell, 2001; Clarke, 2001; Collins, 2001; Gitlin 1985; Hodgson, 2001; Jury, 2001; Powell, 1998, 2001; Sanghera, 2001). In this respect, the CITF rebuttal is likely to prove no less rhetorical than its putative rival.

New Labour and commercial politics

How then do we place this episode in relation to the trajectory of New Labour over its first term (1997–2001) ? Here the picture seems equally unambiguous.

Firstly, it highlights how the 'competitiveness' paradigm constrained and restricted the policy agenda in this arena. The debate began by noting a TV trade deficit, one which was presented as a 'problem' with only one allowable response: namely to 'do better' on the exports side. As we have seen, it soon became apparent that (contrary to initial presumptions by some parties) the scope to 'do better' was wholly marginal.

In effect, the episode was resolved by an un-stated recognition between Government and key industry players that dramatic increases in export performance would require a level of industry reconstruction which would damage its domestic production base.

This degree of 'structural adjustment' was seen as unworkable, and so the 'debate' ran aground. Unable to look at possible strategies on the import side the discussion had nowhere to go conceptually or politically.

Secondly, this policy debacle indicates very clearly that the preliminary stage of identifying the TV BOP deficit as a 'problem' to be solved was a largely rhetorical pretext. In practice, political and corporate decision-makers did not see the TV trade deficit as a significant issue that required or justified significant intervention. Having made some incremental adjustments on the export side the agenda was dropped, and the 'problem' of the TV trade deficit receded from view. Why was this ?

The answer to this question can be found by looking at the wider BOP agenda, and the broader economic trajectory at work. To begin with, all BOP analyses and assessments in practice operate via an over-arching pattern of surpluses and deficits. The 'big picture' issue is the overall pattern, and its prevailing trends and dynamics.

In the case of the UK, the available data assembled by the DCMS suggest that the overall BOP picture for the 'creative industries' mega-sector is that they make a significant net contribution to the UK's trade position.

Of the thirteen sectors which comprise this grouping there is BOP data for eight – all of them in surplus except TV. Looking at the other five, most have a significant export profile and are likely to run a net surplus or, at worst, only small deficits. Taken overall, this complex of sectors can 'afford' a deficit on TV and still make a net contribution to the trade balance.

More broadly, taking the services sector as a whole, the BOP position is also positive. As the Office of National Statistics puts it in the most recent analysis of the long run position, '... a surplus has been recorded for trade in services in every year since 1966' (Office for National Statistics, 2000: 34). In the year 2000 the UK's current account balance on trade in services was in surplus by over £10.9bn (see IFSL, 2001).

Table 2. Creative industries – balance of trade data

Sector	Year	BOP surplus/deficit
Advertising	1999	+ £229m
Architecture	1999	+ £54m
Art/antiques	1999	n.d.
Crafts	2000	n.d.
Design consultancy	2000	n.d.
Designer fashion	1996	n.d.
Film	1999	+£278m
Games – Video/PC	1998	+ £219m
Music	1997/8	+ £526m
Performing arts	2000	n.d.
Publishing	1999	+ £691m
Software & computer services	1998	+£1,378m
TV	1999	–£403
Net BOP position		**+£2,972m**

n.d. = no overall data available. In most cases, data is available for exports, but not imports; Source: DCMS, *Creative Industries Mapping Document,* 2001.

Taking the BOP position on services as a whole, it becomes clear that – in orthodox economic 'competitiveness' terms – the TV trade deficit is a 'non-problem'. Like its US counterpart, the UK enjoys a significant overall competitive advantage in services, and a strong position in the 'creative industries' segments of this broader complex (McRae, 2001).

This underlying position is the key to understanding the fundamentally gestural and short-lived 'export failure' episode outlined above. At a deep structure level political and business elites regard the UK (with some justification) as a newly resurgent commercial power whose 'creative industries' are at the heart of its mercantile success. The existence of trade deficits in a given sector (such as TV) does not threaten this commercial ascendancy. The deficit for TV may be regretted, but policies that would tackle it are not on current agendas, nor likely to become so.

In essence, the prevailing climate of opinion is one which judges that the UK's best prospects in geo-political terms will come from operating within the 'rules' of the 'free trade' agenda, not – as others have argued – from challenging them (see for example, Barlow and Clarke, 2001, Hall, 1998, Lang and Hines, 1993, Scott, 2000)

Acknowledgements: This is an abbreviated version of a paper presented at a Policy Study Day on 28 September 2001 at Birkbeck College, London. The work was funded by the AHRB Centre for British Film and Television Studies as part of the Centre's research strand on 'Public Policy and National Identity'. I am grateful to Professor Sylvia Harvey, Principal Associate Director of the Centre, for the invitation to join the research team and to the Arts and Humanities Research Council (previously the AHRB) for supporting this project.

References

Adamson, C. (2000) 'Who is making millions out of Who Wants To Be A Millionaire?', *Evening Standard*, 1 December.

Anon. (1998) 'UK programmers run up massive trade deficit', *New Media Markets*, 12 November.

—- (1998a) 'Britain: UKTV Blues', *The Economist*, 12 December.

—- [Observer Column] (2001) 'Dream on', *Financial Times*, 12 February.

Barlow, M. and Clarke, T. (2001) *Global Showdown: How the New Activists Are Fighting Global Corporate Rule*. Toronto: Stoddard Publishing.

Barnett, S. & Seymour, E. (1999) *A Shrinking Iceberg Travelling South: Changing Trends in British Television*. London: Campaign for Quality Television.

Barrett, M. (1997) 'New World To Conquer', *Marketing*, 20 February.

Barrie, C. (1999) 'Report condemns television trade gap', *The Guardian*, 8 April.

Bell, E. (2001) 'Dumb luck or good planning ?', *The Guardian*, 28 May.

Blanchard, S. (1989) *Screen Trading: An Audit of the Government's Plans for the Broadcasting Industry*. Manchester: Centre for Local Economic Strategies.

———(2001) *Broadcasting, Citizens Rights and Social Cohesion: A Response To The White Paper 'A New Future for Communications'*, AHRB Centre for British Film and Television Studies, Sheffield Hallam University, Sheffield. Online at: www.bftv.ac.uk/projects/wpresp.htm

Chenoweth, N. (2001) *Virtual Murdoch: Reality Wars on the Information Highway*.London: Secker and Warburg.

Chomsky, N. (1989) *Necessary Illusions: Thought Control In Democratic Societies*. Cambridge, MA: South End Press.

Clarke, S. (1998) 'The Hard Sell', *The Guardian*, 23 February.

——- (2001) 'Competitive tendencies', *FT Creative Business*, 13 February.

Collins, D. (2001) 'Drama and Crisis', *Creation*, May: 35–38.

Davis, A. (2000) 'Public relatios, business news and the reproduction of corporate elite power', *Journalism*, 1 (3): 282–304.

Department for Culture, Media and Sport (1998) *Creative Industries Mapping Document*. London: Department for Culture, Media and Sport.

—- (1999a) *Building a global audience: British television in overseas markets – A report by David Graham and Associates*. London: DCMS.
—- (1999b) *Creative industries: UK television exports inquiry*. London: DCMS.
—- (1999c) *Creative industries exports: our hidden potential*. London: DCMS.
—- (2000) *Action Plan – Response to TV Exports Inquiry (July)*. London: DCMS.
—- (2001b) *Creative Industries Mapping Document 2001*. London: DCMS.
Department of National Heritage (1994) *The Future of the BBC: Serving the Nation, Competing World-wide*. Cm 2621, London: HMSO.
Fisher, M. and Owen, U. (eds) (1991) *Whose Cities ?* Harmondsworth: Penguin.
Gitlin, T. (1985) *Inside Prime Time*. New York: Pantheon Books.
Goodall, C. & Company and Graham, D. Associates (1997) *The Economics of the TV Programme Supply Chain: A Report for the Department for National Heritage*. Taunton: Chris Goodall & Company and David Graham Associates.
Graham, D. (2000) *Speech to the British TV Distributors Association Conference, September 2000, London*. Unpublished paper. London:British Television Distributors' Assocation.
Hall, S. (1998) 'The Great Moving Nowhere Show', *Marxism Today*, November/December 1998, pp. 9–14.
Hodgson, P. (2001) *Commerce and Culture – Regulating Communications. ITN* – European Media Forum Lecture, 12 February. London: ITC.
IFSL [International Financial Services London] (2001) *World Invisible Trade 2001*. London: IFSL.
Jury, L. (2001) 'Switched on to the American dream', *The Independent*, 10 April.
Kelsey, J. (1995) *Economic Fundamentalism*. London: Pluto Press.
Labour Party (1997) *Create the future – A strategy for cultural policy, arts and the creative economy*. London: Labour Party.
Lang, T. and Hines, C. (1993) *The New Protectionism: Protecting the Future Against Free Trade*. London: Earthscan Publications.
Mandelson, P. and Liddle, R. (1996) *The Blair Revolution – Can New Labour Deliver?* London: Faber and Faber.
McArthur, J. R. (2000) *Selling 'Free Trade': NAFTA, Washington and the Subversion of American Democracy*. New York: Hill and Wang.
McChesney, R. W. (2001) 'Global Media, Neoliberalism and Imperialism', *Monthly Review*, 52 (10): 1–19.
McCrae, H. (2001) 'How Harry Potter can work magic on our trading deficit', *The Independent*, 24 June.
Miyajima, H., Kikkawa, T. and Hikino, T. (eds) (1999) *Policies for Competitiveness: Comparing Business-Government Relationships in the 'Golden Age of Capitalism'*. Oxford: Oxford University Press.
Mulgan, G. and Worpole, K. (1986) *Saturday Night or Sunday Morning?* London: Comedia Publishing Group.
Office for National Statistics (2000) *United Kingdom Balance of Payments*. London: The Stationery Office.
Palast, G. (2001) 'Not so fast, Tony. You'll have to earn your keep', *The Observer*, 25 February.
Phillips, M. (2000) *Speech to the British TV Distributors Association Conference, September 2000, London*. Unpublished paper. London: British Television Distributors' Association.
Porter, M. E. (1990) *The Competitive Advantage of Nations*. Basingstoke: Macmillan.
Powell, M. (1998) *Somewhere Over The Rainbow: The Need for Vision in the Deregulation of Communications Markets*. Speech to the Federal Communications Bar Association (New York Chapter), New York, 27 May. Available online at: www.fcc.gov/commissioners/previous/powell/speeches.html
—- (2001) *Speech to British American Inc, London May 24*. Available online at: www.fcc.gov/commissioners/previous/powell/speeches.html
Sanghera, S. (2001) 'Hat Trick have picked the team. Can they score the next big hit ?' *FT Creative Business*, 1 May.

Scott, A. (2000) *Running On Empty: 'Modernising' the British and Australian Labour Parties*. London: Pluto Press.

Shannon, S. (1999) 'Britain's TV shows 'too dull to sell abroad'', *Evening Standard*, 19 April.

Teivainen, T. (2002) *Enter Economism, Exit Politics: Experts, Economic Policy and the Damage to Democracy*. London: Zed Books.

Turner, A. (2001) *Just Capital – The Liberal Economy*. London: Macmillan.

Willis, J. (1999) 'On broadcasting: our transatlantic success story', *The Guardian*, 31 May.

Chapter 4

Indigenous culture and the politics of place: regulation for regionalism in British broadcasting

Sylvia Harvey

This chapter explores some the ways in which one nation state – the United Kingdom – has constructed the categories of national and regional broadcasting, thereby linking this most immaterial of communicative media to the physical and political geographies of place and space. 'Regionalism' is seen as one of the possible sub-categories of the indigenous in cultural production, and the role of the state in regulating for regionalism is examined with reference to selected historical and recent examples. Through these examples the accelerated global traffic in audio-visual products can be placed in a different and perhaps more critical context. The trade in sounds and images between countries and between continents opens up and transforms local cultures, but it can also erase the marks of difference and silence the voices of those who live in the shadows of the metropolis, away from the centres of political and economic power.

The idea of the indigenous and the role of the regional in a transnational world

In a world where the 'big actors' are transnational corporations, it becomes increasingly difficult for nation states and their governments to act in the interests of their citizens. The process of capital accumulation through profitable trading by these corporations is both dynamic and pitiless, despite a growing rhetoric (and sometimes a practice) of social responsibility in business affairs. The quest for profit and a better 'bottom line' is value free and relatively blind to human emotions and aspirations; it has no race, gender or creed; it is the re-fashioned Juggernaut of our times. Faced with the precision engineering and vast resources of this system and required to be supportive of the apparently unstoppable forces of globalisation, elected governments have found their own powers diminished and their sovereignty questioned.

The United Nations (UN) might be seen as the democratic shadow sister of this Juggernaut. The UN rose from the ashes of the Second World War and was created, in part, out of the provisions of the 1941 Atlantic Charter with its aspiration to bring an end to 'fear and want' and designed to create a 'wider and more permanent system of general security' (Sands, 2005: 240–241). Since then, the role of the UN has been radically questioned by powerful players and its resolutions – designed among other things to bring peace with justice in Palestine/Israel – have been routinely ignored. The UN – and Enlightenment – project of dispute resolution through diplomacy and reasoned debate has been overshadowed by the naked show of force. And the principle of national sovereignty and of inviolable borders has been shown to be as much in question in the twenty-first century as in previous eras, as the invasion of Iraq in 2003 appears to demonstrate, albeit with the added complication of new international human rights arguments and obligations.

The nation state has been challenged both from within and without: in the western world by those 'new social movements' that have attacked elite or dominant voices claiming to embody and to represent national culture. In other parts of the world the challenge has come from the brave and often isolated opponents of dictatorial and undemocratic regimes. Moreover, the recent past has seen openly violent disputes about the 'state of the nation', and the spectacle of communal violence in India or of genocide in Rwanda and in Bosnia has demonstrated the continuing and dangerous power of those claiming to speak for or indeed to *be* the nation. The ability of national and transnational broadcasting to reflect and reflect upon the differences of ethnicity, culture, class and religion (differences that sometimes have a spatial or regional specificity) becomes increasingly important, even – or perhaps especially- in those countries where broadcasting is thought of primarily as a medium of entertainment. For, as distinct from the priorities of transnational entertainment and profit-driven television, the 'broadness' of broadcasting suggests a potential for dialogue across otherwise embattled cultural, experiential and faith boundaries.

It has become one of the truisms of the sociology of globalisation that the nation state has been hollowed out, superseded by new realities; and yet it has a strange, continuing and compelling presence even as national boundaries are crossed, in body or in spirit, many times a day. Widespread migration and the new cross-frontier satellite services have, together, created new and transnational communities of belonging as pointed out by Kevin Robins and Asu Aksoy in the case of migrant Turkish and Kurdish communities and as Naomi Sakr has indicated in respect of the new and critical pan-Arab services offered by Al Jazeera (Robins and Aksoy, 2005; Sakr, 2005). But the identification with 'homeland', mother tongue and the place of ones birth remains, and with this some continuing sense of national affiliation.

Saskia Sassen, with her particular interest in the culture and experience of migrants, has observed that what we now see is 'the collapse of sovereignty', noting also – of the newer media of communication – that 'electronic space overrides all existing territorial jurisdiction' (Sassen, 1996: 31 and 6). But the process of change is double-edged, and the future of the nation state is in dispute. For some the loss of national sovereignty is to be mourned and the powers of elected national governments to be fought for and revived as a mechanism of democratic accountability and a means for advancing the interests of the less powerful. For others the future – both culturally and economically – lies with an end to national borders and boundaries.

Chapter 4 • Indigenous culture and the politics of place

And this latter category of commentators itself divides sharply between those who advance the principles of global free trade and economic liberalism and those who organise internationally (for example, to advance the cause of labour or of peace) or who analyse and celebrate the hybrid cultures of the marginalized and dispossessed – whose migrant status is seldom the result of free choice.

Within the academic field of cultural studies the celebration of difference and diversity – and the politically inevitable and necessary challenge to an imposed monoculture of elite minorities – has also emphasised the significance of diaspora and the values of hybridity and heterogeneity. In a world of widespread migration and widespread racism, it has seemed preferable to validate the process of a dynamic mixing or interleaving of cultures. Within this frame of reference the positive advocacy of traditional indigenous culture has come to be seen – by some commentators – as isolationist, exclusionary and regressive. There is some merit in this scepticism given the role of 'send them home' racists, the murderous actions of anti-semites and racial purists and the more recent rise of Islamophobia. In the light of these race and place-based forms of political supremacism, the newer celebration of hybridity and diversity and the refusal of claims of superiority based on the fact of being born in and belonging to 'this place', are welcome and necessary.

And yet the role of the nation state and of indigenous, not imported culture are also worthy of careful attention. This is especially so if we bear in mind the distinction made by Geoffrey Nowell-Smith, elsewhere in this volume, between cultural goods (commodities to be traded in the market) and cultural exchange (the experiences of human beings who pass between cultures). Broadcasting policy in the relatively rich country of Britain has reflected the value placed upon geographically specific modes of representation and has, to some extent, enabled these forms of representation. Thus it has recognised the distinct cultures and experiences of those living in the four nations of the United Kingdom: England, Northern Ireland, Scotland and Wales and the differences also embodied in the regions of England.

This recognition is present in the long policy tradition of making provision for the 'nations and regions' in British broadcasting; a tradition and an associated debate that stretches from the 1920s to the present. The second section of this chapter will explore some examples of the tension between London considered as the hub of broadcasting, of empire, of national politics and of the national economy and the demands of the relatively subordinated nations and regions. From the formation of the BBC in the 1920s, through to the creation of regionally-based commercial broadcasting in the 1950s and to the apparent recognition of a role for regionalism in the early twenty-first century the issue of centre-periphery relationships has been played out across the terrain of broadcasting.

It is one of the more obvious features of modernity that in many, if not most, societies a wide variety of cultural forms are available, mixed or juxtaposed. But it is also the case that the *markets* in cultural goods do not always reflect the full range of cultural experiences and interests and that particular media markets – cinema and television for example – can become dominated by imported goods, leaving little opportunity for the circulation of indigenously produced work. The United Kingdom offers an interesting example of a country where import dominance and the marginalisation of indigenous production can be found on one medium but not in

49

another. Thus the institution of cinema in Britain has – since the 1920s – been dominated by imported films, while the medium of broadcasting has been dominated by indigenously produced programmes.

In 2004 UK films took a 5 per cent share of the value of cinema box office, with an additional 18 per cent share for UK-USA co-productions (UK Film Council, 2005:12). While the output figures for British television in the same year told a very different story. On the two most popular television channels, BBC1 and ITV1, UK-originated programming amounted to – respectively – 82 per cent and 85 per cent of transmission time These high proportions of indigenous material may be largely the result of the cultural preferences of audiences, but they are also underwritten by a distinctive history of institutions and by statutory obligations or regulations requiring original programme proportions of 70 per cent for BBC1 and 65 per cent for ITV1 (Ofcom, 2005a: 219). It is important to note that in British regulation the word 'original' (not 'British' or 'European') is used, but the 'original' programmes referred to are predominantly made within the UK.

In offering here a broadly positive account of public policies designed to protect and to encourage 'indigenous' and more specifically 'regional' production, it is important to have some understanding of the history and use of the term 'indigenous'. The word derives from the Latin and refers to the fact of being born in a country or being native to a place. It can also be traced in relationship to the history of European imperialism and to the terrible history of forced migration represented by the European slave trade conducted between Africa and the Americas. One English dictionary situates the word by citing its use in the work of a mid-seventeenth century writer, Sir Thomas Browne, speaking of South America:

> Although ... there bee ... swarmes of Negroes serving under the Spaniard, yet were they all transported from Africa ... and are not indigenous or proper natives of America. (Oxford English Dictionary, 1989)(OED)

What this citation usefully underlines is the notion that 'the indigenous' only becomes an issue when it is contrasted with that which is not indigenous, with that which has been exported or transported and is therefore found, as it were, in a 'wrong' or unexpected place. It is not surprising, in this respect, to see the word being used in the context of a great historical up-rooting of peoples. By contrast, the idea of the sacred inviolability of place, often linked to natural forces, can be considered in the light of the word 'autochthonous', a term deriving from a Greek adjective meaning 'sprung from the land itself'. An autochthon is a human being 'sprung from the soil' and the term may also denote the 'earliest known dwellers in any country', the original inhabitants or 'aborigines' (OED, 1989). The association of the forces of nature with the specificity of place can have negative consequences as, for example, in providing justification for aggressive nationalism and the parochialism that attacks 'in-comers' or foreigners. But it also has positive aspects linked to the idea of 'mother tongue' and of 'homeland'.

Associated with the word 'native' the term 'indigenous peoples' has also acquired negative connotations, largely as a result of the history of colonialism or as a consequence of the ability of an economic elite to travel in times when poorer people were tied to the place where they were born. The OED refers to an 1823 publication that makes a clear link between 'being native' and 'being backward', claiming: 'the untravelled population of any town, wrapt up in incipient simplicity are natives'. One last link in this web of words takes us to the term 'provincial'. Akin to the negative uses of the word 'native' the term 'provincial' distinguishes between the sophistication of the metropolitan centre and the ignorance or simplicity of those located at a distance from that centre. Thus Samuel Johnson in 1755 spoke of the 'provincial, rude ... unpolished' and the Oxford English Dictionary elaborates on the twentieth century meaning of the term in this way:

> Having the manners or speech of a province ... exhibiting the character, especially the narrowness of view ... attributed to inhabitants of 'the provinces'; wanting the culture or polish of the capital. (OED, 1989)

It is perhaps worth noting in passing here, that whereas the English provinces or regions do not have capital cities, the states of a federal republic – for example Germany or the United States – do have both capital cities and local legislatures for each of their states or *Länder*. Thus the negative associations of the term 'provincial' – by contrast with the culture of the one national capital – may be less apparent.

The term 'region' or 'regional' appears by contrast to be relatively free of the negative judgements associated in the United Kingdom with the term 'provincial'. Regions are also not 'of the centre' or 'of the capital city' but they are defined in a more neutrally descriptive way as: 'tract of land, space, place, having more or less definitely marked boundaries or characteristics' (OED, 1989).

The range of meanings and associations of the term *indigenous* are more-or-less implicit; it requires some effort to excavate the origins and implications of the word. However, there has been more explicit debate about the role of *nations* in the historical construction of the United Kingdom. Indeed the name of the country itself alludes to the various nations or 'kingdoms' that make it up (the nations of England, Northern Ireland, Scotland and Wales) and, if only by implication, to the wars that were fought to create it. Since the beginnings of British broadcasting in 1922, the issue of 'nations and regions' has been recognised as politically sensitive, even though local legislatures have only appeared (or in the case of Scotland re-appeared after a gap of several hundred years) in the recent past. The elected Welsh and Northern Ireland Assemblies were created, respectively, in 1997 and 1998; the Scottish Parliament was established in 1999.

It will be apparent from this brief digression into the use and definition of particular words that the terms 'indigenous', 'provincial' and 'regional' have a history of complex usage and that recent developments in cultural theory have (for understandable reasons) avoided any validation of the concept of the indigenous preferring instead the concept of hybridity. In the next section of this chapter we shall consider examples of three 'moments' in the history of British broadcasting when the idea of regional broadcasting – considered as a positive force, associated with difference and diversity and offering an alternative to the metropolitan vision of the capital city – emerged and was consolidated or challenged.

Regional broadcasting in Britain: Origins

The developments selected for brief consideration here can all be associated with the legislative or quasi-regulatory actions of the British state and, more specifically, with three parliamentary documents: the Ullswater Report of 1936, the Television Act of 1954 and the Communications Act of 2003.

The BBC enjoyed an exclusively licence-fee funded and state-supported monopoly of broadcasting up until 1955 and had, in its earliest days, provided forms of more-or-less local broadcasting. During the 1920s the configuration of transmitters and the provision of local programmes gave to particular localities a sense of ownership of the still very new radio services. And there was also some recognition of the significant link between language and culture with programmes in the Welsh language being broadcast from the main BBC transmitter from 1929 (Scannell and Cardiff, 1991: 298). Although cost was and remains a factor; as a 1926 official Minute recorded: 'The best can only be given where the funds available are spent upon a few good programmes sent ... to many centres rather than diluted to make every centre an originator' (Briggs, 1995b: 284).

When the BBC moved to centralise control of the service in London, closing down some local provision, there was strong opposition. In the period between 1926 and 1928, for example, the civic authorities and Chamber of Commerce in Sheffield conducted a sustained campaign designed to retain a local transmission service. The campaign was lost when the Sheffield station was closed in 1929. This closure was in fact part of a plan to reorganise the transmitter network and to extend choice by offering a regional as well as a national service throughout the UK (Scannell and Cardiff, 1991: 319–320). But this is not how matters were perceived in South Yorkshire at the time, and as the BBC's Chief Engineer had earlier remarked 'relay stations foster a provincial enthusiasm difficult to appreciate in London' (Briggs, 1995b: 283).

Support for local broadcasting and the provision of a space for local voices and concerns remained strong in the pre-welfare state era of the Hunger Marches and there were recurrent tensions between London and the regions. Thus in 1934 the Programme Director of the BBC's North Region insisted upon broadcasting a concert by unemployed musicians in Liverpool rather than a London concert, conducted by a musician of international standing and signalled as a broadcasting priority by staff at head office. In arguing for the importance of giving 'a platform to this Merseyside orchestra' the regional Director took the view that unemployment and its consequences were matters of more pressing interest to local listeners than the relay of a metropolitan event (Briggs, 1995b: 303–304).

This kind of successful intervention on behalf of regional interests was already part of an established tradition, carefully recorded in Scannell and Cardiff's excellent history of broadcasting between the First and Second World Wars. As early as 1927 another northern broadcaster, Ted Living (then Head of the BBC's Manchester station), had expressed concern about the increasing centralisation of broadcasting power and decision-making in London. In a paper providing a positive account of the cultural resources and characteristics of his region, Liveing noted:

> The trend of modern times is to centralize more and more in London the intellectual, artistic and musical life of the nation ... There is now a very significant danger that the provinces will eventually be so heavily denuded of their talent, more particularly in music and drama, that they will become culturally barren and will not continue to supply the capital with the life-blood that it needs (Scannell, 1993: 32)

Chapter 4 • Indigenous culture and the politics of place

The problem was (and is) a general one. And Scotland shared with the English regions a sense of under-development and marginalisation, its Regional Director complaining to London in 1929: 'One's wings are being clipped and one is being debarred from flight in so many directions' (Briggs, 1995b: 298). As we shall see the Parliamentary Ullswater Committee, set up in 1935 to make recommendations on the future of the BBC, was to take seriously such evidence of dissatisfaction in the nations and regions, and to endorse the pro-regional strand of thinking within the Corporation.

The BBC's Director-General, John Reith, was aware of the importance of drawing upon and reflecting the different experiences and cultural resources of Britain and spoke, for example, of the significance of the use of the Welsh language, believing that it constituted a 'bond of enormous value and importance'. In a similar vein he lamented (with a touch, perhaps, of conservative romanticism) the 'immense pity that the whole of Scotland is not Gaelic speaking' (Briggs, 1995b: 298–299). Reith's policy steer is evident in the preoccupations of other key BBC staff of the inter-war period. Thus Roger Eckersley, Director of Programmes and subsequently Director of Regional Relations, noted that the North Region was 'full of programme sources – industrial entertainment – and countryside … The Yorkshire dales, and the Lake District and the Derbyshire hills, have many stories waiting to be told'. In similar vein, a tour of duty in the Scottish highlands triggered the observation that 'there is a special beauty in hearing broadcasts from these remote places, if only as a contrast to the busy lives of the majority' (Eckersley, 1946: 189, 187). Eckersley's duties took him to all the BBC's regions and his Panglossian summary carries also something of the new interest in constructing a national ethnography, highlighted by the Mass Observation movement of the 1930s: 'All over Britain there is material waiting to be tapped, real unspoilt material coming from the heart and roots of the country itself … the core of Regional broadcasting' (Eckersley, 1946: 187).

Eckersley's autobiographical account may be seen to foreground the 'good moments' of regional activity and policy. Certainly he suggested that the days of 'serious friction between head office and the regions' were long gone and, with the classic myopia of the unselfconsciously powerful, attributed any earlier antagonisms to the existence of an 'inferiority complex' on the part of regional staff (Eckersley, 1946: 191).

This complacent view of regional policy and practice does not appear to have been shared by the Parliamentary Committee chaired by Viscount Ullswater and established in 1935 to review the future of the BBC and its Royal Charter. However, in considering at least some of the evidence, it became clear to the Committee that there were already moves afoot within the BBC that could deliver a more regionally and nationally sensitive service. Programme statistics from one sample region were requested from the BBC, and these demonstrated that between 1934 and 1935 the proportion of programmes originated within that region had increased (from 30 per cent to 42 per cent), and the proportion originated in London had decreased (from 38 per cent to 25 per cent), while a further 33 per cent of programmes in 1935 were supplied *from other regions*. These figures excluded 'other centralised types of programmes' such as news, weather, dance music and 'recitals of gramaphone records' but nonetheless appeared to demonstrate a devolutionary trend. Good statistics have a way of magically appearing for parliamentary investigations, but this Committee was sufficiently focused on the need for change to recommend that there should be 'increasing devolution of programme control and an increase in the broadcasting of material of regional origin, performance and interest'. The creation of separate broadcasting regions for Wales and for the north east of England was also supported (Ullswater Report, 1936: 10–12).

For its part the BBC acted to improve head office understanding of regional perceptions and concerns, moving Charles Siepmann – one of the senior figures in the Corporation – from his post as Director of Talks to the newly created position of Director of Regional Relations, even as the Parliamentary Committee was still sitting. By January of 1936 Siepmann had produced his *Report on Regions* and recognised both the 'contrasts in the conditions and attitudes of mind which obtain outside London' and (echoing the earlier words of Ted Living) a 'common pre-occupation with the dangers resulting from the increasing tendency for administrative, cultural and industrial concentration in the London area' (Briggs, 1995b: 272).

As a consequence of Siepmann's detailed analysis, coupled with Parliamentary pressure, the BBC's official *Annual* for 1936 acknowledged the views of the 'gloomy prophets' who had foretold the 'flattening out of regional characteristics under the steam roller of London tastes and ideas' but countered with an assurance that the network of regional stations would succeed in reflecting 'local life and local loyalties' and in strengthening the 'associations and traditions which have their roots in the soil and history of our native countryside' (Briggs, 1995b: 307). Later in the year the BBC's governing body was to accept the critical account offered in Siepmann's report, concurring with the notion that centralisation in the metropolis was a 'bad tendency' and asserting that BBC broadcasting might counter this by 'representing the local point of view and encouraging local talent' (Briggs, 1995b: 311).

The findings of the Ullswater Committee provide a convenient summary for some of the earliest actions of the British state in, at least indirectly, regulating for regionalism. What follows is a brief overview of developments in regional programming since the advent of commercially focused and market-based broadcasting in 1955.

Regional broadcasting: Competition and commercial pressures

By 1965, thirty years after the Ullswater investigations, a head of programmes from BBC West Region was to make the bleak observation that it was becoming difficult for staff to find 'any cogent reason for the existence of the regions, except in political terms of some cynicism'. The same commentator – Desmond Hawkins – had noted that *if* the BBC's famous and long-running television drama series *Z Cars* been produced from within the BBC region where the story was set (that is, in Liverpool, North Region), these same broadcasting regions could have become centres of cultural production and innovation (Briggs, 1995c: 653–654). It was to be 1982 before Liverpool was served by investment in a locally-produced and high profile contemporary drama series, *Brookside*, commissioned when David Rose, an experienced producer from the BBC Midlands Region at Birmingham Pebble Mill, had moved across to become Head of Drama at the new Channel 4 Television.

Chapter 4 • Indigenous culture and the politics of place

When still at the BBC, Rose had produced the politically-charged and abrasively contemporary drama about unemployment in Liverpool in the early years of Margaret Thatcher's premiership: *Boys from the Blackstuff* (1982) and knew something about obtaining funding for innovative and controversial projects. Some years later the writer David Hare was to endorse both the special quality of Rose's skills and the formative part played by regional culture in the honing of those skills. Referring to another BBC drama supported by Rose (*Penda's Fen*, 1974), Hare wrote: 'that is the whole BBC Birmingham culture right there, which was David Rose letting people do what they wanted and nobody in London knowing what was going on' (Cooke, 2003: 119).

So how had the dark mood about the role of the BBC regions, reflected by Hawkins in 1965, emerged? There were at least three reasons for this and for the general downgrading of the role of regional centres in the post-war period: the significantly higher costs of television production (compared with radio production), the emergence of a commercially driven and advertising funded competitor to the BBC in the shape of the new, regionally-based Independent Television companies (ITV), and a renewed centralist philosophy within the BBC, possibly itself the product of the new circumstances of competition but also a consequence of the closure of the regional radio service during the Second World War.

Liverpool might have had to wait until 1982 for significant investment in production, but the old BBC North region as a whole was to be radically transformed as a consequence of the first ITV franchise based in Manchester: Granada Television (1956 to the present). For it was Granada that was to develop – for the national ITV network – two of the most iconic programmes of British television: the long-running and extremely popular drama series: *Coronation Street* (1960 to the present) and the landmark current affairs series: *World in Action* (1963–98) (Finch, 2003).

The 1954 Television Act provided the legislative and regulatory framework for the fifteen companies that were eventually to make up the new ITV network. The main political purpose of the new law was to break the BBC monopoly, introducing choice for television audiences and opportunities for advertisers. But this act of Parliament inherited in some small way the legacy of the Ullswater Committee in requiring the new stations to broadcast 'a suitable proportion of matter calculated to appeal specially to the tastes and outlook of persons served by the station'. The word 'regional' appears not to be used in the law, although the word 'local' creeps into the provisions on advertising (Television Act, 1954: s3 (e); Second Schedule (7)).

In any networked broadcasting system, these regional 'opt-out' programmes, with subject matter of local interest, are expensive to make as funds are in a sense 'diluted' into the production of many rather than a single networked programme – as the 1926 BBC memo noted. However, despite an uncertain beginning, ITV's monopoly of television advertising between 1955 and 1982 was to give it deep economic reserves as well as generally high levels of profitability. In return, the network was to accept the regulatory challenge or burden of making dedicated opt-out programmes for each nation and region. As early as 1962 the regulatory body, the Independent Television Authority (ITA), was able to point out with pride that the ITV companies supplied some 80 per cent of all UK programmes 'of local interest for local use', with the clear implication that the BBC now fulfilled a minor role in this sector (Sendall, 1982: 387).

However, ITV's thirty-year role as the powerhouse of regional production was threatened by the very principle of competition that had created it. From 1993 it lost control of the sale of Channel 4's airtime and many more television competitors were to emerge in the course of the decade, challenging ITV's share of audience and of advertising revenue. In the ten years between 1993 and 2003 its share of the national audience nearly halved, dropping from 40 per cent to 23.7 per cent (BARB, 2006: TV Facts). The same period saw increased concentration of ownership with the two largest ITV companies – Carlton and Granada – merging in 2004 (Johnson and Turnock, 2005: 29).

The process of increased competition stemming from the deregulatory policies of the Thatcher and Blair governments had the effect of undermining the viability of regional provision in the commercial sector. This became explicit in 2005 when the new regulatory body, Ofcom, reduced by 50 per cent the amount of 'non-news' regional programming required from each of the ITV licencees in England, lowering the provision from three hours per week to one and a half hours. In the nations or 'national regions', however, higher levels of locally specific material were still required. This policy differentiation was justified in part on the grounds that Scotland, Northern Ireland and Wales had a 'culture and heritage' that led audiences to expect more extensive, dedicated programming provision (Ofcom, 2005b: 95, 101). Thus the Ullswater principle of an even-handed approach to making programmes that embodied the 'character and culture of a region' was effectively rejected. And, paradoxically, this rejection happened in an era when the dominant political rhetoric claimed an end of scarcity in the channels of broadcast communication.

This contemporary coda to the brief history of regulation for regionalism has, however, one more significant theme. The deregulatory principles embodied in the Communications Act of 2003 still embraced elements of public intervention, notably in respect of the requirement that public service broadcasters, including some commercial providers, should invest significant sums in the production of programmes 'outside the M25 area'. The M25 is the motorway that encircles London and this is perhaps the first time that a broadcasting law has enshrined a road name as the indicator of implied cultural objectives. The purpose is stated more clearly in a section that requires Ofcom to ensure that services include:

> A sufficient quantity of programmes that reflect the lives and concerns of different communities and cultural interests and traditions within the United Kingdom, and locally in different parts of the United Kingdom (Communications Act, 2003: s264 (6) (i) and (j)).

It remains to be seen in what ways the regulatory body will ensure that British television programmes, whether network or opt-out, fulfil this requirement for locally produced, indigenous material.

Acknowledgements: I would like to thank the Arts and Humanities Research Council for supporting the research for this chapter as part of the 'Public Policy and National Identity' project within the AHRB Centre for British Film and Television Studies. Thanks are also due to colleagues and friends in Sheffield and elsewhere who have worked to sustain a pluralism of resources within the UK nations and regions.

References

BARB (2006) URL: http://www.barb.co.uk/TVFACTS (accessed 24 January 2006).

Briggs, A. (1961/1995a) *The History of Broadcasting in the United Kingdom. Vol. I The Birth of Broadcasting 1896–1927*. Oxford: Oxford University Press.

Briggs, A. (1965/1995b) *The History of Broadcasting in the United Kingdom. Vol. II The Golden Age of Wireless 1927–1939*. Oxford: Oxford University Press.

Briggs, A. (1995c) *The History of Broadcasting in the United Kingdom. Vol. V Competition 1955–1974*. Oxford: Oxford University Press.

Communications Act, 2003.

Cooke, L. (2003) *British Television Drama. A History*. London: British Film Institute.

Finch, J. (ed) (2003) *Granada Television. The First Generation*. Manchester: Manchester University Press.

Eckersley, R. (1946) *The BBC and All That*. London: Sampson Low, Marston and Co.

Johnson, C. and Turnock, R. (eds) *ITV Cultures. Independent Television Over Fifty Years*. Maidenhead: Open University Press.

Office of Communications (Ofcom) (2005a) *The Communications Market 2005*. London: Ofcom.

Office of Communications (Ofcom) (2005) *Ofcom Review of Public Service Television Broadcasting. Phase 3: Competition for Quality*. London: Ofcom.

Robins, K. and Aksoy, A. (2005) 'Whoever Looks Always Finds: Transnational Viewing and Knowledge Experience' in J. Chalaby (ed) *Transnational Television Worldwide. Towards a New Media Order*. London: I.B. Tauris, pp. 14–42.

Sakr, N. (2005) 'Maverick or Model? Al-Jazeera's Impact on Arab Satellite Television', in J. Chalaby (ed) *Transnational Television Worldwide. Towards a New Media Order*. London: I.B. Tauris, pp. 66–95.

Sands, P. (2005) *Lawless World. America and the Making and Breaking of Global Rules*. London: Allen Lane/Penguin Books.

Sassen, S. (1996) *Losing Control? Sovereignty in an Age of Globalization*. New York: Columbia University Press.

Scannell, P. (1993) 'The Origins of BBC Regional Policy' in S. Harvey and K. Robins (eds) *The Regions, the Nations and the BBC*. London: British Film Institute.

Scannell, P. and Cardiff, D. (1991) *A Social History of British Broadcasting. Vol. I 1922–1939 Serving the Nation*. Oxford: Basil Blackwell.

Sendall, B. (1982) *Independent Television in Britain. Vol. I Origin and Foundation, 1946–62*. London: Macmillan.

Ofcom (2005) *The Communications Market 2005*. London: Ofcom.

Oxford English Dictionary (1989) Oxford: Clarendon Press.

Television Act, 1954. Current Law Statutes.

UK Film Council (2005) *UK Film Council Statistical Yearbook and Annual Report 2004–05*. London: UK Film Council.

Ullswater Report (1936) *Report of the Broadcasting Committee, 1935*. Cmd. 5091. London: HMSO.

SECTION II:
National Industries: Global Currents

Introduction

The six chapters in this section explore the complex interweaving of national interests and imagery with the interests of multi-national companies and the expectations of national and international audiences.

For the two small countries of Lebanon and Scotland Dima Dabbous-Sensenig and Duncan Petrie explore, respectively, the opening out of national markets to imported film and television programming and the development of local policies designed to facilitate modest export activities in film. Dabbous-Sensenig identifies a history of policies adopted by Arab states to regulate trade flows in the audio-visual sector, seeing these as motivated 'more by authoritarian tendencies and a desire to control the flow of information ... than by any genuine interest in protecting and promoting local culture'. However, Lebanon is an unusual case in being the first Arab country to introduce legislation to create and regulate private broadcast media. And this legislation includes requirements for the promotion of locally-produced programmes; though most of this local output is in the cheaper genre of the talk show. In the cinema sector by contrast, and where no national content quotas exist, some 90 per cent of films screened are American with most of the rest coming from France. The public story-telling that the genre of drama provides is thus massively dominated by tales from other cultures. In a further contrast, Petrie points to some recent successes for Scottish films screened at festivals abroad, arguing that these effectively present – for audiences both at home and abroad – 'various aspects of contemporary Scotland and its distinct cultural, social and geographical formations'.

Other chapters address some of the complexities of cross-border traffic and the ways in which emerging national industries may rely for their development on the intervention of experts in other countries. Thus Lúcia Nagib identifies the powerful role of international sponsors and investors in delivering 'international hits' for the

TRADING CULTURE

New Brazilian Cinema and contrasts this with a continuing 'auteurist trait' that serves as a 'national contribution to a transnational language under construction'.

Albert Moran and Michael Keane further advance an examination of the cross-border theme but in relationship to the growth of markets within the global region or 'territory' of the Asia-Pacific. Their particular focus is on the growth of 'copy-cat TV' as television formats are increasingly traded across this large and diverse area. John Sinclair considers multi-lingual developments within what is probably the single most valuable market in the world – the United States – tracing the consolidation of Spanish language television within this market and its sub-sectors.

Finally, Manjunath Pendakur considers the changing configurations of the film and television industries in India, exploring both the increasing popularity and financial value of Bollywood films sold abroad and the increasing liberalisation (and class stratification) in the delivery of an expanding cinema sector at home.

Chapter 5

Ahead of the bandwagon: Lebanon's free media market

Dima Dabbous-Sensenig

Introduction

With the launch, in May 2005, of another intergovernmental meeting of experts working on a second draft for a UNESCO proposed Convention on Cultural Diversity, the issue of trading culture is, once again, placed high on the international agenda. One of the main motors behind such heightened interest in a convention – and not merely another 'declaration' – on cultural diversity is the need to create a legally binding international agreement 'to implement the principle that culture cannot be reduced to a commodity', in recognition of the twofold nature – economic and cultural – of cultural expressions (UNESCO, 2005). This new instrument, more importantly, would allow states to respond to 'specific threats to cultural diversity in the era of globalization', by allowing 'each country to exclude its cultural policies, including 'audio-visual services'... from 'free trade' deals like the WTO'.* In other words, potentially, such a convention would allow member states of the World Trade Organisation (WTO) to maintain or establish policies that can promote cultural diversity – such as supporting public service broadcasting, non-profit, and community media – against the liberalizing agenda of the WTO, and without fear of retaliation. It would also allow them to impose local ownership requirements, language requirements, and quotas for local films and music; and to grant support for local artists among other measures.** The need for such a convention can only be fully understood against the backdrop of the decisive incorporation, nearly a decade ago, of the cultural industries into the framework of free trade negotiations within the WTO. At the time, this incorporation was achieved with the establishment of the General Agreement on Trade in Services (GATS) during the Uruguay Round of trade talks concluded in 1994, when a specific reference was made to 'communication services'. With this first multilateral trade agreement covering services, new obligations could now be imposed on member states in the audio-visual sector. These include, among others, minimizing

---

*   See 'UNESCO convention on cultural diversity: key documents', available online: http://www.mediatrademonitor.org/taxonomy/page/or/44 (accessed on 28 May, 2005).

** See 'Coalition for cultural diversity comments on UNESCO draft', available online: http://www.mediatrademonitor.org/node/view/168 (accessed on 10 February, 2005).

domestic regulation (e.g. content and ownership requirements) and avoiding the 'trade-distortive' effects of subsidies (Freedman, 2003: 286).

The launch of the process of liberalizing services (including cultural products) was, however, far from smooth. Indeed, the talks were nearly derailed by the anti-liberalization or 'protectionist' camp led by France which sought to exclude audio-visual products from the treaty, through what was eventually, though erroneously, known as 'the cultural exception clause' (Torrent, 2002). The rationale behind such a position was that any lifting of state support for culture (tariffs, quotas, or subsidies) would tip the trade balance towards 'the fittest'; i.e. those countries or players with a comparative advantage (mainly the US in this respect) and would lead to an 'inundation' of world markets (especially those of smaller, poorer countries) with American cultural products, and consequently to the 'Americanization' of the world's cultures (Tomlinson,1997: 120–129).

In the present chapter, I will examine the implications (or likely effects) of liberalizing 'culture' within the framework of GATS on Lebanese cultural production and exchange, and the extent to which the fears of the 'protectionist' camp are justified or applicable to the Arab context. To that effect, I will assess existing Arab cultural policies in the area of film and broadcasting, taking Lebanon as a case study. This will be done by studying Lebanon's national cultural policy vis-à-vis film and broadcasting, and by quantifying, as much as possible through original research and interviews with key national players (keeping in mind the alarming lack of any officially released data on cultural trade), production and distribution in the area of film and broadcasting. Moreover, special importance will be given to Lebanon's recent WTO accession talks (namely its June 2004 *Offer on Specific Commitment in Services*). These negotiations not only reveal much about the state's policy on culture, they might also have a bearing on the future state of culture in the country and the region.

Finally, an assessment of the cultural production and exchange in both the film and broadcasting sectors in Lebanon will be made, by making use of and reflecting on theories of international communication, namely the theory of 'cultural imperialism' which is particularly relevant for this type of study. I will use the data collected in this chapter to 'test', in the Lebanese context, the effectiveness of this thesis which addresses the issue of imbalance in the international flow of cultural products and ultimately underlies the position of those opposed to liberalizing trade in culture (Tomlinson, 1997: 119–120).

Arab cultural policies or lack thereof

Alarm about the stark imbalance in the international flow of information (news and entertainment) was already sounded by UNESCO, with the publication in 1980 of the McBride report, *Many Voices, One World*. The objective of this landmark study was not only to document and raise awareness about such imbalances on an international scale, but more importantly to recommend measures to bring balance and equity to the existing lopsided information order. At the time, the response of several Western countries, led by the US, was that the report was anti-Western, pro-communist and seeking to curtail democracy internationally (Smiers, 2003:

174). Unfortunately, in the quarter of a decade since then, Arab cultural policies only managed to give credence to US led criticism. It seems that the measures adopted by Arab countries to rectify the imbalance in the flow of information and cultural products were motivated more by authoritarian tendencies and a desire to control the flow of information than by any genuine interest in protecting and promoting local culture. Indeed, a quick review of the changing regulatory environment since the McBride report shows that Arab cultural policies resulted almost exclusively in the setting up of a range of national and regional news agencies (Al-Deek, 1993). By contrast, hardly anything was done to enact cultural policies that could ensure the promotion and protection of local artistic life or to introduce legislation on private national audio-visual media, with a public service mandate that could help achieve, however partially, this goal. Moreover, whereas renewed interest in protecting local culture in Western Europe, especially in the wake of the introduction of GATS in the mid-1990s, found its most logical expression in the upholding of the public service ideals of publicly owned channels (PSB), such a discussion on the crucial role that can be played by PSB was entirely absent from official and public discourse in Arab countries. As private Arab satellites started proliferating as of the early 1990s and eventually challenged state control of the media in many Arab countries, criticism of their utterly commercial programming by both academia and civil society rarely if ever was informed by an understanding of the advantages, however limited or contested, that are normally linked with public service broadcasting in the West. Indeed,

> the practice of PSB in the Arab world is nonexistent, a missing link in the history of the evolution of broadcasting in the region: in less than a decade, the Arab world witnessed an abrupt shift from a situation of tight state control over terrestrial broadcast media to a situation where new private satellite channels were a dime a dozen. Questions over how to best deal with the changing environment in order to ensure fair representation, pluralism and diversity of content hardly ever surfaced in policy debates. (Dabbous-Sensenig, 2005: 141).

As I will argue later, it is precisely this lack of an enlightened, public-oriented approach to policymaking in the area of culture that undermines, among other things, any serious attempt to curb the liberalizing effects of GATS during accession talks by many Arab countries, including Lebanon.

The case of Lebanon

Lebanon stands out among all other Arab countries as being the first to have introduced legislation to regulate the private broadcast media, as early as 1994. Not only that, but, rather uncharacteristically in the Arab context, this legislation contains stipulations for the promotion of local cultural products (Article 7, paragraph 3). The Guidebook for Operating Conditions goes even further, giving a breakdown of the types and quantities of local content required by law (Dabbous-Sensenig, 2002: 37). By contrast to this distinct interest in promoting, on a legal basis, local culture on private radio and television, Lebanese cinema totally lacks state support. The only existing piece of legislation related to cinema is solely concerned with the physical aspect of movie theatres, such as size and safety measures (Decision no. 509 dated 19/12/1939).

In the following sections, I will study the existing regulatory framework for audio-visual media, and the current state of local cultural production and distribution in the area of television and film. The purpose of such a study is to examine both the position of the state on the issue of culture and the existing reality on the ground. Such an appraisal would help us assess the potential danger, if any, for Lebanese culture of liberalizing trade in culture in the wake of joining the WTO.

The Lebanese broadcasting scene: law vs. reality

Lebanon boasts of having a state broadcaster (Tele-Liban or TL) operating alongside four private television stations (FTV, NBN, LBC, and NTV), licensed since 1996. The operation of these stations is regulated by the Broadcasting Act of 1994. Concerning the production of local programming, Article 7 (Paragraphs 3 and 4) of the 1994 Act stipulates that the granting of a license to an applicant is conditional, among other things, upon the applicant's commitment to develop the national cultural industry (by hiring local talent) and, more specifically, upon the fulfillment of quotas for local production as specified in the accompanying Guidebook for Operating Conditions (or Decree 7997).

When compared with the quotas for local programming fixed by other 'protectionist' countries, the Lebanese quotas pale, to the extent of looking ridiculous indeed (Dabbous-Sensenig, 2002). This is especially true because the Lebanese Broadcasting Act was repeatedly sold as being modelled after the French audio-visual law (Dabbous-Sensenig, 2003). For instance, not only are the Lebanese quotas negligible by comparison to the French quotas, the Guidebook for Operating Conditions, unlike its French counterpart, is totally silent on the issue of *new* productions and scheduling time. Thus, Lebanese stations are allowed to schedule exclusively 'old content' or re-runs, and they can do so outside of prime time hours with impunity. In sum, the local content requirements are lax in more than one way, making it possible for private stations to dismiss the requirement to generate local content or to support the local artistic scene.

Having said that, it is still worth examining the breakdown of the percentage of local content required by law, since such a breakdown is revealing with respect to the state's policy toward culture. I will deal specifically with Lebanese dramatic production, since drama or fictional programming is the genre that most aptly reflects the cultural heritage and social norms and concerns of a given society. It is, moreover, the television genre which is most capable of engaging and providing employment to a wide range of artists (scriptwriters, actors, composers, etc). It can reflect local societal issues while having direct economic consequences for local talent and local cultural industries. The 1994 Act indeed acknowledges this importance in principle but fails to enforce it in any material or practical terms. According to the Guidebook of Operating Conditions, of the total annual compulsory 730 hours of local programming, thirteen hours should be dedicated to drama or fictional programming, be it 'inspired by Lebanese, Arab, or international history and literary heritage'. Since these thirteen hours are not exclusively about Lebanese cultural heritage, the Guidebook adds that 'the percentage of Lebanese programmes should make up at least 40 per cent of these hours'. In other words, a licensed private television station is required by law to produce no less than five hours and twelve minutes of locally

Chapter 5 • Ahead of the bandwagon

Table 1. Percentage of Lebanese local television production, Fall 2004–5

Average broadcast time: 16 hours per day★ (or 5840 broadcasting hours per year)	Future TV	LBC	Yearly quotas for local production as required by law (or 730 hours of local programming per year)
Local news	20.8%	8.8%	Not specified
Local variety shows, public affairs programming, political and social talk shows	46.1%	48.5%	2.8% of yearly programming (or 166 hours per year)
Local game shows	7.2%		1.5% of yearly programming (or 90 hours per year)
Local reality programming	1.8%	7.8%	Not specified
Locally produced drama with Lebanese issues or content	3.7%	3.9%	0.1% of total programming (or 5.2 hours per year)
Total local programming per year	79.7% (or 4508 hours of local programming per year)	68.9% (or 4156 hours of local programming per year)	12.5% (or 730 hours of local programming per year)
American programs (news and entertainment)	5.7%	15.5%	
Mexican drama series (telenovelas)	4.6%	12.1%	
Egyptian drama series	10%	3.5%	
Total foreign programming per year	20.3% (or 1147 hours per year)	31.1% (or 1876 hours per year)	

The percentages in this table are calculated by the author, based on the Fall 2004/2005 grid as published in the *Al-Mustakbal* daily newspaper between 3 January and 9 January, 2005. According to FTV and LBC programme managers, this grid, except during the month of Ramadan and periods of major political events, is subject to minor changes throughout the year (around 5 per cent). The calculations exclude overnight programmes (scheduled roughly between 12:00 a.m. and 7:00 a.m.) which consist of re-runs and contain no advertisements.

produced drama *about* Lebanon and Lebanese national heritage *annually*. This compulsory number of hours, for a station broadcasting sixteen hours per day, would roughly make up 0.1 per cent of its total broadcasting time per year. It is difficult, considering this very low required percentage, to see how existing regulation of the audio-visual sector would contribute to the development of local culture and local cultural industries.

A cursory look at the breakdown of programming on FTV and LBC allows us to make the following observations regarding actual local television output in Lebanon, and to contrast this output with the percentages fixed by law. Firstly, programming on these top-rated television stations is still predominantly locally produced. Secondly, almost half of this local programming (an average of 47 per cent of total yearly programming on LBC or FTV) is dedicated to cheaply produced talk shows (social, political, or entertainment), while Lebanese drama (consisting mostly of comedy and parody sketches and little 'serious' social drama in the present breakdown) is barely present on the screens (an average of 3.75 per cent of the yearly output on each station). On both stations, the production of games and reality shows is almost three times the production of local drama. Thirdly, FTV airs almost three times as many Egyptian dramatic series as it airs local drama (10 per cent of yearly output), while the same can be said about LBC with respect to Mexican *telenovelas* (12.1 per cent of yearly output). Finally, American programming is generally not very visible on these stations, though there are noticeable differences between the two stations (5.6 per cent on FTV vs. 15.5 per cent on LBC). This relatively modest American 'presence' is further reduced by having American programs scheduled either early in the morning (between 7:00 a.m. and 10:00 a.m.) or very late at night (after 10:30 p.m.).

In sum, it can be said that the quotas fixed by law are so low that de facto all local television stations are actually 'over-fulfilling their quota'. Indeed, the stations included in this study, FTV and LBC – which are also the two most watched and most profitable stations, both locally and regionally (Le Pottier, 2003: 56–63) – exceed the quotas fixed by law in all areas of local programming. In the aggregate, they provide six times as much local programming as is required by law (local programming on FTV and LBC is 80 per cent and 69 per cent respectively, or an average of 74 per cent, compared to a required 12 per cent), and their meagre yearly output in locally produced drama with Lebanese content (3.7 per cent for FTV and 3.9 per cent for LBC) is still dramatically higher than the legal quota (0.1 per cent). Even if one were to consider the quota related to drama in general (i.e. dramatic series that are locally produced but do not have to deal with Lebanese issues or themes), the existing output in local drama on FTV and LBC (an average of 220 hours a year for each station) is still at least 17 times as much as what the law requires (i.e. 13 hours a year).

The Lebanese film sector

In contrast to the broadcasting sector, where the state enacts (however ineffectively one might argue) some form of regulation to protect local culture, the film sector is entirely left 'on its own'. Except in the area of physical ownership of the movie theatres, where ownership – as a general rule applying to all acquisition of property – has to be Lebanese, Lebanese cinema suffers from the absence of state intervention or support (while censorship is duly exercised through the Sûreté Générale or internal police, as stipulated in the Law of 27 November 1947). Whereas local television stations, which also broadcast on satellite, create and give regional visibility to Lebanese programming, as we have already seen, Lebanese cinema is hardly ever produced or distributed locally or regionally. There are less than three feature films being produced annually, with only twelve made since 1990. Of these, hardly any are exhibited in local cinemas for the broad Lebanese public.

Chapter 5 • Ahead of the bandwagon

The problems facing the film sector in Lebanon are multi-faceted. To start with, there is a serious issue of funding, whether coming from local producers or the Ministry of Culture. In 2001, the Ministry of Culture finally introduced, for the very first time, a financial plan to support Lebanese cinema. The total sum allocated by the Ministry was $200 000, to be distributed among ten different films. Considering that a single fiction film can cost up to half a million dollars, and that such state subsidies barely cover five to ten per cent of the cost of a feature film, Lebanese

Fig. 1. Doing the deer dance in Verve *(Nigol Bezjian, Lebanon 2002).*

filmmakers have had to look for other sources of funding to make their films. With the lack of interest or mere absence of local producers, such funding has so far been predominantly provided for by the EU (through public service broadcasters such as ARTE or Channel Four or through the EuroMed Partnership agreement) (Dabbous-Sensenig, 2002).* Some filmmakers, especially those working on documentaries or short fiction films using digital cameras, were able to circumvent the funding problem altogether by producing what they call 'no budget' films. Nigol Bezjian, for instance, made an experimental short film about Armenian dance titled *Verve* for exactly $90, and admitted that it cost him more money to send the film abroad to participate in festivals than to make the film itself. Such very low production costs are of no surprise in Lebanon, with many dedicated filmmakers engaging a whole team of volunteer actors, editors, composers, cameramen, and so on, while they themselves perform multiple functions such as writers, directors, producers, and even distributors. Moreover, their video equipment is often made freely available

---

* Of the twelve feature-length Lebanese films made in the last fifteen years, 75 per cent are co-productions benefiting largely from EU, mostly French, money.

67

Fig. 2. 'Muron' carried out for blessing (Nigol Bezjian, Lebanon 2001).

by the institutions they work for, be they television stations or universities (Bezjian, 2005; Fouladkar, 2005).

While the difficulties of getting films made are innumerable, they are not insurmountable. The major problem is lack of distribution. Very few films ever get made, however even fewer films are shown to Lebanese audiences, including films that are award winning, both regionally and internationally. *When Maryam Spoke Out* (2001) is one such film. The director, Assad Fouladkar, who is also the screen writer and producer, had to add the double hat of promoter/distributor when trying to find an outlet for his film in Lebanon (Fouladkar, 2005). The fact that the film had collected several awards, including an award for best actress at the Cairo Film Festival, did not seem to have a positive influence on its distribution. Quite the contrary, Fouladkar actually believes festival awards make a Lebanese film less attractive to local exhibitors, who tend to associate these awards with elitism or high-brow art, and prefer the predictable popularity and profitability of Hollywood films.

Whatever the reasons that push Arab or local exhibitors to shun local films, the end result is that these films are not shown to local audiences. *Maryam* was thus neither shown in cinemas in Egypt (where it won a prestigious award), nor shown in multiplexes throughout Lebanon, the way a Hollywood movie would be. Its director finally managed to have it shown in two movie theatres, only one of which was located in the capital Beirut (Sodeco 6). Eventually, and despite the success of the film in Sodeco 6, *When Maryam Spoke Out* had to be removed to make way for a European production, since the owners had an EU contract allowing them to receive cash subsidies in return for showing European films for at least 40 weeks per year

Chapter 5 • Ahead of the bandwagon

Fig. 3. When Maryam Spoke Out *(Assad Fouladkar, Lebanon 2001).*

(Fouladkar, 2005). It should be noted here that movie distribution and exhibition in Lebanon is a duopoly involving two major circuits, Empire and Planète, that successfully introduced multiplexes to Lebanon in the mid-1990s. Out of a total of 82 movie theatres in Lebanon, Empire owns 37 theatres, Planète owns 28, while the remaining seventeen are independent. Between the two of them, Empire and Planète attract 89 per cent per cent of Lebanese moviegoers (Eid, 2005). It is this duopoly in the area of film distribution, more than the absent role of the state or lack of funding, which has been denounced by many local artists, and considered to be a major hindrance to the visibility of Lebanese cinema on Lebanese screens.* The result of all these adverse circumstances is that Lebanese cinema is largely absent from Lebanese screens, making up barely one per cent of the total number of movies exhibited per year. By contrast, 90 per cent of the films played are American, while the remaining nine per cent are French.**

These results echo, if not surpass other results worldwide, and especially in Europe, where, on average, 80 per cent of all movies played in Holland, Britain, or Germany are American (Smiers, 2004: 60–62). One reason for the increasing dominance of American films on European screens, in addition to the rise in the number of multiplexes (Smiers, 2003: 31), is attributed to the powerful distribution structures and methods of major US studios. Local exhibitors are forced, as part of a package deal, to rent blockbusters on the condition that they will show other American films of less commercial value from the same distributor. As a result of this 'block booking'

---

*   *Al-Anwar* newspaper, 20 June 2005, p. 17.

**   These percentages are derived from a total of about 240 films exhibited yearly in Lebanon (Eid, 2005).

practice, local screens are usually saturated with American films, leaving little or no space for other, non-American films.

Interestingly, whereas this explanation may be true in the case of European exhibitors, major Lebanese exhibitors operate under entirely different conditions. These companies are vertically integrated with major Hollywood studios (e.g. Columbia, Fox, MGM and Disney), through an arrangement that provides them with a regular, uninterrupted supply of 'free' films throughout the year, in return for a 50 per cent share of box office sales that go to the US studios with which they are affiliated. As such, only the few existing independent local exhibitors end up having block-booking enforced on them (Eid, 2005).

In sum, Lebanese films, *when* they are made, are made against incredible odds. To start with, they lack state support and local sources of funding (the market is too small to be attractive for local investors and producers). Even if digital video and personal initiatives and volunteerism have made it possible to produce high quality films that often make it to international festivals and collect awards, the major problem is still distribution. Indeed, as Smiers duly warns, 'the real war ... is over *the control of distribution channels worldwide* '(Smiers, 2003: 30, emphasis in original).

Lebanon's accession to the WTO

Perhaps equally revealing of the Lebanese government's position on culture is the way it is conducting its accession talks with the WTO, specifically regarding the General Agreement on Trade in Services (GATS). An observer country since April 1999, Lebanon submitted its *Offer on Specific Commitments in Services* in June 2004 (Makki, 2000). Unlike the offer of several other Arab countries who are either already WTO members or in the process of accession, Lebanon's offer does not include the audio-visual sector (Makki, 2005). The sector is instead part of the 'List of Article II exemptions'. Such an exemption allows Lebanon to request the extension of preferential access and treatment – both measures prohibited by Article II of GATS (Most-Favored-Nation Treatment) – 'to audio-visual works originating from countries with whom Lebanon is a party to bilateral or plurilateral agreements' for the purpose of promoting 'cultural links with the countries concerned'.* Though by doing so Lebanon joins a long list of WTO members who have made use of the MFN exemptions in order 'to opt out of non-discrimination commitments' (Freedman, 2003: 289), such a decision on culture should not be construed as being symptomatic of an active state policy to maintain the regulation and protection of Lebanese national culture. As we have already seen, no such policy in film or broadcasting truly exists in the first place to justify such a position. Quite expectedly, the exemption of the audio-visual sector is the result of the EU putting pressure on Lebanon, which may lead to Lebanon losing its accession to the WTO by antagonizing the American negotiators, should this exemption be maintained (Makki, 2005). Moreover, according to Fadi Makki, Director General of the Lebanese Ministry of Economy and head of the negotiating team, the entire negotiations are

---

* See Lebanon's Offer on Specific Commitments in Services on the Ministry of Economy and Trade website: http://www.economy.gov.lb/MOET/English/Panel/Trade/InternationalTradeAgreements/WTO.htm (accessed 20 May 2005).

being conducted single-handedly by the Ministry of Economy and Trade, without any input whatsoever from the Ministry of Culture (for cinema), and much less from the Ministry of Information (for broadcasting). As he further explains, the negotiating team is operating in a statistical vacuum, especially in the area of cultural production and exchange, and receives no specific recommendations or proposals concerning its negotiations on culture – 'just complaints' from local anti-globalization NGOs. Though Makki is keen on 'opening up carefully', through the establishment of 'joint ventures' and co-productions that 'make good business sense', Lebanon will most probably end up 'parachuting' offers (in the audio-visual sector). In the end, under constant pressure from the US and Japan 'which are aware of and resentful of EU pressure', Lebanon will probably have no choice but to make commitments in its audio-visual sector if it ever hopes to join the WTO, which it considers inevitable (Makki, 2005).

What's GATS got to do with it? Concluding theoretical comments on Lebanon's trade in culture

This study set out to assess the impact on Lebanon of liberalizing culture in the wake of joining the WTO. It seeks to answer the following questions: To what extent can one speak of imbalanced cultural flow in the case of Lebanon? In case this imbalance does exist, to what extent has the country been able to enact legislation to correct it? Does GATS threaten to scrap these 'corrective' policies should they exist? This assessment can not be carried out without first understanding what cultural policies have been introduced in Lebanon, and how effective these policies are in protecting and promoting local culture. This chapter started out by mapping, very roughly, cultural policies in the Arab world, and argued that, individual differences notwithstanding, national debate on cultural regulation in the Arab world is generally impoverished. Cultural policy is marked by the absence of a tradition of public service broadcasting and of a comprehensive approach to legislation that can actively promote the production and distribution of national culture. Conclusions will now be drawn regarding Lebanon exclusively. The Lebanese case cannot be said to be representative of the situation in other Arab countries, mainly because it stands alone with its legalized, private national terrestrial broadcasting sector that has also been successfully marketed regionally. Syria, for instance, allows no private broadcasting, but has a thriving state and private sector for the production of Syrian television drama, and offers state funding for the production (but not distribution) of film through its National Film Foundation. Concluding remarks will therefore be based on the Lebanese specificity and the (likely) effects on local culture of WTO-imposed liberalization in the audio-visual sector, even though some of these remarks may be applicable to other Arab countries.

Concern with the imbalances in the international flow of cultural products and with the consequences of such imbalances on national expression of identity and the democratic process continues to be at the heart of the ongoing debate on liberalizing culture. Particularly relevant for this debate is the concept of 'media imperialism', which, as early as the 60s, was advanced by leftist researchers who pointed out the existence of the imbalance in cultural trade and the injustice suffered by developing countries because of this imbalance. Increasingly, however, this theory of international communication has been challenged by many scholars. It has been found to be 'totalitarian', 'untested', undifferentiated, and problematic, for instance, when equating 'presence' of American cultural products' with 'influence', since such an equation presumes that viewers' agency 'no longer matters' (Boyd-Barrett, 1998: 157). This does not mean, however, that the concept of 'media imperialism' is a 'dead concept', or that it does not have much to offer as an analytical tool when 'modified for application to the present time' (Boyd-Barrett, 1998: 157).

Particularly relevant for the present study, which is strictly limited to studying cultural policies and trade in culture in Lebanon, Boyd-Barrett's definition acknowledges the 'multi-dimensionality' of media forms and activity, and 'recognizes that imperialism could vary between different media, and between different levels, dimensions or spheres of activity within any one sector of the media industries' (Boyd-Barrett, 1998: 163).

Indeed, in the case of Lebanon, it is very difficult to speak outright of American or Western cultural dominance, though many local artists and intellectuals readily do so. The picture is significantly more complex than the one put forth by the traditional media imperialism thesis, and reflects, among other things, significant changes in the audio-visual landscape since that thesis became increasingly popular in the 1970s. Firstly, the American (or more generally Western) dominance in Lebanon is predominantly *sector-specific*, being very strongly felt in one sector (film) – with 99 per cent of films being American and/or European – and comparatively negligible in the broadcasting sector (10 per cent of programming is American and almost none is European). With three quarters of the programming on FTV and LBC being locally produced, Lebanese TV is still very much local, proving that 'content scarcity' (Galperin, 1999) or the need to fill increasingly available airtime space with cheaply available American programming is not applicable in the Lebanese context. More importantly, it proves that 'cultural distance' (Galperin, 1999) is indeed the best market barrier against the uneven flow of 'foreign' programming, and that it is undoubtedly more effective in protecting and promoting local culture than any quotas on local content that might be imposed by the state regulators. It is so effective, in fact, that 'price' ceases to be a major criterion for the purchase of some television programmes and, in some cases, not even foreign programming that is free of charge is attractive to television programmers (Bezjian, 2005).

Secondly, in addition to being sector-specific, this Western 'dominance' is also, though to a lesser extent, *'channel-specific'*, with noticeable differences in local vs. foreign content between the two major terrestrial Lebanese stations studied. First, LBC has 50 per cent more foreign programming than FTV, with an average of 30 per cent a year (FTV averages 20 per cent of foreign programming a year). One further qualification is required here, since an undifferentiated definition of 'foreign' could influence results when mapping the international flow of cultural products. In other words, it is important, analytically, to distinguish between different types of 'foreign programming'. Interestingly, while 'foreign' at LBC is predominantly 'American' *and* 'Mexican', with Egyptian drama lagging behind, the picture is the reverse when it comes to FTV. 'Foreign' at FTV is predominantly 'Egyptian' (10 per cent of total programming), and only secondarily 'American' and 'Mexican' (5.7 per cent and 4.6 per cent respectively). These channel-specific differences cannot be simply explained in economic terms (cheap vs. expensive products), or even cultural ones ('cultural distance' vs. 'cultural proximity'). Rather, the explanation seems to lie with corporate image, with LBC, despite its regional Arab outreach, successfully maintaining a strongly 'Western' image compared to the more 'conservative', 'less Westernized' FTV (Le Pottier, 2003).

Thirdly, when dealing exclusively with television dramas, it should be noted that the dominant 'foreign' dramas featured on Lebanese television do not originate at all from the developed countries, and here of special significance is the US. In this particular area, local drama is eclipsed by Egyptian drama on FTV (10 per cent vs. 3.7 per cent) and Mexican *telenovelas* on LBC (12.1 per cent vs. 3.9 per cent). This illustrates what Smiers refers to as 'marginal imperialism', where regional (as opposed to international) players capable of taking 'local characteristics into account' come to dominate certain markets (Smiers, 2003: 110). In the Arab regional context, Egypt certainly came to play this dominant role both in the area of broadcasting and film, so much so that 'Arabic', as in 'Arabic film', has long become synonymous with 'Egyptian'. In the area of film, Egyptian dominance has been easily secured because of lack of competition and the meager output, to date, by all other Arab countries.[*] In the area of broadcasting the Egyptian state has been following a more aggressive policy of production and distribution of television drama series, in an attempt to block out the (relatively recent) competition from Syria among other countries. Just as Hollywood internationally swamps movie theatres with American movies through the practice of 'block-booking', Egypt tries to swamp regional television screens with 'forced package deals' that seek to drive out independent productions (Bezjian, 2005).

Finally, it should be born in mind that any definition of 'local' is bound to be conceptually problematic, and should be used with skepticism, especially when trying to 'quantify' what is local and what is not, as this study has attempted to do (Martin-Barbero, 1993: 180–181; Nederveen Pieterse, 1997: 134). For instance, a significant part of the local programming on FTV and LBC is comprised of games and reality shows. These shows, to use the parlance of Lebanese television production managers, are 'format' shows that are merely a local 'variation' or 'adaptation' of international shows acquired from the US, UK, France and Holland, and whose conformity with the original Western format is diligently monitored by the copyright holding company (Hammoud, 2005). The yearly output of these 'format' shows is relatively high, more than twice the yearly output in local dramatic production. To what extent these locally produced format shows can be considered 'local' has yet to be determined.

In sum, the Lebanese 'global-local mix' is indeed complex, to paraphrase Boyd-Barrett (1998: 169). As the present research has shown, differences in local/foreign programming are sector-specific, channel-specific with some of these differences being constantly blurred depending on the adopted definition of what is 'local'. Moreover, different markets of origin dominate different national audio-visual sectors, with Egypt or Mexico exercising on a regional level and in the broadcasting

---

[*] According to one estimate, Egyptian films make up three fourths of all films produced by the Arab world. See Darwish, Mustafa 'A Portrait of Egyptian Cinema' available on
http://www.egyptianfilmclassics.com/egyfilm/portrain/pormain.htm (accessed on 25 February 2004).

sector (with respect to television drama) what Hollywood does internationally in the area of film. This composite picture, interestingly, is totally independent of the regulatory environment which is, at present, quite ineffective in influencing local cultural production and distribution in Lebanon. As this study has shown, the audio-visual sectors in Lebanon are, whether *de jure* or *de facto*, already liberalized. To ask what kind of influence joining the WTO will have on Lebanon's culture may, under these circumstances, be just the wrong kind of question to ask. This question only makes sense in countries where aggressive, comprehensive cultural policies exist in the first place, such as Canada or South Korea.* This also means that, for better or for worse, making commitments in the audio-visual service during the GATS negotiations is not likely to alter the picture for Lebanese filmgoers or television audiences. You can't lose what you don't have in the first place.

References

Al-Deek, I. (1993). *Al-Yunesco wal Seera' al-Douali hawla al I'ilam wal Thakafa* [UNESCO and the international struggle over communication and culture]. Beirut: Al Mu'assassa al-Jami'iyah.

Bezjian, N. (2005) Manager of Program Acquisition at FTV, personal interview, 21 May.

Boyd-Barrett, Oliver (1998). 'Media Imperialism Reformulated,' pp. 157–176 in D. Thussu (ed) *Electronic Empires*. Arnold.

Choung Byoung-Gug (2004) 'Korean Audiovisual Industry & the Importance of Cultural Diversity. Focusing on Korea's Screen Quota System'. Paper presented at the Universal Forum of Cultures conference on *Global Broadcasting, Cultural Diversity and Regulation,* Barcelona 28–29 May.

Dabbous-Sensenig, D. (2002) 'From Defending "Cultural Exception" to Promoting "Cultural Diversity": European Cultural Policy and the Arab World.', *Quaderns del CAC*, issue on 'Globalisation, audiovisual industry, and cultural diversity', published by the Audiovisual Council of Catalunya, Spain, No. 14, September-December: 33–44.

Dabbous-Sensenig, D. (2003) *Ending the War? The Lebanese Broadcasting Act of 1994*. Unpublished doctoral dissertation, Sheffield Hallam University, UK.

Dabbous-Sensenig, D. (2005) '"Lost in Translation' dans le Monde Arabe", *MediaMorphoses*, special issue, June: 135–143.

Dickinson, M. and S. Harvey (2005) 'Public Policy and Public Funding for Film: some recent developments in the UK', *Screen*, 46(1): 1–9.

Eid, B. (2005) Empire production and distribution manager, personal interview, 7 May.

Fouladkar, A. (2005) Lebanese film-maker, personal interview, 13 May.

Freedman, D. (2003) 'Cultural Policy-Making in the Free Trade Era: an Evaluation of the Impact of Current World Trade Organization Negotiations on Audio-visual Industries', *International Journal of Cultural Policy*, 9 (3): 285–298.

Galperin, H.(1999) 'Cultural Industries in the Age of Free-Trade Agreements", *Canadian Journal of Communication*, 21(1). Available online: http://www.wlu.ca/~wwwpress/jrls/cjc/BackIssues/24.1/galperin.pap.html (Accessed on 5 May 2004).

Hammoud, I. (2005) Director of Production Department at FTV, personal interview, 16 May.

Le Pottier, G. (2003). 'Alloubnanyyoun wa Dawrahoum fi Tanmyat Alam Al-Talfaza Al-Fada'yya' [The Lebanese and their Role in Developing the World of Satellite Television], pp. 55–84 in F. Mermier (ed) *Al-Fada' Al-Arabi* [The Arab Space]. Damascus: Qadmus.

Makki, F. (2000) *Ma Bayna Algatt wa Munazzamat al Tijara al-Alamyya* [between GATS and the WTO]. Beirut: Al-Markaz al-Lubnani lil-Dirasat.

---

* For details of the Korean success story, see Choung Byoung-Gug, 2004.

Makki, F . (2005) Director General of the Ministry of Economy and Trade, personal interview, 12 May.

Martin-Barbero, J (1993) *Communication, Culture and Hegemony*. London: Sage Publications.

Nederveen Pieterse, J. (1997) 'Multiculturalism and Museums: Discourse About the Other in the Age of Globalization', in *Theory, Culture & Society*, 14 (4): 123–146, p. 134.

Smiers, J. (2004) *Artistic Expression in a Corporate World: Do We Need Monopolistic Control?* Utrecht: Utrecht School of Arts.

Smiers, J. (2003) *Arts Under Pressure: Promoting Cultural Diversity in the Age of Globalization*. London: Zed Books.

Tomlinson, J. (1997) 'Internationalism, Globalization and Cultural Imperialism', pp. 118–153 in K. Thompson (ed) *Media and Cultural Regulation*. London: Sage Publications.

Torrent, R. (2002). 'The "Cultural Exception" in the World Trade Organisation (WTO): the Basis of the Audiovisual Policy in Catalonia', *Quaderns del CAC*, published by the Catalonia Broadcasting Council, September–December: 17–24.

UNESCO (2005) 'Towards a Convention on the Protection of the Diversity of Cultural Contents and Artistic Expressions', available online: http://portal.unesco.org/culture/en/ev.php-URL_ID=11281&URL_DO=DO_PRINTPAGE (accessed 15 May 2005).

Chapter 6

Trading genie out of the bottle: global currents in India's film and television industries

Manjunath Pendakur

Indian popular cinema, often called Bollywood, has finally arrived in North America's capitalist media and has been accorded, somewhat grudgingly, the status of a competing film industry.* *Variety*, Hollywood's major trade publication, has started to heap accolades on Indian movie stars, offered industry news, film reviews, and has even made space in its Box Office Report to recognize the success of Indian films imported into the North American market. Major critics such as Richard Corliss of *Time* magazine have now become fans of Hindi cinema which used to be dismissed by the critics as melodramatic family dramas, dripping in sentimentality and filled with songs and dances. Andrew Lloyd Webber, the leading impresario of musical theater, composer, and owner of many theatres and variety halls in London and New York worked with A.R. Rahman, a leading film music director from India, and created *Bombay Dreams*, which had a successful run on New York's Broadway. Just a few years ago, both the form and content of Indian popular cinema met with the usual disdain in the West that it was 'escapist' and technically not on par with Hollywood. All that appears to have changed because major Indian stars are now featured on successful television shows such as *Oprah*, *60 Minutes*, *Nightline*, *Lateshow with David Letterman*, et cetera. Even the prestigious jury at the Cannes International Film Festival, a preserve of 'art' cinema critics and film-makers, invited Aishwarya Rai, one of the leading actresses, to adjudicate the festival in 2003. The honor to be on the jury this year went to another talented Indian actress, Nandita Das. This chapter does not address the cultural shifts, if any in the West regarding Indian cinema, but examines the political economic issues that might help us understand the larger forces that are reshaping India's feature film and television industries since the 1990s. Contemporary issues related to global trends in India's film and television industries might be better understood if we take a brief historical detour.

I will begin by contrasting two images that refuse to go away from my memory. In

---

* An earlier version of this chapter was presented as a keynote address at the 'Trading Culture' Conference, Sheffield Hallam University, Sheffield, England, 17 July 2002.

Fig. 1. Aishwarya Rai on CBS' 60 Minutes

my view, they are compelling images that recount history, economy, and culture. The first image is a huge oil painting that decorates one of the walls in the Victoria and Albert Museum in London, England, a museum that houses large collections of the loot from different parts of the British Empire. The painting is predominantly red and blue and depicts the royal court of the Mughal Emperor, Shah Jahan (r. 1628–1658), who is remembered primarily for his contributions to Indian art and architecture. Among the many monuments and forts he built, the Taj Mahal and the Red Fort are certainly the most beautiful. The Emperor ought to be remembered for something equally important in terms of the politico-economic history of India and its future for centuries to come. The painting depicts a critically important moment in India's history when a representative of the East India Company is receiving permission from the Mughal Emperor to establish his British trade in India.* By then, the Portuguese, among others, had traded with Indian merchants for nearly two hundred years. The French had already established their trading outposts on the East Coast. The English mercantilists, who had been given the monopoly right to trade with India by the British Court, arrived a bit late on the subcontinent but endured for more than a hundred years since Shah Jahan gave them his approval to trade. They became the most important power brokers between the warring, vassal kings who were tearing at the edges of the vast territory held by the Mughal Empire. The East India Company was forced by the British Parliament in 1843 to give up its control over the subcontinent when Queen Victoria declared India as a formal colony of Britain. Going back to the allegorical painting, the officer of the East India Company obtaining permission from the Mughal Emperor is on his knees and the Emperor is sitting on the famous Peacock throne.

Let us flash forward to the year 1994. It is the chilly month of February in New Delhi. Rupert Murdoch, the principal owner of NewsCorp, one of the largest media conglomerates in the world by then, arrives in New Delhi with an entourage of

---

* In 1617 Sir Thomas Roe presented himself to Emperor Nuruddin Jehangir, Shah Jahan's father, and the first warehouse of the East India Company was established in 1639 at Fort St. George, Madras.

Chapter 6 • Trading genie out of the bottle

Fig. 2. Rupert Murdoch, Chairman and CEO of NewsCorp.

managers and technical experts that was large enough to occupy a whole floor at the Taj Intercontinental Hotel. Having acquired a controlling interest in the pan-Asian satellite network called STAR-TV in 1993, which had given him access to a large part of the Asia-Pacific region, Murdoch needed to negotiate his space in the changing Indian political economy. The Narasimha Rao government in Delhi rolled out a red carpet welcome to Murdoch and gave the visitor the high priority which is reserved for a head of state or royalty. The President, the Prime Minister, and the leaders of the opposition political parties received Murdoch in private meetings. While the state thus embraced him, the English language press featured Murdoch on the front page, thereby giving the story high status.

The irony could not be missed. Here was an international capitalist whose only priority was to seek entry into the growing Indian economy and feature entertainment produced by his vast holdings in the US and elsewhere with as few constraints as possible. Here also was the political establishment, which, not too long ago, had debated issues of cultural imperialism in the Parliament, giving him a warm welcome. Joining the cacophony of voices were also the Hindu fundamentalists, who call themselves 'nationalists', led by Lal Kishan Advani, whose concerns about Murdoch's MTV were represented in the media as 'nationalist' and anti-imperialist. The king of global media reportedly assured Advani that MTV would be appropriately censored to suit the Indian conditions. Following Murdoch, other international giants in the media business – Time Warner, Universal, Paramount, Disney, the Turner Group – announced their own plans to set up production facilities in India. Obviously, the whole policy context had changed in a very short period of time – from national autonomy to the dogmas of neo-liberalism (liberalization and privatization) – which necessitated a different outlook, a 'new' perspective on investment, including in the complicated area of culture. The Indian industrialists lined up at the doors of the transnational enterprises in the West following Murdoch's visit to Delhi. The indigenous, small capitalists who created the cable television industry since 1988 were at his feet requesting the media mogul to help them convince the government of India to regulate the emerging cable industry in their favor.

Current changes in India's media landscape began in 1984. This is not an Orwellian hint but the fact that in that year the government of India gave Rajiv Gandhi the power and the money to expand the national television network and to introduce color television transmission. Sponsored programming to fill the hours and advertising revenue to pay for program production, both important conditions for the development of a profit-based television industry, emerged then. I have argued elsewhere that the whole system was put at the service of the ruling Indira Gandhi family dynasty, the advertisers, and the advertising agencies (Pendakur, 1988). The state turned away from the earlier policy of using the media for educational purposes to bolster egalitarian values in a highly class-caste ridden society to create markets and to aggressively reinforce the hegemony of the Congress Party. As one author has noted accurately,

> If they didn't have enough to eat, no clean drinking water to quench their thirst, no clothes to wear or no roof over their heads, they could watch on TV the best ice creams, Maha soft drinks, instant coffee, designer clothes and international quality paints reminding one of Marie Antoinette and the French revolution. If the deprived didn't have drinking water they could have a taste of thunder* (Thomas, 1990: 7).

Satellite television networks, controlled by private corporations, emerged in the 1990s and have been enormously successful in gaining audiences. Some 250 million viewers, almost the size of the entire population in the US, were created by mass oriented television development in India, which is clearly attractive to national and international investors in production, distribution, and marketing of programs, goods and services.

Some recent trends and issues

The entertainment industry in India consists of theatrical film, television broadcasting, cable television, newspapers, magazines, billboards, music, radio, advertising, live entertainment, and event management. Due to lack of space, I will focus on film and television industries, which are closely tied together in a number of ways. In fact, what gets the attention of the television audience are the film-related entertainment programs, film stars, their lifestyles, song and dance numbers from popular Indian films, and even contests related to singing and performing such songs on national television.

One of the important trends is the growth of the entertainment sector in the 1990s. In March 2001, the Federation of Indian Chambers of Commerce and Industry estimated the size of the entertainment industry at about Rs. 96 billion.** It was expected to grow rapidly to about Rs. 286 billion by 2005. Another report by Arthur Anderson Associates projected even higher revenue growth, as can be seen in the

---

*   The author of this quotation is making reference to a cold drink called 'Thumbs Up'.

**   The exchange rate in 2001 was approximately Rs. 47 to 1 US$.

chart below. The Swiss-based research firm KPMG's estimates, however, differed but still predicted that India's burgeoning entertainment industry is set to grow by 18 per cent each year to 2010.

According to this projection, television will be the main growth driver, accounting for 62 per cent of revenue (Pearson, 2005: 21).

Table 1. Indian entertainment industry revenues (estimated).

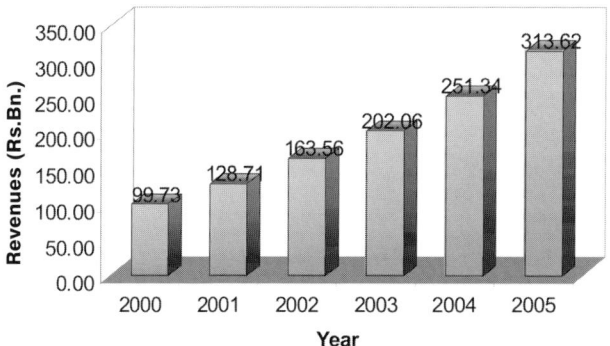

Source: *The Indian Entertainment Industry: Strategy and Vision.* New Delhi: Federation of Indian Chambers of Commerce and Industry, 2000.

Such spectacular growth may be fuelled by several factors. Principal among them are a population of more than one billion people, a large middle class hungry for commodities, the expansion of state-controlled television to cover most of the country, and the privately controlled cable television and satellite delivery services catering especially to linguistic minorities. Additionally, the willingness of the state to accommodate private investment in certain sectors of the industry, particularly in satellite broadcasting, is a key factor in this dramatic expansion of revenues.

The theatrical film sector, measured in terms of investment in film production, distribution, exhibition, and marketing is estimated around Rs. 13 billion.* Estimates vary widely because truthful accounting and reporting hardly exist. Many companies keep two sets of books and what they report to the government may only be a fraction of what is going on. This is particularly the case in the film business where unaccounted money circulates widely. That aside, it is clear that the film sector has seen an unprecedented growth of 10 per cent per year in the last five years and some estimates suggest that total investment in the film sector will reach Rs. 50 billion in 2005. That is indeed remarkable for a country with 40 per cent of its population below the poverty line.

Entrepreneurial capital dominates all sectors of the industry, while the so-called 'black money', a predominant feature of the Indian political economy, heavily

---

* This sector has historically been in private hands, except for specific periods in history when the state made attempts to support the film industry by way of grants and subsidies, etc. State funding for feature films varies widely across the country as the provincial governments have also become involved in aiding local production, etc. See Pendakur, 2003: 59–92).

Fig. 3. Cable television operators with satellite dishes. [Photo: M. Pendakur.]

influences the film industry as well.* Three years ago, when Bharat Shah, a prominent producer of Hindi films, was arrested, it was revealed that he had financed 100 of the 300 pictures in production that year. The source of his funds was noted to be illegal trade in diamonds, land, and other goods with deep connections to the smugglers in Karachi and Dubai. There have been murders, death threats to prominent stars, producers, etc. by these underworld financiers, all of which has been widely reported in the Indian media.

To break this stranglehold on the film industry by criminal elements, in 2000 the government recognized the film business as an 'industry', thereby making it possible for legitimate filmmakers to apply for bank financing. This policy was also led by the belief that film businesses would transform into modern corporations, thus getting away from moneylenders who charged usurious rates of interest. All indications are such attempts have failed so far (Chopra, 2005: A2). What draws entrepreneurial capital into the film industry is that it is relatively easy to launder money in this field and all the major participants (meaning stars, producers, directors) accept unaccounted money.

The film industry employs an estimated 2.5 million people in production, distribution, and exhibition. Some 13 million tickets are sold every day in the approximately 13,000 theaters in the country. The actual attendance may be much higher, even three times that, but exact data are unavailable. Theaters, particularly in small towns and medium size cities, do not report actual sales figures to the distributor or the government. The theater owner, the distributor, their agents, the government officials – all seem to collude to keep this system of cheating the treasury going.

---

* In my view, war profits and capital from large land-owning farmers flowed into the film industry after 1945, thereby boosting production in all languages.

Chapter 6 • Trading genie out of the bottle

Fig. 4. Movie theater in a small town. [Photo: M. Pendakur.]

Approximately 1,000 feature films are produced in the nation's many production centers in various Indian languages, including some in English. For example, in 2003, the latest year for which reliable data are available, the Central Board of Film Certification approved 877 feature films in 23 languages (Central Board of Film Certification, 2005). These films are made primarily for audiences at home but circulate in other countries, an issue which we will explore in some detail later in the chapter.

One of the most interesting aspects of Indian film exhibition and perhaps unique is the touring cinema also known as 'tent' cinema. It is literally a tent with a 35 mm film projector, sound system and foldable chairs. Most of the people, the masses, sit on the floor to watch a three-hour extravaganza of songs, dances, fights, all of which make the package called the Indian masala film.* In 1997, there were approximately 3,918 such tent cinemas. Although that number represented a decline from 4,641 in 1985, the tent cinema may not go the way of the drive-in theaters because new theater construction in rural areas, where 75 per cent of India's burgeoning population is living, is not keeping pace with multiplexes in big cities.

The theatrical market is divided into A, B, and C centers, a classification system devised by the distributors based on population data. Large cities with more than one million people are 'A' centers, big towns with 100,000 and above population are called 'B' centers, and small towns are classified as 'C' centers. Within each city, because of the severe shortage of theaters,** there is no system of first run, second run, etc., a distribution system that is followed in North America that creates a

---

* For a thorough discussion of the narrative structure and ideology of the masala film, see Pendakur, 2003: 95–117

** By various accounts I have seen, India has 12.5 screens per one million people as opposed to the US which has 117 screens per million people (Parekh & Parikh, 2001: 1).

hierarchy of desirable and not-so-desirable theaters in any market. In the Indian context, if there is a wide release of a film with hundreds of prints, the film makes its way from 'A' centers downwards to the small towns. There are more than 500,000 villages in the country. If there is no tent cinema in their village, people travel by cart, bicycle, or whatever means available to the nearby town to watch a movie.

In this situation of viewing, the masses and the classes have to mingle. Inside the theater, space is divided along class lines or one's capacity to spend money. The balcony is the most expensive and the front rows are the least expensive seats. Whether one is sitting in an expensive seat or the cheapest, the theater is a noisy, performative space in India. Audiences laugh loudly, talk among themselves, clap, cheer, boo, and some even get up on the stage to dance to a song. Some times, a fight may break out as well.

The pattern of ownership of theaters in India is unlike in North America where vertically integrated oligopolies dominate. Single theater owners are common. There are a few chains in the country and more are developing now given liberalization of the economy. I will outline one company's development to illustrate the larger question of change in the theatrical exhibition market in the globalization context.

Multiplexes for the 'Gold Class'

PVR Cinemas – catering primarily to a middle class audience – began its operation in 1997. The launch of one theater in Delhi with four screens was followed by rapid growth to a total of 75 screens nationally. The company's business plan was to offer better quality screening facilities in a high tech environment to the up market audience. 'Located around the cinema, in the same complex are a number of up-market restaurants, pubs and fast-food restaurants making it a popular hangout for teenagers, and indeed an entertainment experience for the entire family', boasts the company's web site (PVR Cinemas, 2005). One of the results of liberalization of the economy was the rise of the shopping malls. PVR Cinemas have become an attractive destination for young consumers with nearby outlets like Reebok, TGIF, Pizza Hut, McDonalds, Nirulas, Barista, Benetton, Modern Bazaar, Wills Lifestyle and the like.

PVR's 'discerning audience' in Gurgaon, Hyderabad, Mumbai, Bangalore and other cities can enjoy custom built, plush reclining seats with double arm rests and ample legroom. The company web site claims that the choice of movies will be 'an eclectic mix of tastefully chosen niche Indian films, internationally acclaimed films as well as Oscar winning Hollywood films' (PVR Cinemas, 2005). The red carpet treatment given to the patrons of Europa or the Gold Class Cinema in Bangalore is clearly aimed at the small but relatively wealthy populations, particularly the younger generation which has grown up on MTV and the Hollywood imports, speaks English and aspires to seek opportunities abroad.

High cost of entry* and the kind of films played in these multiplexes will certainly

---

* In March 2005, each ticket at the Bangalore multiplex in 'Gold Class' cost Rs. 500, which included food. Beverages cost extra. A domestic worker earns about that much in a month's time. Obviously, such entry costs keep the workers out of these theaters.

Chapter 6 • Trading genie out of the bottle

Fig. 5. Five-star treatment in a Bangalore multiplex theater.

attract the 'classes' (as the Indian film industry refers to them) and keep out the noisy, often exhibitionist, vulgar, 'masses'! In other words, the whole viewing experience that has existed for the last 100 years, which was about families of different classes going to see a film in the same theater, is dramatically changing. It is possible to argue that different kinds of films will be made for this audience in India, quite likely in the English language with much more liberal doses of sex. There is a already a crop of films coming out of Bombay and other cities with titles like *Jism* (2003), *Girl Friend* (2004), *Shabd* (2005), *Black* (2005), *Raincoat* (2004). In the short run, these films appear to be setting a trend, away from the big budget extravaganzas that have been popular with the domestic and international audiences for decades.

Growth of Indian entertainment markets abroad

While Bollywood has become emblematic of India these days, just as Darjeeling tea or the Taj Mahal have been for some years, feature films from India have circulated in Africa, Asia, Latin America, and parts of Europe for more than 50 years. Until the 1990s, all foreign territories constituted about 15–16 per cent of total revenue for Hindi language films (Pendakur, 2003: 40–44). The estimates these days are 33–40 per cent of the total expected box office for Hindi cinema is earned abroad. Yash Chopra's *Dilwale Dulhaniya Le Jayenge* (Hindi, 1995), a hugely successful film, reportedly earned Rs. 200 million internationally against Rs. 500 million domestically. This success clearly established that there was a great appetite for film and television entertainment abroad. By 2001, Bollywood films were exported to nearly 95 countries (Parekh & Parikh, 2001: 2).

Fig. 6. PVR Cinemas' lobby.

Another leading producer-director in Bombay, Subhash Ghai, openly advocates making films for the growing international audience for Bollywood films by tailoring them to their tastes. With the success of *Pardes* (Hindi, 1997) and *Taal* (Hindi, 1999), Ghai grew bolder in his tactics. His latest film called *Kisna* (Hindi and English, 2005) is declared to be a mainstream film to appeal to the 'masses and the classes', but the English version is deliberately trying to cater to not only South Asians living abroad but also white British audiences:

> We have two cuts of *Kisna*. The English version, *The Warrior Poet*, is a two-hour cut, and the Hindi film is two hours, 50 minutes. I hired a British editor, with British sensibilities for the film, in order to craft it to be something they like. He didn't cut all the songs. Seven songs in Hindi have been cut to three-and-a-half songs in the English version because he loved the songs and the picturisation. When I asked him why should the Western audience watch this film, he replied, 'Because it's a trip to India' (Rediff, 2005: 2).

Ghai's films attempt to define what and how the diaspora should desire in terms of family, culture, homeland, and their relationship to India. They are loaded with feudal notions of family, women's role in the home and outside, devotion to gods and goddesses, and an idealistic representation of India in the throes of modernity or even postmodernity. In *Pardes* for instance, Ghai throws in a long song and dance number which takes the viewer through a tour of Hindu and Muslim monuments, pays tribute to the harmonious ideal of a joint, Hindu family, and even a boat trip on the river Ganga. The unabashedly titled song, 'I love my India', offers a mishmash of nostalgia for the 'homeland' and patriotic notions, all well contained within patriarchy. The dominant men of Hindi cinema still rule the plot, but the good natured, Hindu woman wins them all in the end by her selfless devotion to family and true love.

These instances should be seen as patterns of representations that are emerging in

Chapter 6 • Trading genie out of the bottle

Fig. 7. Subhash Ghai's films in North American markets on DVD.

a new Bollywood cinema that is trying to balance between what the filmmakers see as the needs and demands of the domestic market and the growing markets abroad. In many films, Bombay as a location has simply disappeared while foreign locations – be it European, North American, or Australian – stand for India. They are, however, subjected to change if financial and other conditions change (Kapur and Pendakur, 2005).

The distributors generally agree that the US-Canada market constitutes about 40 per cent of the total global market for Hindi language cinema, the UK about 25 per cent, the Middle East about 20 per cent, and the rest of the world about 15 per cent. An estimated 60 pictures are released theatrically these days in the US and UK markets. Major films may be shown in 60 major cities such as New York, Chicago, Toronto, Vancouver, Los Angeles, Dallas, and Houston, in one or two theaters, often coinciding with the film's release in Bombay. The US market for Indian cinema is also organized as A and B centers. There were some 25–30 'A' centers and 25 'B' centers in 2000 (Sharma, 2000). Smaller cities, which used to be referred as 'C' centers, disappeared because of video and DVD. By 2002, estimated revenue from film, music, and video distribution in North America had reached the high mark of $100 million (Naqvi, 2002: 1).

The Indian government abolished taxes on income earned abroad to help these companies to expand globally. A few Indian-owned film companies have set up distribution offices outside the country to seek markets directly. For example, following the success of *Dilwale Dulhaniya Le Jayenge*, Yash Chopra launched Yash Raj Films to distribute films, videos, and recorded music in New York and London. Yash Raj Films joined other Indian-owned distribution firms – Eros and Video Sound – which had been in international marketing of Indian entertainment for

Fig. 8. Los Angeles multiplex features Indian imports. Photo: M. Pendakur.

some years. *Kabhi Khushi Kabhi Gham* (Hindi, 2001), a star-studded, extravagantly shot film with six major stars, European and Indian locations, gigantic sets, designer costumes, broke previous box office records in North America in December 2001 for a week. It was reportedly the first Indian film to make it to *Variety*'s top ten list. The film ran on 70 screens and grossed $3 million in its first month (Naqvi, 2002: 1). Such instances of box office bonanza have drawn considerable attention in the US mainstream and ethnic media.

Inevitably, such successes attract attention from the US entertainment industry giants. The Hollywood Majors, such as Twentieth Century Fox, Sony, and Walt Disney have made significant forays into India and are beginning to compete abroad also with Indian entertainment. Sony Entertainment followed suit by opening an office in New Jersey with exclusive marketing rights for *Mission Kashmir* (Hindi, 2000). Sony also set a precedent by buying foreign theatrical and ancillary rights for the highly successful *Lagaan* (Hindi and English, 2001).

Indian-owned corporations in television production and distribution have also set up joint ventures and partnerships in many countries to lure the viewers to their programs (Pearson, 2005a: A6). Large industrial corporations such as Hindujas, Modis, Tatas, and Birlas have entered the fray. Their strategic partnerships with some of the large international corporations create their own version of global companies to compete in the growing entertainment industry abroad. For example, B4U is such a satellite pay-TV operation based in London, England, which is available to cable audiences on both sides of the Atlantic. The government of India has encouraged digital technologies and the creation of up-linking hubs from India to reach foreign markets. Eight Indian corporations have been allowed to set up up-linking hubs in the country and 36 channels have been permitted by the government to uplink their programs abroad.

What drives all these strategic moves is the size of the South Asian diaspora and the fact that South Asians have the desire to consume and spend their leisure dollars on cable subscriptions, movie tickets, entertainment events, and so on. Approximately 11 million Indians live, work, and study abroad (Fredriksen, 2002). According to the 1990 census, the American Asian population totaled 6,908,638, a dramatic 99 per cent increase over the 1980 census count. Asian Indians constituted 11.8 per cent of the total of Asians in the US with the second highest per capita income of $17,777. Asian Indians also surpassed the total US population in terms of educational attainment (US Department of Commerce, 1993: 2, 4, 7).

The numbers of potential viewers of Indian films is larger than Asian Indians if one accounts for all South Asians, East Asians, people of the Middle East; East Africa, West Africa, the Caribbean, and even some Central and Latin American countries. CBS News claimed that Bollywood films reach a global audience of five billion (CBS News, 2004). An article in the *National Geographic* estimated the global audience for Indian cinema at around 3.6 billion, or a billion more than Hollywood's global audience (Mehta, 2005: 57). Hype or not, such potential to reach a large, global audience is propelling Indian and foreign-owned entertainment corporations to look to profitability around the world.

Zee TV, a leading media firm in Bombay and a contender in this emerging global entertainment business for Indian entertainment, claims that it has more than 1 million viewers in the UK and about the same in the US-Canada markets. Zee reportedly can access fewer than a million viewers in the Middle East, and about 1.5 million in South East Asia. If Africa and the Pacific regions are added, Zee claims to have built up a viewership of half billion in ten years. Murdoch's STAR distributes television programs in seven languages – including Mandarin, English, and Hindi – and claims to reach more than 300 million viewers across 53 Asian countries. STAR, however, lags behind Zee in India. Zee TV claims 40 million households in India. Sony Entertainment Television claims to reach 40 million households throughout India, Pakistan, Sri Lanka, Bangladesh, and the Middle East (Pearson, 2005a: A6). These data are, however, difficult to verify.

Hollywood in India

The US film industry, with its historic strategy to expand into territories around the world, often with financial and strategic assistance from the US government, has maintained a foothold in the Indian market for almost 50 years.[*] Prior to 1989, the Majors had a deal with the government of India for exclusive distribution of English language cinema into the country. No company, other than members of the Motion Picture Export Association of America (MPEAA), the US motion picture industry cartel, was allowed to import feature length films into India.[**] In exchange, the

---

[*] For historic research on the U. S. film industry from a political economy perspective see, Guback (1969), Wasko (2003), Miller et al (2001), and Pendakur (1990).

[**] The MPEAA was registered as a trade association in 1945 under the Webb-Pomerene Export Trade Act, 1918. Created to lobby governments abroad in order to preserve the Majors' market dominance, the MPEAA membership is restricted only to the Hollywood Majors.

government won restrictions on the number of films to be imported, which was fixed at 100 films annually, and also placed restrictions on the repatriation of hard currency. Much of the $5 million earned annually by the Majors had to be spent on buying goods and services (Pendakur, 1985). When other governments complained about the exclusive deal with the MPEAA, India gave similar concessions to the Soviets and the French. In those years, only about 150 screens in the country showed imported films. The Soviet and French films did not receive wide release in the country, except at international film festivals.

All of this began to change when the Indian government openly embraced market liberalization in 1991.* First, the government of India began to license Indian owned companies to import films from abroad in addition to lifting all the restrictions on the Majors. This meant all sorts of product – from *Cannibal Girls* to *Jurassic Park* could be seen in the country. Available data indicate that the market for imported product has grown dramatically in the 1990s. The trickle of box office revenue in 1992 was at Rs. 38 million for Hollywood imports which is reported to have grown to Rs. 400 million by 2000, while attendance for these films has grown from 8 million in 1988 to 47 million in 1992. *Titanic, Independence Day, Godzilla, The Mummy, Tomorrow Never Dies*, etc. have had huge appeal with the Indian audiences (Indian Express, 2000). The number of prints released for imported films is also an indicator of how Hollywood sees the market potential. In the 1980s, the typical release consisted of 5–10 prints whereas since 2000, it is not uncommon to find a blockbuster getting a wide release with 100 prints. Columbia Pictures sent out 163 prints of *Godzilla* and 100 prints of the *End of the Day*. But the Majors are not satisfied with the upscale, urban audience for their films. Action packed as they often are, Hollywood imports may attract even those who do not speak English. When that fails, Hollywood has actively pursued that audience by releasing dubbed versions in regional languages simultaneously with the original English version. This is done to maximize on the promotion and advertising campaigns mounted to reach a wide audience. I saw *Twister* (1996) dubbed into Kannada in a rural theater that would not have otherwise screened a Hollywood import. These strategies to compete for local audiences in Bollywood's own backyard appear to be paying off as each of the Majors is now releasing more dubbed films in the country.

The second major change in policy was made in the mid-1990s when the Foreign Investment Promotion Board approved Sony Pictures Entertainment's application to produce and distribute Indian films in the domestic and international markets. The government's goal was to encourage foreign investment in production, enhance employment opportunities for local talent, and import advanced film production equipment into the country. Duncan Clark, President of Columbia TriStar Film Distributors International, a subsidiary of Sony Pictures, was ecstatic about this change:

> India has a rich and prolific film history. We at SPE recognize the potential and importance of the Indian market and welcome the opportunity to team up with the Indian film industry (Sony Pictures, 2005).

---

* One policy the government has kept intact is the power to regulate the market by way of censorship on all films shown in the country. Excessive sex and violence often face the censor's scissors, as does anything that would be perceived by the bureaucrats as 'political'.

Such dramatic shifts in national policy are consistent with the goals of neo-liberalism and what is clearly observable in the short term at least is further integration of the Indian film and television industries into the global market.

Conclusions

I began this chapter on India's film and television industries by recounting a visit by Rupert Murdoch in 1994 and will end it by an account of his latest visit to Delhi in 2005. This time his ambition was not simply to pry open the market but to expand NewsCorp's operations by launching Space TV, a direct-to-home satellite television co-venture with Tata, a corporate giant in India with interests in steel, automobile, and other industries. He met with Prime Minister Manmohan Singh and Information and Broadcasting Minister Jaipal Reddy. Apparently, not getting the expected approval during his visit, Murdoch stated,

> India is slow to accept the idea of foreign investment; I think it's changing. It's always very complicated here. There is a lot of bureaucracy, the rules change from time to time, but we have to step into it. Media is changing all over the world, and in a country like India it is a great and huge opportunity (Pearson, 2005b: 21).

He then went on to declare, 'In India, the TV sets are only in half the homes. So with full electrification, higher education, better standard of living, all of which are coming fast, the television market will at least double in this country' (Pearson, 2005b: 21). Michael Eisner, Chief Executive Officer of Walt Disney Corporation, also went calling on India's Prime Minister with plans to build a Disney theme park (Intercot, 2005). In December 2004, Disney had successfully launched two 24-hour channels – Toon Disney and Disney Channel. The theme park would be a logical progression to further consolidate Disney's entry into one of the largest entertainment markets in the world.

India's film and television industries are clearly caught up in the maelstrom of globalization. The patterns of change analyzed in this chapter demonstrate how government policy shifts have refracted the global currents and also how Bollywood's leading filmmakers are trying to take strategic advantage of them. The inroads made by the Hollywood Majors into the Indian market would be difficult to alter in the future because the government of India would have to face the wrath of the US government that does not hesitate to use its clout when it comes to preserving the power of Hollywood in global markets.

There are at least two unpredictable factors that will define future change in this matrix of power – the audience and the various elements of capital. It is not guaranteed that their interests will coalesce in the future. Whether the audience will be enamored by the seductive power of capital and its media is hard to tell. The success of ventures such as PVR Cinemas to lure the upper and middle classes into their theaters suggests that a small but powerful section of the Indian population identifies with these changes. In fact, a new genre of film has emerged which is commercial in its orientation but has none of the pretenses to art. That is a welcome development in this complex situation.

It is the 'masses' (in the nomenclature of the industry) that are unpredictable. I would suggest that a cinema that caters to their tastes will continue to be made because of their sheer numbers and also because Indian audiences still desire to see their own heroes and heroines on the screen bringing stories that are familiar to them or at least in a familiar form. There appears to be a thorough understanding of this fact within the corporations that produce and distribute film and television productions, whether they are Indian owned or not.

Big capitalists, including industrial powerhouses such as the Birlas and the Tatas, have invested in the entertainment sector with market liberalization. Their interests can easily collide with those of the small capitalists, moneylenders, and money launderers who are often tied to smuggling and racketeering. How that will be sorted out is anyone's guess. The state will have to mediate those power relations in the future as the industry further globalizes and corporate practices get even more entrenched. At the present moment, government policy for the most part favors investment in certain sectors of the industry and collaboration of international capitalists with national capitalists. These relationships predictably will bring many pressures on policy makers to open other areas to competition by international capitalists. News and public affairs, for instance, could be difficult genres for future privatization, engendering ideological conflicts.

Liberalization and privatization, the twin prongs of the policy of globalization, however, appear to be well entrenched in the Indian political economy. Some of the ruling elites in Delhi may have trepidations about this historic process and might want to approach it with caution, but the genie is out of the bottle. There appears to be no way to put it back.

References

CBS News (2004) http://www.cbsnews.com/stories/2004/12/29/60minutes/main63862.html

Chopra, A. (2005) 'Suits Stumble at B.O. Corporations fail to produce blockbusters', *Variety*, 28 March – 3 April, p. A2.

Ciecko, A. (2004) 'Into the Sc(re)nery: Bollywood Locations and Docu-Diaspora', *Asian Cinema*, 15 (2), Fall/Winter.

Central Board of Film Certification, Government of India (2005) http://www.cbfcindia.tn.nic.in/statistics/statistics-page-2003-31.htm (retrieved 21 May).

Federation of Indian Chambers of Commerce and Industry (2000) *The Indian Entertainment Industry: Strategy and Vision*, New Delhi: Federation of Indian Chambers of Commerce and Industry.

Fredriksen, J.E. (2003) 'Some Notes on Bollywood movies hitting big abroad', http://xent.com/pipermail/fork/2002-August/04165.htm (retrieved 04 August).

Guback, Thomas H. (1969) *The International Film Industry: Western Europe and America since 1945*. Bloomington: Indiana University Press.

Indian Express (2000) http://www.indianexpress.com/ie/daily/20000707.ien06044.html (retrieved 07 July).

Intercot (2005) http://www.intercot.com/boards/cgi-bin/ultimatebb.cgi?/topic/8/5876.html (retrieved 22 April).

Kapur, J., and Pendakur, M. (2005) 'The Strange Disappearance of Bombay from its Own Cinema', *unpublished manuscript*, 2 May.

Mehta, S. (2005) 'Welcome to Bollywood', *National Geographic*, February.

Miller, T., Govil, N., McMurria, J. and Maxwell, R. (2001) *Global Hollywood*. London: British Film Institute Publishing.

Naqvi, M. (2002) 'Indian filmmakers look west', Columbia News Service, 7 July.

Parekh, A. and Parikh (2001) 'Bollywood v. Hollywood: Legal & Business Practices. A Comparative Analysis', *Interim Report*. Mumbai & Palo Alto.

Pearson, B. (2005a) 'Zee leads race to capture diaspora', *Variety*, 28 March – 3 April, p. A6.

Pearson, B. (2005b) 'Murdoch gazes into Space for his new India venture", *Variety*, 28 March – 3 April, p. 21.

Pendakur, M.(1985) 'Dynamics of Cultural Policy Making: The US Film Industry in India,' *Journal of Communication*, 35 (4), pp. 52–72.

Pendakur, M. (1988) 'Indian Television Comes of Age. Liberalization and the Rise of Consumer Culture,' *Communication*, 11 (1) Summer, pp. 177–197.

Pendakur, M. (1990) *Canadian Dreams and American Control: The Political Economy of the Canadian Film Industry*. Detroit: Wayne State University Press.

Pendakur, M. (2003) *Indian Popular Cinema: Industry, Ideology and Consciousness*. Creskill, N.J.: Hampton Press.

PVR Cinemas (2005) http://www.ipan.com/clients/pvr/pvr.htm (retrieved 22 May).

Rediff. (2005) 'You will relate to *Kisna*!', http://in.rediff/com/movies/2005/jan/19raja.htm (p. 2, retrieved 22 May).

Sharma, J. (2000) CEO, Yash Raj Films, USA. *Personal interview*, New York, 8 November.

Sony Pictures (2005) 'Sony Pictures welcomes the government of India's decision to allow production and distribution of Indian films', http://www.Sony.co.in/movies-press.htm (retrieved 20 May).

Thomas, T. K.(1990) *Autonomy for the Electronic Media. A National Debate on the Prasar Bharati Bill, 1989,* New Delhi: Konark Publishers, Pvt. Ltd.

US Department of Commerce (1993) Economics and Statistics Administration, Bureau of Census, *We the Americans*, September, pp. 2, 4, 7.

Wasko, J. (2003) *How Hollywood Works*. London: Sage Publications.

Chapter 7

Going global: the Brazilian scripted film

Lúcia Nagib

'*Central Station* is the story of a film searching for a country'.
Walter Salles

This article departs from the assumption that a certain section of world cinema, usually defined as 'independent', has been evolving on the basis of good scripts.

Between the late 1980s and early 1990s, there has been a boom of new cinemas in the world, such as the new Iranian, Taiwanese, Japanese, Mexican, Argentine and Brazilian cinemas. A significant part of this production shows a renewed interest in local and national peculiarities of their respective countries, going against the grain of globalisation and its typical cultural dilution. Most of these films are also engaged in reassessing narrative cinema, as a kind of reaction against the deconstructive work carried out by postmodern cinema of the 1980s.

Recent new cinemas are supported by a combination of local and international resources, derived from public and private sponsors at home, and funding agencies, festivals and TV channels abroad. In most cases funds are granted after the film script has been analysed and approved by commissions of experts. Thus hundreds of scripts are annually submitted to the scrutiny of institutes, festivals and TV channels, such as the Sundance in the US, the Hubert Bals Fund, connected with the Rotterdam Film Festival in Holland, Arte Channel in France, Canal+ in Belgium and Fabrica in Italy. The control of a film from its birth as a script, exercised by international sponsors, has proved extremely effective in terms of delivering international hits, of which some recent examples are the Argentinian *La Cienaga* (Lucrecia Martel, 2001), Uruguayan *Whisky* (Jan Pablo Rebella and Pablo Stoll, 2003), Palestinian *Divine Intervention* (Elia Suleiman, 2002), Bosnian *No Man's Land* (Danis Tanivic, 2003) and Mexican *Y tu mamá también* (Alfonso Cuarón, 2001).

The New Brazilian Cinema, or *cinema da retomada* as it is locally called, has been enormously affected by this scheme, which has even caused a 'script boom' in Brazil in the past decade. From the mid-1990s, after the passing of laws of cultural incentive and the Audio-visual Law, script courses and young scriptwriters have emerged everywhere in the country. Syd Field, 'the guru of all screenwriters', as CNN once called him, has been in Brazil several times, offering lectures and workshops, and his books have been published in Portuguese and become fashionable. Another notable case is that of film professor, critic and historian Jean-Claude Bernardet, who stepped down from his academic career to devote himself entirely to writing screenplays and offering script workshops. Bernardet's collaboration as a scriptwriter with director Tata Amaral has resulted in at least one important film of the New Brazilian Cinema, *Starry Sky* (1997), based on an original story by Fernando Bonassi. Bonassi, in his turn, initially a playright, has become so involved with the production of original stories and scripts for films, that his name has become central to the New Brazilian Cinema.

Once local sponsorship has been secured, the next necessary step for any independent Brazilian film with international ambitions is to seek for co-production abroad. The script will thus be submitted to prospective funding agents who, after analysing it, will often invite selected scriptwriters to laboratories in which they will fine tune their work under the supervision of specialists. Such is the case of the Sundance Institute, founded by actor and director Robert Redford, which has been training scriptwriters from all over the world since 1981. The support offered by Sundance is intended to create the so-called 'vertical integration', which, as in the case of mainstream cinema, ensures distribution and exhibition to the final product from its inception. Indeed, Sundance's guidelines offer assurances that 'after leaving the Labs, international Fellows continue to receive both creative and practical support as they work to bridge the gap between development, production and distribution' (2005).

It is not mere coincidence that several of Brazil's most successful films abroad, such as *Central Station* (Walter Salles, 1998)*, Me You Them* (Andrucha Waddington, 2000) and *City of God* (Fernando Meirelles and Katia Lund, 2002), have received Sundance support for their scripts. *Central Station* was the first screenplay in the world to receive the Sundance/NHK International Filmmakers Award, created in 1996 to celebrate 100 years of cinema. This was the beginning of a long series of awards collected by the film, including the Golden Bear for best film and the Silver Bear for actress Fernanda Montenegro at the Berlin Film Festival in 1998, the American Golden Globe and the British BAFTA. This lavish critical reception boosted the film's commercial career through international screens and homevideo.

Apart from Sundance, Brazilian films have been backed by several other international sponsors, such as Fabrica, owned by Benetton and directed by filmmaker Godfrey Reggio*,* which helped finance and train the staff of *Brainstorm* (Laís Bodanzky, 2001), and French TV Channel Arte, which commissioned *Midnight* (Walter Salles and Daniela Thomas, 1999).

The emphasis on the script which characterises current Brazilian cinema as well as other independent cinemas in the world, qualifies it both as beneficiary of, and contributor to, a new transnational cinematic aesthetics, intended to satisfy the aspirations of an audience whose profile is equally new. I am referring to the enlightened middle classes, not necessarily motivated by the imperatives of the old left, but imbued with politically correct principles, who prefer instructive and constructive films to commercial action movies. They feel comfortable in multicultural environments and are used to hearing foreign languages and reading subtitles,

Chapter 7 • Going global: The Brazilian scripted film

though not always ready to brave the difficulties posed by outspokenly experimental or auteurist films, such as those by Godard or Manoel de Oliveira.

The task of the new cinemas is therefore to offer an intermediate product between art and entertainment, which requires scripts made to measure. Thus, films from the most diverse origins have been trying to honour a formula, so far proved effective, which basically combines the following elements:

(1) Local colour. Globalised societies, including their filmmakers and scriptwriters, bored with the repetition of the same in the universe of consumerism, long for untouched cultural reservoirs often identified with national identity. Thus new cinemas try to connect or reconnect with the culture of their home countries, in order to convey a sense of belonging provided by local specificities.

(2) Realism. The use of real locations in the home country and of non-professional or unknown casts supplies these films with the feel of authenticity required to inform spectators about original or picturesque aspects of a given society. The result is the production of a documentary backdrop to the film, thanks to which audiences from the UK or Canada will get acquainted with life in Bosnia, Mongolia, Georgia, Iran, Mexico or the backlands and shantytowns of Brazil.

(3) The private hero. To such realist backdrop a fictional plot is applied, with the aim of producing entertainment and launching the process referred to in film studies as 'identification' and 'illusionism'. At this point, the screenplay must connect to some basic rules of classic narrative cinema, since, unlike auteurist or experimental cinemas, the fragmentary, improvised, enigmatic or unfinished are not allowed here. Thus, the formation and singularisation of a hero with well defined psychological features becomes indispensable. Because realist narratives, unlike the epic tale, focus on common people, and not gods or super-heroes, the rule here is to concentrate the action on an ordinary individual, subjected to extraordinary events, which he/she eventually overcomes.

(4) The improbable but convincing event. These events, often improbable in real life, become convincing thanks to the well-constructed script, whose main challenge is to make the fictional plot naturally emerge from a situation recognised as real. This is made possible by the enclosure of the story within the hero's restricted, private realm, where his/her individual truth is exempt from the factual requirements of the outside world.

A good example of the use of this formula is *Central Station,* whose script was carefully elaborated by Marcos Bernstein and João Emanuel Carneiro, and refined with the help of the Sundance lab, director Walter Salles himself and the crew, including Swiss producer Arthur Cohen. Here cultural and national references are obvious, starting with the title, which, in Portuguese, *Central do Brasil,* suggests a train station which is the very core of the country, and continuing with careful depictions of Brazilian daily habits and religious traditions.

The film begins with location shots focusing on a series of illiterate Brazilians, chosen from Rio Central Station's real-life passengers, who dictate letters to a scribe, Dora (Fernanda Montenegro). These representatives of the populace soon monopolise the camera's attention, which closes in on their faces, of various shades of skin colour, all calmly smiling. This array of faces of common people plays an important part in setting the films realistic, documentary-style backdrop. Not by chance, the first speaker, a woman called Socorro Nobre, who weeps as she dictates the letter to be sent to her husband in jail, is an ex-convict in real life and the subject of a documentary made by Walter Salles. The sequence, responding to the woman's verbal metaphors ('I'll remain locked outside here, waiting for you'), includes a series of shots from behind large gates and rows of columns, creating a station full of fences. This effect is further amplified by the sound mixing of gates slamming without any reference in the diegesis. The idea behind this is to create a natural fusion between the film's realistic base and the fictional aspects imposed on it, without alienating the audience. Two of the protagonists, Ana and her son Josué, are singled out from the many faces that shape the ordinary Brazilian, and are given, as if naturally, more time, more makeup and more elaborate lines.

The follow-up is a series of improbable events made credible by the ingenuity of the script. Ana is run over and killed by a bus at the station exit. Josué, who strangely enough has no other friends or relatives in the world, falls into the hands of Dora, who, due to another series of unexpected circumstances, is forced to take the boy back to the Northeast in search of his father, thus causing the documentary shots to be prolonged across Brazil's dry hinterlands. At the end, after all external or political causes of Josué and Dora's misfortunes have been left back at the central station, they are duly consecrated as private heroes. Josué adapts to life with his half-brothers retrieved in the Northeast, thus reversing the natural logic of Northeasterns migrating to the south. Dora, in her turn, returns to Rio re-humanised after having experienced the 'true' Brazil, that is, the archaic *sertão* (backlands).

A similar narrative schema can be found in a number of recent world films. For example, in the Georgian-French film *Since Otar Left* (Julie Bertucelli, 2003), an international success financed by TV Arte, an elderly woman, filmed with documentary-like authenticity in her native Tbilisi, lives on the letters sent by her son Otar, now residing in Paris, which are read (or made up) to her by her grand-daughter. The frail lady ends up undertaking a most improbable expedition to Paris to search for her son. In *Whisky* (Juan Pablo Rebella and Pablo Stoll, 2004), another award-winning Uruguayan film, also financed by the Sundance/NHK scheme, an elderly Jew, owner of a small factory, unexpectedly asks his life-long employee to pretend to be his wife, when his brother comes for a visit. The three of them go on a leisure trip together, giving the camera the opportunity to document a decadent Uruguay. Trips, opening up for the description of local landscapes; letters of distant relatives highlighting affective links; and extraordinary events, leading to the private life heroes' triumph, appear in all these films, revealing themselves as script devices aimed at producing likeliness and entertainment. In all cases it is the child or the elderly, performed by non-professional or unknown actors, who provide proof of authenticity to the heroic feat.

The recipe of the private hero, in a national cultural context, who goes through the experience of the improbable made convincing by a wisely constructed script generates interesting questions of authorship and nationality which deserve further investigation.

Chapter 7 • Going global: The Brazilian scripted film

Discovering Brasil

Central do Brasil epitomises the passionate rediscovery of Brazil, and was celebrated internationally as the landmark of the Brazilian film revival. With its reconciling ending and harmonious mingling of races and creeds, despite the violence that victimises its poverty-stricken population, it certainly tends to confirm what Marilena Chauí called the 'Brazilian foundational myth', according to which: 1) Brazil has a peaceful, orderly, generous, happy and sensual populace, albeit one that suffers a great deal; 2) Brazil is a country devoid of prejudice against race or belief, and practices the mingling of races as a means of strengthening its profile (2001: 8).

However, the enclosure of the drama in the private sphere reduces the nation to an ornamental accessory, incapable of satisfying the requirements of a national project such as preached by Glauber Rocha and his early Cinema Novo colleagues, to whom the film pays homage with its locations in the northeastern backlands. Walter Salles significantly refers to *Central Station* as a 'film searching for a country' (Costa, 1998: 5–7). It is indeed as a foreigner that he rediscovers Brazil after the adventures of *High Art* (1991), an international production spoken in English, and *Foreign Land* (1995), about Brazilians in exile, shot in Brazil, Portugal and Cape Verde.

In *Central Station,* the need to retrieve a home country on the part of the filmmaker, running parallel to the character's search for his father in the story, indicates that the narrator is situated outside the narrated realm. The stunning images of Brazil's poor areas, captured in glorious colours by celebrated director of photography Walter Carvalho, have something strange, even uncanny, about them. The advertising chic of these images prompted Ivana Bentes to develop, with reference to the New Brazilian Cinema, the concept of 'cosmetics of hunger', as opposed to Glauber Rocha's 'aesthetics of hunger' (Bentes, 2003: 121–137). Though he draws on his documentary experience to capture the film's real life characters, Salles' poverty is so clean and aestheticised that one immediately senses the narrator's remoteness.

The great achievement of *Central Station* is to have represented nostalgia for the national (or 'Brazilianness', in the director's word) (1998) at a moment when the world was awakening to the problems of globalisation and the monotony of cultural dilution in a transnational world. Whilst expressing disillusionment with urban modernity, the film, thanks to a skilful script, confers credibility on a pre-capitalist, naturally democratic and harmonious paradise, depicted over a documentary backdrop, but withdrawn into the private sphere and devoid of links with reality. The director himself, however, has already moved on from this phase of national longing, having recently filmed with the same passionate gaze several Spanish speaking South American countries, in *Motorcycle Diaries* (2004). He has also just finished shooting a horror movie in the US, which is a remake of the Japanese commercial hit *Dark Water* (Hideo Nakata, 2002).

Another interesting example of the scripted film is *City of God,* the greatest Brazilian international success of all time, also focusing on Brazil and its society. Filmmaker Fernando Meirelles adopted a different solution from Salles' for the problem of a director who is foreign to the story he wants to tell. A São Paulo native and owner of an advertising company, Meirelles from the beginning acknowledged that the film, for him, was a means to discover the lower classes, Rio de Janeiro and

99

ultimately Brazil (Mantovani, Meirelles and Muller, 2003: 9–10). He then decided to find the means to establish an insider's point of view, as is achieved in the original story by Paulo Lins, the favela author of the novel *City of God*. To that end, he asked for the support of Katia Lund, who had long experience with filming the favelas and became the film's co-director. Further to that, he put together a cast with favela inhabitants, delegating the task of training them to specialists familiarised with such communities.

The resulting film, entirely convincing with its perfectly integrated realist settings and cast, does not fail to rely partly on the artifice of the private hero exposed to extraordinary and improbable events. Unlike Paulo Lins' novel, the film is structured upon a centralising point of view represented by the character Rocket, who directs the plot with his voice-over. In the film, Rocket is the sole favela inhabitant granted access to the upper classes, when, by mere chance (that is, thanks to the tricks of the script), one of the photos he takes is printed on the front page of *Jornal do Brasil*.

City of God's sophisticated formula, which I have commented on in detail elsewhere (2004), was even more successful than that of *Central Station*, being partly responsible for the currently fashionable status of Brazilian culture abroad, particularly in the UK. Three years after its international launch, further developments from the film continue to flood the market, such as the recent success of Seu Jorge, a member of the film's cast, who is also a singer and composer and a current hit in the UK.

Questions of authorship

The emphasis on the script, as well as the delegation to others of some of the director's tasks, as seen in the case of *City of God,* raises interesting questions of authorship. Fernando Meirelles is somebody used to collaborative work. His long feature films prior to *City of God* were also co-directed by others. As to the script, adapted from Paulo Lins' extremely complex book, it was commissioned from Bráulio Mantovani, a beginner at the time, who produced no less than twelve versions of it before the shoot. During this time, he received various contributions, resulting from discussions with Meirelles, Lins, Walter Salles and other members of the latter's production company, Videofilmes, besides, of course, the improvements suggested at the Sundance lab. The celebrated American screenwriter Alexander Payne became deeply involved with the film, to the point of hosting Mantovani in his own house in Los Angeles and following the film's development up to its world première in Cannes, as recounted by Meirelles (Mantovani et al., 2003: 11–12).

Meanwhile, Walter Salles and Videofilmes have become a veritable school for filmmakers and scriptwriters willing to approach Brazilian social issues. Salles has built around himself a strong nucleus of collaborators, including his brother, João Moreira Salles, Katia Lund and Karim Aïnouz, who are at the core of Brazil's film revival. Scriptwriters such as João Emanuel Carneiro, Fernando Bonassi, Di Moretti and even novelist Marçal Aquino, frequent collaborator of Beto Brant, have become essential pillars of contemporary Brazilian cinema.

One could therefore ask who the actual authors of current Brazilian films are, since

Chapter 7 • Going global: The Brazilian scripted film

Fig. 1. Ilha da Flores *(Jorge Furtado, Brazil, 1989).*

the importance attached to the script challenges the basic principle of auteur cinema, that is to say, the mise-en-scène. When young François Truffaut launched his *politique des auteurs,* which would subsequently inspire the French *nouvelle vague,* his attacks were directed precisely against the scripted cinema, based on adaptations of celebrated literary works and responsible for keeping the *tradition de qualité* of post-war French films (Truffaut, 1954). Glauber Rocha, who always wrote his own scripts, defined the cinematic auteur, that is to say, the director, as a 'totalising noun', with exclusive rights to creativity (2003: 36). In the new transnational Brazilian cinema and its decentralised creative system, would there be any room for authorship?

As an indicative answer I would like to comment on an interesting case. *City of God's* insightful narrative style draws to a great extent on a technique under development for more than a decade in Brazil. Its origin goes back to the short film *Island of Flowers* (Jorge Furtado, 1989). In a dark period for Brazilian Cinema, when production of feature films was reduced to nearly zero, the short film experienced a sudden burgeoning. The Casa de Cinema de Porto Alegre, which gathered a group of talented filmmakers including Jorge Furtado, was one of the most active nuclei at that time, and *Island of Flowers* its main product. The film won at the Berlin Film Festival in its category, receiving a standing ovation only comparable to *Central Station's* success nine years later at the same festival. The Golden Bear in Berlin was just one of a series of awards collected by *Island of Flowers* in Brazil and abroad. Among the general international accolade, I would like to highlight Rober Stam's

101

TRADING CULTURE

Fig. 2. City of God *(Fernando Meirelles/Katia Lund, Brazil, USA, France 2002)*.

comment that the film 'brings the "garbage aesthetics" into the postmodern era, while also demonstrating the cinema's capacity as a vehicle for political/aesthetic reflexion' (1998). The film's reception was especially favourable in France, where it received awards at the Clermont-Ferrand and Saint-Paul festivals and inspired followers.

The narrative peculiarity of *Island of Flowers* resides in the combination of different materials, such as photographs, newspaper and magazine clippings, citations from encyclopaedias and poems, all edited together in quick montage and accompanied by voice over commentary, spoken by celebrated gaucho actor Paulo José. The film follows the trajectory of a tomato, since its cultivation by Japanese farmer Suzuki, until its collection by paupers at the rubbish dump of Island of Flowers. The parodic style, entirely in tune with the postmodern fragmentary superficiality in vogue at that time, includes a critique of the trite didacticism practiced in newsreels, school books and TV programmes, deconstructing the official discourse in a country marked by economic inequality. But it is not exactly a novelty in itself, as it had been utilised in Brazilian cinema as far back as in 1970, in Nelson Pereira do Santos' *How Tasty Was My Little Frenchman*. *Island of Flowers'* originality resides in the radicalisation of this method, turning it into a curious predecessor of the music video and self-reflexive advertisement and TV programmes. Not accidentally Jorge Furtado is one of the most successful authors of TV series in Brazil, including episodes of *City of Men,* a series produced in the wake of *City of God* and exported to various other countries, including the UK.

I would like to stress the itinerant trajectory of this auteurist trait, which, in the international context, has acquired the quality of a national contribution to a transnational language under construction. One of the most successful films of recent French cinema, *Amélie* (Jean-Pierre Jeunet, 2001), utilises an identical narrative technique, even though, of course, with much more sophisticated means. If

Island of Flowers ridicules positivist scientific discourse, beginning with information on the exact latitude and longitude degrees of Rio Grande do Sul, *Amélie* opens with the information, also conveyed by voice over, that a 'bluebottle fly, capable of 14,570 wing beats a minute, landed on Rue St. Vincent, Montmartre' at a given time and date. It is followed by the entirely parodic description of Amélie's birth, with all the artifices of stills, freeze frames and didactic material once employed in the Brazilian short.

Island of Flowers and its parodic didacticism also resonates in *City of God,* in Rocket's voice over, when, for example, he gives a lecture on cocaine processing and drug traffic hierarchy.

Island of Flowers, if not a direct contribution to, is certainly a predecessor of the narrative style, again with voice over and parodic didacticism, of a film such as *Y tu mamá también* (Alfonso Cuarón, 2001). Here, two irresponsible adolescents, driving about the streets of Mexico City, bump into political demonstrations and corpses of workers killed in the traffic, which, for them, are nothing but traffic obstacles, leading to ironic self-reflexive voice over commentary.

I believe that the development of such narrative techniques, which reflect an acute awareness of the problems of the contemporary world, makes room for the expression of authorship, but of democratic auteurs, convinced of the benefit they can gain from collaborative work and dialogue with international partners.

References

Bentes, I. (2003) 'The *sertão* and the *favela* in contemporary Brazilian film', in L. Nagib (ed) *The New Brazilian Cinema*. London and New York: I.B. Tauris.

Chauí, M.(2001) *Brasil – mito fundador e sociedade autoritária*. São Paulo: Fundação Perseu Abramo.

Costa, J.F. (1998) 'Um filme contra o Brazil indiferente', Interview with Walter Salles, in *Folha de S. Paulo, Mais!*, 29 March, pp. 5–7.

Ewald Filho, R. (1998) Interview with Walter Salles available on the DVD of *Central Station*.

Mantovani, B., Meirelles, F. and Muller, A.L. (2003) *Cidade de Deus – o roteiro do filme*. Rio de Janeiro: Objetiva.

Nagib, L. (2004) 'Talking Bullets – the Language of Violence in *City of God*', in *Third Text*, Vol. 18, No. 3, pp. 239–250.

Rocha, G.(2003) *Revisão crítica do cinema brasileiro*. São Paulo: Cosac & Naify.

Stam, R. (1998) In *Estudios Interdisciplinarios de America Latina y el Caribe,* 9 (1), June.

Sundance Institute Web Page (2005). http://institute.sundance.org

Truffaut, F. (1954) 'Une certaine tendance du cinéma français', *Cahiers du Cinéma*, 31, January, pp. 15–29.

Chapter 8

Copycat TV and new trade routes in Asia and the Pacific

Albert Moran and Michael Keane

> Many foreign reality TV programmes have content that just could not work in China, such as expensive prizes, voyeurism, nudity and sex, as well as glamorous looking people cheating each other in order to attract viewers.
> Chen Qiang, Producer of the Chinese reality show *Into Shangrila*; interview with authors, 12 October 2003).

Over the past few years Asian cinema has gained a higher profile in global markets. Successes – including *Crouching Tiger, Hidden Dragon* (Director Ang Lee: Taiwan), *Hero*, *The House of Flying Daggers* (Zhang Yimou: P.R. China), *Old Boy* (Park Chan-wook: South Korea) – have shown that creativity is flourishing outside of the established Hong Kong and Bollywood movie clusters. These successes are just the tip of an iceberg of creative content moving westwards. However, this considerable presence and its potential contributions into GDP have been underestimated in major audio-visual industry reports.[*]

Content *is* 'a growth industry' in Asia. In emphasising this, we can point to the following: the rapid growth of the Indian satellite television market; the high adoption rate of 3G mobile phones in South Korea, Taiwan, and China; the availability of express broadband capability in South Korea that allows audiences feedback into production of games and television; and the rapid distribution of cut-price DVDs in China, Hong Kong, and Indonesia, often through black markets (Keane, 2004; Chin, 2003).

Recent attention by television researchers to geo-linguistic regions, or 'cultural continents', as significant mediators of a worldwide reach of broadcasting suggests a middle level of investigation between the global and the local (Barker, 1997; Cunningham and Jacka, 1996a; Goonasekera and Lee, 1998; Straubhaar, 1997; Sinclair, Jacka and Cunningham, 1996). In this chapter we examine how Asian television industries are responding to media industry internationalisation in the first decade of the 21st century. We show how growth in local content aligns with

---
[*] An OECD report (1998) as well as a report commissioned by the UK Television Exports Enquiry DCMS (1999) provide limited recognition of the dynamism of non-English markets.

changes in global media practices, primarily multi-channelling and the increasing proclivity on the part of producers to adapt and exploit successful formulas. We base our claim that Asian content is more *tradeable* from our research into national and international television program formats.*

In attempting to categorise regional differences we have broadly distinguished three cultural continents: East Asia (Japan, South Korea, Taiwan, Hong Kong, and the People's Republic of China), South Asia (India, Singapore, Indonesia, and the Philippines) and Oceania (Australia and New Zealand).

The new content trade routes

Cultural traffic is on the increase as information superhighways expand in many directions. As nation states lose capacity to control the flow of information into their borders, they look to strategies to send out their ideas and images to the world. The export of creative content is necessary – not so much for its obvious tangible economic dividends, but for its intangible outcomes. Export success can offset the negative effects of sophisticated imports from the centres of global production. When sold at prices that local markets can afford, 'foreign' programming becomes an impediment to local industry development, as well as a source of nationalist discomfort for many. While media industries in many parts of the globe have attempted to copy international genres and organisational models, there are ways of making programming, assuring finance, and securing distribution that devolve from local knowledge. In this environment of increased trade in programming the TV format provides a vehicle for ideas to be transferred (Keane, Fung and Moran, 2006).

Local television industries have always existed in relationships of dialogue – internally, among themselves, and externally, with industries elsewhere. Three different forms of exchange control this interaction (1) the licensing of programmes for broadcast elsewhere; (2) international co-productions; and (3) the adaptation of TV programme production ideas from one place to another. Licensing and syndication of programming is well known and has been extensively researched while co-productions have attracted the attention of scholars. The third kind of exchange is less recognised, although a moment's reflection enables us to call to mind recent instances, such as the various national versions of 'international formats' including *Survivor*, *Idol*, *The Weakest Link*, *Big Brother* and *Who Wants to be a Millionaire?* In the Asian television landscape we identify a rapid rise in formatting activity. In south and south-east Asia we observe how these international quiz and game show formats are reworked into hybrid versions, while in East Asia the popularity and reach of Japanese formats are evident in shows such as *Happy Family Plan*, *Iron Chef*, and *Future Diary*, to name but a few.

---

*   In 2000 we undertook two pilot projects; this was followed in 2001/2 by a larger study of Australia, India, Indonesia, Japan, New Zealand, The Philippines, The People's Republic of China, Hong Kong, Singapore, South Korea, and Taiwan. The areas we observed contain a variety of broadcasting industries that are qualitatively very different from each other, not least in their attitude to formats as intellectual property. By examining eleven different television systems, it was possible to track a series of different format flows, economic and cultural chains that link national industries together.

Landscapes of abundance and adaptation

Television is undergoing a sustained shift, away from oligopoly-based scarcity associated with broadcasting towards a more differentiated abundance or saturation associated with the proliferation of new and old television services, technologies and providers. One major consequence of these changes is likely to be a falling audience for any particular television show, no matter how fashionable it seems to be. With so many channels and technologies of distribution and circulation, it is increasingly impossible for any hit show, no matter how popular, to register the kinds of ratings achievable in earlier phases of television. In turn, several responses to this situation are now evident. One of these is stagnation, if not a drop, in the system's demand for more expensive forms of prime-time programming. In the UK and Australia, for example, there has been a decline in demand for both drama and current affairs programming in prime time (Brunsdon et al., 2001). In other words, in characterising the present era as one of abundance, it has to be borne in mind that this tendency only occurs with certain programming genres, and it occurs at the expense of other types of content.

What then is the motor or source of this differentiated abundance? How does it register as a phenomenon and how does it come about? The significant dynamic of the present era in television seems to be one of adaptation, transfer and recycling of narrative and other kinds of content. Not surprisingly, this tendency is not limited to television but instead is characteristic across media and cultural industries. Nor is it unique to the present epoch. However, in the present age of international media conglomerates, recycling and adaptation of content across different media platforms is rapidly multiplying to the point of marginalising, if not extinguishing other economic and cultural practices.

Many of these different kinds of adaptations are familiar. Films become television series just as television series trigger feature films. Remakes are equally common although these are sometimes known under other names such as the sequel, the spin-off, or even the prequel. And this general phenomenon of a content-genealogy does not end there. Narratives can span several media – theatrical film, television, video, DVD re-release, video games, CD soundtrack, radio, comics, novels, stage shows, musicals, posters, merchandising, and theme parks. Fanzines and Internet web sites further spin out these contents. Individually and collectively, this universe of narrative and content constitutes a loosening of the notion of closure and the self-contained work of art.

Behind this proliferation of transfers, this ever-expanding recycling of content, is a set of new economic arrangements designed to secure a degree of financial and cultural insurance not easily available in the multi-channel environment of the present. Adapting already successful materials and content offers some chance of duplicating past and existing successes. Media producers, including those operating in the field of television, attempt to take out financial and cultural insurance by using material that is in some way familiar to the audience. Having invested in the brand, it makes good business sense to derive further value from it in these different ways. And, of course, in turn, this tendency of recycling is further facilitated by the fact of owning the copyright on the property in the first place.

In the age of multi-channelling and adaptation, there is a clearly identified need to derive as much financial mileage out of an ownership as possible – hence the idea of Intellectual Property. Despite rhetoric to the contrary, rights are not innate or inherent. Rather, they are constructed aspects of the competition between different programme producers, local and international, and between different users of program content and 'brands' – broadcasters, cable, radio, telephone and internet. The interests in rights held by television companies – both producers and broadcasters – are not defined abstractly but change with commercial circumstances. For example, the income generated from the licensing of a TV programme into public usage has to be measured against its use as a means of promotion. As Frith has pointed out, copyright is generally used to make money rather than to control use (Frith, 1987).

Adaptation through formats: globalisation in another guise?

This emphasis on rights helps secure the general conditions for the process of selling the same content over and over again across a series of different media. The TV format is now a crucial mechanism in regulating the recycling of programme content across different television systems. In contradistinction to general use of the term and even its specific application in radio, a television format is understood as that set of invariable elements in a programme out of which the variable elements of an individual episode are produced; or, as a more homely explanation for would-be format-devisors would have it:

> A format sale is a product sale. The product ... is a recipe for re-producing a successful television program, in another territory, as a local program. The recipe comes with all the necessary ingredients and is offered as a product along with a consultant who can be thought of as an expert chef . (Bodycombe, 2002)

In the recent present, the process of international adaptation of TV programme ideas has been deliberately systematized and formalised through a series of related measures. These include the deliberate generation of value-adding elements under the name of the format (such as the format Bible), format marketing arrangements (industry festivals and markets), licensing processes and a form of self-regulation within the newly formed, Cologne-based Format Registration and Protection Association (FRAPA). This new situation and arrangement formalises what was once casual and spontaneous as a means of deriving financial benefit, most especially from overseas adaptations. Now TV programmes are not simply devised and produced for local buyers with the (often faint) hope that they might sell elsewhere in the world. Instead, they are consciously created with the deliberate intention of achieving near simultaneous international adaptation. Additionally, increased communication and company linkages around the world have meant that unauthorised appropriation of TV programme formats, especially in the larger international metropolitan centres of population, are less and less likely to go unchallenged.

Within the East Asian continent Japanese television industries play an influential role, circulating content that is 'already local'. In Hong Kong, Taiwan and China local producers 'cleanse' imported formats according to cultural values. Countries such as India, Singapore, and Malaysia exhibit greater porousness to English-language programming in contrast to Japan, Korea, Taiwan, and the People's Republic of China (PRC), whose audio-visual products do not attract a great deal of competition from English programming. Linguistic isolation works to the advantage of local content production in East Asia as they are able to make local language versions. In South Asia Hindi, Malay, Chinese, and Tamil constituencies allow multiple versions of formats to be made; in many instances these are unlicensed copies of popular 'brand' formats (Thomas and Kumar, 2004). Indonesia and the Philippines in turn demonstrate a rapid uptake of the format mode of production (Kitley, 2004; Santos, 2004).

This process is not dissimilar from what is occurring in Australia and New Zealand, However, certainly so far as cultural and economic trade is concerned, Australia and New Zealand are part of a different 'cultural continent' whose geographical centre is located in the Northern Hemisphere. In other words, despite some recent claims about Australia becoming more open and oriented to East Asia, the fact seems to be that both these regions of white, settler societies remain firmly within a Western Anglophone region whose centre is the US, the UK and western Europe.

East Asia: information challenge shows and soft reality

In order to contextualise the maturity of content industries in East Asia, we need to recognize that cultural borrowing, combined with a range of trade and industrial policies, encouraged the growth of high-tech and capital intensive industries in the region, allowing countries like Japan, Singapore, Taiwan, and South Korea to become competitive during the mid-1980s, and regional centres like Hong Kong to establish cluster advantages. The confidence derived from competitiveness asserted itself in cinema and television production during the 1990s.

The East Asian mediascape was of interest to us because of its economic dynamism, shared values, and extensive history of cultural flows. Japanese influence remains particularly strong and is filtered through a variety of popular cultural genres, often using Hong Kong and Taiwan as a conduit (Iwabuchi, 2002; Yeh and Davis, 2002). Television consumption practices in Taiwan and South Korea have for some time reflected Japanese influences and styles – although in recent years both South Korea and Taiwan have managed to develop their own distinctive aesthetic.

The most conspicuous format newcomer in Asia is the 'winner-take-all' quiz show. While quiz shows have been a staple diet of audiences in Japan, China, Hong Kong, Taiwan, and Korea for some time, the sudden emergence and licensing of the international brand format *Who Wants to be a Millionaire?* (produced by UK-based company Celador) created a new benchmark for quiz show makers. Quiz shows became information challenges, and became more exciting and riveting. Part of the mystique and attraction of the Celador format is the magic lure of becoming an instant millionaire. *Who Wants to be a Millionaire?* was first broadcast in Singapore in August 2001, initially in English, then in Mandarin Chinese. A Cantonese version was unveiled in Hong Kong in May 2001 while versions followed in India (Hindi); The Philippines (Filipino), and Indonesia (Bahasa) (see below)

Until the arrival of *Who Wants to be a Millionaire?*, large payouts were not permitted on television in China, Japan or Korea. Japan's version had already made its entry into the market by 2000, creating a surge in ratings for Fuji Television (Iwabuchi,

2004). In Japan the maximum prize for a single contestant still remains 2 million yen (10,800 GBP). While this amount might appear insubstantial in comparison with the UK and US payouts, there is the proviso in Japan that a maximum prize of 10 million yen (54,000 GBP) can be shared among five team members: the person answering questions and nominated 'phone-a friend' team members. In Hong Kong, where there is no limit on prizes, the success of the Celador 'franchise' was partly attributed to a yearning for material success in a time where the Asian economic crisis had hit hard (Fung, 2004). With people losing their hard-earned savings in the crisis the idea of instant wealth created a 'Millionaire fever'. Reports estimated that ATV had to pay Celador, the UK franchising company a license fee around HK$2 million in total, and around HK$20,000–30,000 for each subsequent episode of *Who Wants to be a Millionaire?* (Chau, 2001).

In China Celador optioned the format to Shanghai Television (STV) but local producers felt that its viability in the Chinese marketplace was compromised by the focus on individualism and the excessively large prize payout. Reluctance to commit, however, had more to do with the cost of buying a format license, a mode of programme exchange which at the time was foreign in China. The Hong Kong company entrusted with distributing the format in China, Fengyu, meanwhile attempted to persuade local stations of the viability of the format deal, comparing it to the brands of KFC and MacDonalds (Keane, Fung and Moran, 2006). In the interim, however, the Beijing-based national broadcaster China Central Television (CCTV) had noticed the international appeal of *Who Wants to be a Millionaire?*, and moved quickly to gain the first mover advantage with its own programme *The Dictionary of Happiness* (*kaixin cidian*). The similarity between CCTV's winner-take-all quiz show and *Millionaire* was more than just serendipitous, although the producer of *The Dictionary of Happiness*, recognising the economic value of the show, distanced themselves and CCTV from accusations of plagiarism. Despite Celador claiming a trademark on its '50:50', 'Phone A Friend' and 'Ask The Audience', the CCTV version heavily exploited these key elements. Even the background, set design, and use of heartbeat background sounds during questions, are strikingly similar.

A sub-category of winner-take-all formats in East Asia is the elimination reality game show or elimination quiz show. The most recognizable-profile international models are *The Weakest Link* and *Survivor*. While these programs have been criticised as being too individualistic and materialistic for Asian audiences, there have nevertheless been several attempts to utilise the fundamental premise on which these shows are based. This is the prisoner's dilemma, a gambit that necessitates contestants forming strategic alliances with other players in order to progress in the game. This makes for a complex game in which viewers have the pleasure of anticipating alliances. However, despite these intricacies, *The Weakest Link* failed to impress Taiwanese viewers, where it was localised as *The Wise Survive* (*zhizhe shengcun*). The stern manner of the quizmaster was adjudged to be inappropriate for a culture intent on maintaining face. In Hong Kong the format rights for *The Weakest Link* (*yibi OUT xiao*) were purchased by TVB in 2001 to counter the success of *Who Wants to be a Millionaire?* on rival network ATV (Fung, 2004). In Japan the format had a brief but unspectacular lifespan during 2001, again introduced in the wake of *Millionaire* success. By the time *The Weakest Link* was introduced in mainland China, it was retitled *The Wise Rule* (*zhizhe wei wang*), and the host, an attractive woman called Shen Bing, well-known as an investigative journalist, offered words of encouragement rather than berating, cajoling, and humiliating contestants. Interestingly, ECM, the distributors of *The Weakest Link*, had offered the franchise to Shanghai Oriental Television, who declined the opportunity, again citing the fact that it was not culturally appropriate for Chinese viewers. Meanwhile Nanjing Television, a smaller station, took up the ECM franchise. Following this, Shanghai Oriental Television went ahead and made an unlicensed knock-off version called *The Examination Room of Riches* (*caifu da kaocha*) with a high prize of 220,000 RMB (21,500 Euro) (Keane, 2004b; Keane, Fung and Moran, 2006).

The reality game show, *Survivor*, the first format to utilise the prisoner's dilemma as its mainstay, has achieved great success from its strategy of locating its contestants in 'hostile' oriental settings such as Borneo, Thailand, and more recently Pearl Islands. However, attempts to localise the format in Asia have met with disapproval by audiences. Japanese *Survivor* commenced in April 2002 (Tokyo Broadcasting System) with a great deal of promotional activity, only to struggle with its own survival. Reluctance to countenance the key elements of the *Survivor* format has also resulted in localisation according to more 'collectivist' values of cooperation in Mainland China. A Chinese version called *Into Shangrila* (*zouru Xianggelila*) was made in 2002. According to the producer, Chen Qiang, this was a great leap forward for Chinese programming:

> At the beginning, we needed to promote an idea and a concept. We did not start from the programming. We had to tell (audiences) that this was not a TV drama, not a documentary, not a variety program, and not a talk show. It is a reality TV show. What is reality TV? It is about real people and events. It was being made for the first time. Nobody knows what will happen and what will be the result. It can make common people into heroes, common people can have leading roles, and viewers become the adjudicators. These kind of slogans were used to promote and market the format. The aim is that we wanted ordinary people to understand how to enjoy the format and play along together with it. So we had to chart a course that was more problematic than the West. Our audiences were on a different level than western audiences. (Interview with producer, 17 October 2003)

Filmed in the foothills of the Himalayas in Sichuan province, it offered Chinese viewers a chance to identify with members of two teams – the sun and moon teams – striving for an ultimate glory (no cash prize) and testing their mettle in a series of challenges, against the elements and against themselves. The programme announces itself as documentary: an anthropological and sociological examination of people's relationships, rather than the dog-eat-dog nature of the international *Survivor* formats. The promotional material for the program closely echoed its international cousins. The opening credits even saw the word 'China' burning across the ground, a branding strategy reminiscent of the opening credits of the Western versions.

Into Shangrila attempted to generate publicity through its novelty. Apart from national propaganda campaigns of the revolutionary past, nothing like this had been attempted before in China, certainly nothing of this scale. The preparations for the adventure were linked to national web-sites and people could follow the events unfold. The show was itself responsible for coining a new Chinese term – *zhenren*

TRADING CULTURE

Fig. 1. Into Shangri-la, *an independent Chinese production echoing the global* Survivor *format: Challenges are overcome through cooperation. [Image courtesy of Chen Qiang, Weihan Cultural Production.]*

xiu – literally 'real person show'. By the time the show was broadcast the term reality television had become part of the vernacular and new ways of blending reality with documentary were being offered to station officials.

South Asia: the multi-racial format

For the purposes of our research the south Asian cultural continent includes India, Singapore, Indonesia, and the Philippines. In many respects programming is more diverse in these areas due to a multiplicity of language groups. Linguistic variation generates format abundance as multiple language versions are possible; many of these are economically viable as such linguistic communities are vast. In India for example there are seventeen major languages, aside from Hindi and English (Thomas and Kumar, 2004). Singapore, while being usually identified as a Chinese city, endorses a policy of multi-racialism and television is broadcast in English, Mandarin, Tamil, and Malay. While Indonesia is a Muslim country, it has a recent history of importing programming, including localizing Chinese and Indian drama scripts. In the Philippines most programming is in Filipino, although English is understood by many of the elite classes.

Format activity has increased in south and south-east Asia in recent years as international game show formats, both licensed and unlicensed, have displaced to some extent a former reliance on finished programming. In Indonesia local content increased significantly during the period from 1994 to 1999 on all television stations (see Kitley, 2004: 142). Licensed formats have become part of the business of broadcasting during this period. In 1994 the broadcaster Indosiar had taken advantage of a contractual arrangement with Hong Kong's TVB to adapt 800 Chinese

Chapter 8 • Copycat TV and new trade routes in Asia and the Pacific

television drama scripts, thereby reducing the strain on local scriptwriters, but in the process creating an industrial furore tinged with racism (Kitley: 147). Even earlier during the 1970s and 1980s children's game show formats such as *Romper Room* had been licensed from the Australian company Becker Entertainment. Shows that were licensed in Indonesia in recent years include *Who Wants to be a Millionaire?* (Celador), *Family Feud* (Fremantle Media), *Russian Roulette* (Columbia Tristar), and *Newlywed Games* (Becker Entertainment).

In Singapore shows such as *Who Wants to be a Millionaire?* and *The Weakest Link* became mainstream hits, replicating trends elsewhere and precipitating widespread debates in the print media as to the effects of formats (Lim, 2004). The trend towards exploiting this new mode of media globalisation and avoiding paying license fees has led to a 'copy and be damned' attitude in places such as China and India in particular. In India opportunistic cloning merged with multi-lingual diversity, resulting in what Thomas and Kumar (2004) have called 'clones of clones'. This is the practice of making local versions of copies of international formats. For instance, the massive and sudden popularity of the licensed version of *Who Wants to be a Millionaire?* (*Kaun Banega Crorepati*) spawned copies including Zee TV's *Sawal Dus Crore Ka* and Sony ET's *Chapar Phadke*. However, the only clone of *Millionaire* that managed to compete with the original was one produced in the Tamil language by Sun TV, a South Indian channel (Thomas and Kumar 2004, 133).

The Philippines presents a case study of where the foreign format *Who Wants to be a Millionaire?* encountered a strategic opponent. *Millionaire*, along with *The Weakest Link*, and *The Price is Right*, had established a formidable presence in viewing schedules. The Filipino *Millionaire* was a cheaper version of the original with money saved on sets. Nevertheless, it was effective in winning ratings for the government sequestered Channel 13. ABS-CBN, the dominant network, having felt the tide turn, moved to up the ante with a counter program, *Are You Ready for the Game?* (*Game Ka Na Ba*), which drew on many of the key elements of Celador's original such as a modernistic set with visual aids. However, there was the added lure of prizes and jackpots exceeding those of *Who Wants to be a Millionaire?* Josefina Santos (2004) notes that the lesson learnt from *Are You Ready for the Game?* is that local versions can compete and defeat international formats. The comparative advantage here was that by avoiding paying the significant license fee ABS-CBN was able to shift its production expenses into providing big prizes, a tactic that won the day.

Oceania: the Anglo-American/ European main street

The cultural continent in which the least amount of 'tweaking' is required is arguably Oceania or the Pacific Rim. As these names suggest, the latter is not a part of Asia no matter how proximate. Additionally, the vast area of the region is mostly composed of water dotted by islands. Of the latter, Australia and New Zealand have the largest populations followed by many underdeveloped countries with small populations including Papua New Guinea and Fiji. Australia and New Zealand are therefore the main television markets in this region and formed separate case studies in our project. Given the fact that these country's economic foundations, political institutions, and cultural patterns mark them as part of an international Anglo-American diasporic formation, one of the many sites of a global English geo-linguis-

TRADING CULTURE

Fig. 2. Three contestants examine the day's strategies.
[Image courtesy of Chen Qiang, Weihan Cultural Production Company.]

tic configuration, it might be predicted that the two television industries would look well beyond the television infrastructures of their geographically close neighbours for the television ideas and techniques that can help underwrite the start up of new programmes. These countries are avowedly not part of the Asian geo-linguistic region, despite the fact that from time to time, cultural researchers – including those concerned with media – have claimed their 'Asianisation' (cf. Cunningham and Jacka, 1996b). In both the Australian and New Zealand television schedules TV format trade is of central importance in producing many of the 'headline' programmes that dominate programming. More formats come in rather than go out. Where they come from is the Anglo-American/European main street of international television. The Australian and New Zealand television producers and broadcasters almost universally draw their format imports from the US, the UK, The Netherlands, Germany and one or two other European industries. Television formats do not come from Asia to these 'major minors'.

English-language programming emanating from the UK and America finds a comfortable fit within Oceania, at least in Australia and New Zealand. Format traders such as Endemol, BBC, Fremantle Media, ECM and Distraction have managed to secure distribution and partnerships in Australia and New Zealand. The most notable of these to date has been Endemol's collaboration with Southern Star to co-produce the Australian version of *Big Brother*. The latter was first licensed to the Ten Network in 2001 and each succeeding year has seen another series licensed by the same broadcaster. In turn, both because the New Zealand television market at less than 4 million viewers is deemed to be too small for a local version and because

New Zealand appeal can be built into the Australian version, the same programme is broadcast in the two markets.

This instance of a common Australasian version of *Big Brother* is one example among several of convergences between these neighbouring television industries. As always, the traffic has been two-way. Budgetary matters are often decisive, particularly with formats imported from the UK and Europe. For example, New Zealand could not afford the requisite production budget (including licensing fees) for such overseas hit formats as *Survivor*, *Big Brother*, *Who Wants To Be A Millionaire?*, and *The Weakest Link*, and had to make do with sharing in the versions produced primarily for the Australian market.

On the other hand, New Zealand has acted as a format incubator and was the source of the format of *Popstars* (Lealand, 2004). First broadcast on New Zealand television, the idea was acquired by the Australian company Screentime (now with additional offices in Auckland, Dublin and London). The Australian production subsequently became the prototype for this very successful international format. Another point worth mentioning is the recent history of programme ideas and formats that have made the leap from New Zealand to other places. Most recently, as Geoff Lealand documents, Touchdown Productions had consciously chosen to bypass Australia with a new format, *The Chair*, and instead struck a deal with CBS for the first adaptation. The show went to air after its devisor attempted to secure a court injunction against what seemed like a clumsy attempt by a rival broadcaster Fox to produce its own clone called *The Chamber*.

Concluding remarks

As mentioned in the beginning of this chapter, the adaptation of already successful materials and content offers a means of duplicating successes. Media producers are in effect taking out financial and cultural insurance by using material that is in some way familiar to the audience. As this chapter has suggested, the media incubation effect in Asia is occurring not only at the level of technological hardware take-up but also in the area of software provision. The latter shift aligns with important changes in global media practices not least in television multi-channelling and the rationalisation of content generation through format adaptation. With increasingly efficient and rapid distribution mechanisms in place globally, broadcasters and producers in the region of study have been quick to exploit successful programming blueprints developed both elsewhere in the region and in other industries across the world. However, as our study also confirmed, this part of the world is not geographically, economically, politically or culturally homogeneous. Instead, it has been necessary and convenient to decompose the area into a series of 'cultural continents' to obtain a sharper, harder grip on the complex reality of television programme format flows there. Hence, our major determination is that there are indeed new cultural trade routes in operation in Asia and the Pacific and that copycat TV is now a main avenue to this district of commerce and culture.

Acknowledgements: We would like to thank the Australian Research Council for supporting this project in its two incarnations. The main research was conducted as part of a three year project, The Economic, Cultural and Legal Dynamics of Television Format Flows in the Asia Pacific. Chief investigators were Albert Moran, Michael Keane, Amos Owen

Thomas, and Justin Malbon. We would also like to acknowledge the extended team: Koichi Iwabuchi (Japan), Anthony Fung (Hong Kong), Lee Dong-Hoo (South Korea), Liu Yu-Li and Chen Yi-Hsiang (Taiwan), Keval J. Kumar (India); Philip Kitley (Indonesia) Josefina Santos (The Philippines), Tania Lim (Singapore), Geoff Lealand (New Zealand). Unfortunately our research was not able to encompass all countries. Pakistan, Malaysia, and other Muslim locations such as Brunei will undoubtedly provide grounds for future revelations. We should point out that the study did not canvass audience reception. The methodologies we employed were a combination of interviews with producers, distributors, and television format industry agents. This was supported by documentary research.

References

Bandhu, P. (1992) *Black and White of Cinema in India*. Thiruvananthapuram: Odyssey.

Barker, C. (1997) *Global Television and Cultural Identities*. Buckingham, UK: Open University Press.

Bodycombe, D. (2002) 'So You Want to Create a Game Show: A Guide for the Budding Quiz Devisor'. Available at http//:www.tvformats.com/formatsexl2lained.htm

Brunsdon, C., Johnson, C., Moseley, R. and Wheatley. H. (2001) 'Factual Entertainment on British Television: The Midlands Research Group's 8–9 Project', *European Journal of Cultural Studies*, 4 (1): 29–63.

Chao, M. (2001) 'Chan Chi-wen: Nobody Should be Responsible', *Ming Pao Weekly*, 17.11: 58–59.

Chin S.Y. (ed) (2003). *Digital Review of Asia Pacific*. Penang: Southbound Press..

Cunningham, S. and Jacka, E. (1996a) *Australian Television and International Mediascapes*. Melbourne: Cambridge University Press.

Cunningham, S. and Jacka, E. (1996b) 'The Role of Television in Australia's 'Paradigm' Shift to Asia' , *Media Culture and Society*, 18 (4): 619–638.

DCMS (1999) *UK Television Exports Inquiry: The Report of the Creative Industries Task Force Inquiry into Television Exports*, London, DCMS.

Frith, S. (1987) 'Copyright and the Music Industry', *Popular Music*, 71: 57–75

Fung, A. (2004) 'Coping, Cloning, and copying: Hong Kong in the global television format business', A. Moran and M. Keane (eds) *Television across Asia: Television Industries, Programme Formats and Globalization*. London: Routledge Curzon, pp. 74–88.

Goonasekera, A. and Lee, P.S.N. (eds) (1998) *TV Without Borders: Asia Speaks Out*, Singapore: AMIC.

Iwabuchi, K. (2002) *Recentering Globalization, Popular Culture and Japanese Transnationalism*. Durham and London: Duke University Press

Iwabuchi, K. (2004) 'Feeling Glocal: Japan in the Global Television Format Business' in A Moran and M. Keane (eds) *Television across Asia: Television Industries, Programme Formats and Globalization*, London: Routledge Curzon, pp. 21–36.

Keane, M. (2004) 'Bringing Culture Back in', in J. Howell (ed) *Governance in China*. Lanham: Rowman and Littlefield, pp. 77–96.

Keane, M. (2004a) 'A Revolution in Programming and a Great Leap Forward for Production', in A. Moran and M. Keane (eds), *Television across Asia: Formats, Television Industries and Globalization*. London: Routledge Curzon, pp. 88–104.

Keane, M. (2004b) 'It's all in a Game: Television Game and Reality Formats in East Asia', in K Iwabuchi, S. Meucke, and M. Thomas, (eds), *Rogue Flows: Trans-Asian Cultural Traffic*. Hong Kong: Hong Kong University Press, pp. 53–72.

Keane, M., Fung, A. and Moran, A. (2006) *New Television, Globalisation and the East Asian Cultural Imagination*. Hong Kong: Hong Kong University Press.

Kitley, P (2004) 'Closing the Creativity Gap – Renting Intellectual Capital in the Name of Local Content: Indonesia in the Global Television Format Business', in A. Moran and M. Keane (eds) *Television across Asia: Television Industries, Programme Formats and Globalization*. London: Routledge Curzon, pp. 138–156.

Lealand, G. (2004) 'An Export/import Industry: New Zealand in the Global Television Format Business, in A. Moran and M. Keane (eds) *Television across Asia: Television Industries, Programme Formats and Globalization*. London: Routledge Curzon, pp. 185–196.

Lee, Dong-Hoo (2004) 'A Local Mode of Programme Adaptation: Korea in the Global Television Format Business', in A Moran and M. Keane (eds) *Television across Asia: Television Industries, Programme Formats and Globalization*. London: Routledge Curzon, pp. 36–53.

Lee, Dong-Hoo (2004) 'The case of Yojolady', paper presented at the JAMCO Symposium, Tokyo, February 2004.

Lim, T. (2004) 'Singapore Slings into Action with Game Show Formats' in A. Moran and M. Keane (eds) *Television across Asia: Television Industries, Programme Formats and Globalization*. London: Routledge Curzon, pp. 105–121.

Moran, A. (1998) *Copycat TV, Globalization, Program Formats and Cultural Identity*. Luton: University of Luton Press)

Moran, A. and Keane, M. (eds) (2004) *Television across Asia: Television Industries, Programme Formats and Globalization*. London: Routledge Curzon.

OECD (1998) *Content as a New Growth Industry Working Party on the Information Economy*, Paris: OECD.

Santos, J, (2004) 'Reformatting the format' in A. Moran and M. Keane (eds). *Television across Asia: Television Industries, Programme Formats and Globalization*. London: Routledge Curzon, pp. 157–168.

Sinclair, J., Jacka, E. and Cunningham, S. (1996) 'Peripheral Vision', in J. Sinclair, E. Jacka and S. Cunningham (eds) *New Patterns in Global Television: Peripheral Vision*. New York: Oxford University Press.

Straubhaar, J. (1997) 'Distinguishing the Global, Regional and Local in International Communication', in A. Sreberny-Mohammadi, D. Winseck, J, McKenna and O. Boyd-Barret (eds) *Media in Global Context: A Reader*. London: Arnold, pp. 284–298.

Thomas, A.O. and Kumar, K. (2004) 'Copied from Without and Cloned from Within', in A. Moran and M. Keane (eds) *Television across Asia: Television Industries, Programme Formats and Globalization*. London: Routledge Curzon, pp. 122–137.

Yeh, Y.Y. and Davis, D. (2002) 'Japan Hongscreen: Pan-Asian Cinemas and Flexible Accumulation', *Historical Journal of Radio, Film and Television*, March. Online version available at http://www.findarticles.com/cf_0/m2584/1_22/84409366/print.jhtml

Chapter 9

From Latin Americans to Latinos: Spanish-language television and its audiences in the United States

John Sinclair

While it may be a truism that cultural identity is socially constructed rather than any given essence, it has to be constructed out of something. In the case of the various peoples who constitute the so-called 'Hispanics' of the United States, that 'something' is their common origin in Spanish-speaking countries. Even if we reject this category 'Hispanic' as an artefact of governmentality and marketing, and accept instead the term with which many of these people now prefer to identify themselves generically, 'Latino', and/or 'Latina', it is still their putative Spanish-speaking, or 'Latin' origin which unites them. This paper will outline the diversity amongst the peoples of Spanish-speaking origin in the US, and examine how, even in spite of their various efforts to forge cultural identities on their own terms, the institutions of government, media and marketing have ascribed to them a common cultural identity for them to assume within the mainstream. On the other hand, by reference to the Spanish-language television industry in particular, the paper also offers a case study in how institutions are having to adapt to the pressures they face in an era of increased cultural diversity within the nation-state and movement of peoples across its borders.

Diversity and diaspora

Leaving aside the fact that the speaking of Spanish in the Americas is the legacy of the first phase of European colonialism (and some would say, the beginning of globalization), the entry point in accounting for the diversity of peoples of Spanish-speaking origin in the US today is provided by the Chicano activist and film director Luis Valdez when he says, 'We did not, in fact, come to the United States at all. The United States came to us' (1972: xxxiii). This serves as a sharp reminder that the US incorporated thousands of Spanish-speaking people when it took over what are now its Southwestern states from Mexico after 1848, so that some Mexican-Americans in those areas can trace back their family histories there for over a hundred years, while others are arriving right now.

Thus, length of residence in the US is one major dimension of diversity. Yet it is not just a matter of when, but of the historically specific circumstances under which a certain people arrive which makes a difference. For example, the very fact that the Cubans (and the first Dominicans also) were political refugees from a crisis nation of the Cold War era has always put them in a quite different light to the Puerto Ricans, who are born as Spanish-speaking American citizens, since Puerto Rico is a possession of the US (Sullivan, 2000: 6); even within a given group of common origin, there is differentiation (apart from the usual race, class and gender). The Cubans thus distinguish between the 'golden exiles', the business and professional people who fled to Miami at the very beginning of the Cuban Revolution, and all subsequent waves of refugees (Soruco, 1996: 5–10).

The Puerto Ricans and the Cubans are the second and third largest groups of Hispanics identifiable by national origin, by far the largest being the Mexicans. According to the 2000 Census, Hispanics of Mexican origin amounted to 58.5 per cent of the 35.3 million Hispanics then in the US. Those of Puerto Rican origin were 9.6 per cent and Cuban 3.5 per cent. However, there were also significant totals in the aggregated categories of Central American, 4.8 per cent, South American, 3.8 per cent, and 'All Other Hispanic', 17.3 per cent. For the Central American category, the largest groups were Salvadorians and Guatemalans, and for South America, it was Colombians, Ecuadorians and Peruvians (US Census Bureau, 2001a). As for 'All Other Hispanic': since the terms 'Hispanic' and 'Latino' are intended to be non-pejorative and non-racial (the latter being used for the first time in the 2000 Census), many people seem to have obligingly identified themselves with those categories when they have been offered for statistical purposes. The fact is, however, they are more likely to think of themselves in terms of their national origin: that is, as Mexican or Mexican American, and so forth (Sullivan, 2000: 2–8).

Thus, in addition to time spent and the circumstances of arrival in the US, Hispanic groups are differentiated by the cultural and linguistic differences which tied them to their regional and/or national origins, just as surely as English-speakers recognize differences within and between the US, UK, Canada, Australia and New Zealand. Yet the presence of such large numbers of people in the same country who have a common language, but come from diverse origins, has no parallel in the English-speaking world. Rather, the US Spanish-speaking population more resembles, in an inverse way, the huge diasporic overseas populations of Chinese, Indians, and Arabs, who, like the Hispanics, have been cultivated as international markets for television in their own languages and cultures (Sinclair et al., 1996; Cunningham and Sinclair, 2001).

That is, to the extent that a 'diaspora' can be extended to mean a series of mass deterritorializations from various countries, whether occurring at finite historical stages or continuing into the present, as distinct from a single or continuous dispersal of people from the same origin, then the dispossessed Mexicans, the Cuban exiles, the Salvadorian and Guatemalan refugees, and the endless waves of Latin American 'economic refugees', whether documented or not, who are all now resident in the US, can be considered collectively to form a diaspora. More strictly speaking, they form a diaspora in reverse, since a traditional diaspora is the flow of people from one country into many, but these people have come from many countries into one: A neat ideological fit with the classic motto of the US, *E Pluribus Unum*.

Our interest here is in how such a diaspora can be shaped into a television audience. If we set aside the development of Spanish-language print and radio in the US and concentrate on the television era, decade by decade, it is possible to trace the emergence of an audience for Spanish-language television in the same process as collective identities were being formed by other forces, including their own intrinsic dynamics. However, there has remained a tension between the collective identities that various groups have chosen and asserted for themselves, and those which have been chosen for them by media and marketing interests.

The 1960s – Chicanos, SICC and SIN

Spanish-language television broadcasts in the US began as early as 1955, but it was not until 1961 that there were the beginnings of a network. In that year, the Spanish International Communication Corporation (SICC) launched its first station in San Antonio, followed by stations in other strategic locations over the next ten years, namely Los Angeles, New York and Miami. Programming was supplied by the Spanish International Network (SIN) from Mexico, the principal in these companies having been the founding father of the Azcárraga dynasty subsequently associated with Televisa in Mexico, although their manager was René Anselmo, a US Hispanic. The crude but durable economic model was that entertainment programming generated for a commercial audience in Mexico and already paid for and proven there, could do double service by attracting a culturally and linguistically similar audience in the US. This has since become a fundamental strategy for Latin American producer/distributors in the US, but it did not meet with immediate success. The prime reason for this was that an audience was still in the process of formation, and further, that advertisers had yet to be convinced of the very existence of that audience. According to Stephen Gaymont, Creative Director, Marketing and Communications, of Univisión in Miami, advertising sales staff for SICC had to carry a portable set to tune in and prove to prospective advertisers that they were not being scammed (personal communication, 1 August 2001).

It is interesting to note that US Hispanics were becoming conscious of themselves as a group and beginning to mobilize politically during much the same period that television was first seeking to cultivate them as an audience. This is not to suggest that there was a causal relationship in either direction, but just to observe the 'elective affinity', as Max Weber might have called it. In particular, amongst Mexican-Americans in the Southwest in the 1960s, mobilization occurred around the Chicano movement. The choice of the name is instructive in itself, especially in relation to the term 'Hispanic'. According to one cultural activist, 'Chicano' is a corruption of 'Meshicano', which although once derogatory, serves as an affirmation of both the Native American and the Hispanic origins of the Mexican people (Burciaga, 1992: 49). So, SICC/SIN were starting up their network while the Chicanos were struggling for rural labor reform in the Southwest, and at the same time, the 'golden exiles' from Cuba were setting themselves up as the establishment in Miami, and the Puerto Rican and Dominican communities were becoming concentrated in New York (the West Side, but that's another story).

TRADING CULTURE

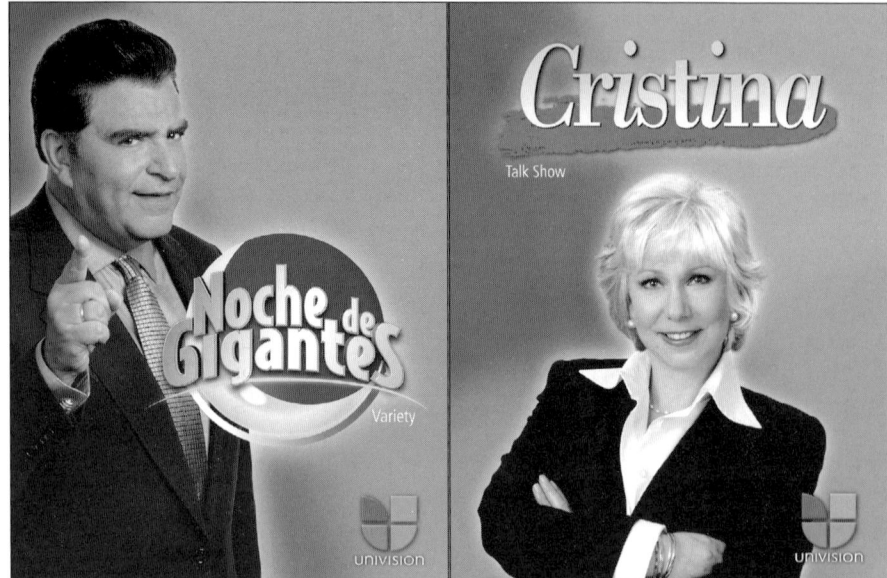

Fig. 1. Don Francisco, host of Sábado Gigante, a Saturday night variety show which he launched decades ago in his native Chile. Now produced at Univisión's studios in Miami, it has become an institution for audiences throughout the Spanish-speaking world. [Univision.]

Fig. 2. Cristina Saralegui, Cuban-born host of El Show de Cristina, the most popular talk show amongst Spanish-speaking audiences in the US, and widely seen outside the US, enjoying much the same status as Oprah does within the English-speaking world. [Univision.]

The 1970s – a narrowcast national network

'Prior to the 1970 census, the concept of Hispanics as a group barely existed' (Davis et al., 1983: 5), even for demographic purposes, let alone in cultural terms. As well as the diversity of socio-economic and national origins, sheer geographic dispersion militated against any sense of 'imagined community' (Anderson, 1991). However, before the end of the decade, SICC/SIN had built itself into a truly national network through the innovative application of the satellite as a new signal distribution technology, which was ideally suited to incorporating these dispersed people into one audience. In 1976, it fully interconnected all its stations and affiliates via satellite so that they could air the same programming at the same time – programming which itself was being transmitted via satellite from Mexico. This innovation put SICC/SIN ahead of the mainstream networks, ABC, CBS, and NBC, in being the very first network to be nationally interconnected via satellite, although SICC/SIN was pleased to follow the mainstream networks' practice when it then instituted a 'must carry' regime. This meant that SIN could oblige all the stations, as a national network, to carry the satellite feed, including commercials, beamed up from Mexico.

This is what we would now call 'global narrowcasting', delivering the signal over a very large territory, but to a small, specialised and widely-dispersed audience, in this case distinguished and united by Spanish as their lingua franca. Neither the size of the communities reached nor their distance apart mattered, as satellite coverage meant that they could be sold to advertisers as a national audience. However, the linguistic and cultural dimension was crucial to the constitution of that audience. Univisión (as SICC/SIN came to call itself in the 1980s) thus acquired a vested interest in cultivating the conception that all peoples of Spanish-speaking national origin in the US had been formed into a vast diaspora, and asserting this as the natural constituency of their network. Anselmo declared that Univisión's 'mission' was 'to unite the Puerto Rican in New York, the Cuban in Miami, the Mexican in San Antonio and the Chicano in Los Angeles through their common Spanish heritage' (Quoted in Bagamery, 1982: 99). But clearly, they had to do that on the economic basis of the predominantly Mexican programming to which they had low-cost access. As Arlene Dávila has argued, this has inclined Univisión to foster Mexican Spanish as the hegemonic standard, and at the same time, to cultivate a sense of common, pan-Hispanic 'Latinidad' (2000). The degree to which actual audiences identify with this is another question – Cubans, for example, are particularly resistant to being incorporated under such Mexican hegemony.

The 1980s – commercialization and competition

If the 1970s closed with the technical basis established for a national television audience, the 1980s saw the beginning of the ever more intensive commercial formation of that audience. This process involved advertising agencies and market research companies, as well as the advent of Telemundo, a rival network to Univisión, backed by mainstream 'Anglo' capital. Government also played a role to the extent that the 1980 Census yielded more reliable data than previously had been available. Whereas the 1970 Census had notoriously undercounted Hispanics, relying as it did on Spanish surnames, national origin, and whether Spanish was spoken at home, the 1980 Census introduced the method (basically that still being used) of asking people if they identified themselves as being 'of Spanish/Hispanic origin or descent' (Davis et al., 1983: 6–7).

The Census brought out the kind of demographic patterns that marketers like to see: the Hispanic population was young, growing, and concentrated in geographical regions. This in turn precipitated a whole commercial discourse about 'the Hispanic market', including the first market research studies (Yankelovitch et al., 1981; Guernica and Kasperuk, 1982), and the arrival of advertising agencies, such as Sosa and Associates in San Antonio (Sosa, 1998), that specialized in 'marketing to Hispanics', as a regular feature of the leading trade journal *Advertising Age* came to be called. Roberta Astroff has referred to these intermediaries between advertisers and the market as 'cultural brokers' (1997), who are themselves Hispanics, or Latinos, but there is a class difference which emerges here, to the extent that these people are college-educated and in a position to capitalize on their ethnicity by delivering Hispanics to advertisers, the mass of whom are 'racially non-White, linguistically Spanish-speaking, and socio-economically poor' (Rodriguez, 1997: 284–285).

Indeed, the generally lower levels of education, income and occupational status of Hispanics made many potential advertisers reluctant to embrace them as a new market, as it still does, but these characteristics have always been downplayed in the discourse. Relative to their countries of origin, US Hispanics have been claimed to be 'the wealthiest Hispanics in the world' (Guernica and Kasperuk, 1982: 59), and

TRADING CULTURE

Fig. 3. Publicity stills from Cara o Cruz ('Heads or Tails'), a telenovela produced for Telemundo by Argos Comunicación, an innovative production house in Mexico. This one was controversial for its theme of one woman commanding the love of two men. [Telemundo Inc.]

in any case, are reported to have other characteristics bound to endear them to advertisers. In particular, they spend much more of their disposable income on food and packaged goods than the general population, and are very conscious of brands, and loyal to them (Strategy Research Corporation, 1986).

We have seen that SIN/SICC/Univisión, the only Spanish-language national network in the US prior to 1986, had a close connection to Mexico, and thus, authentic credentials as being at least one major kind of 'Hispanic'. What was striking about Telemundo, the second network which emerged as its rival at that time, was the fact that it was backed by mainstream capital from Wall Street. Small independent Spanish-language stations in all the key markets were acquired and formed into a network. Experienced Hispanic managers were recruited, and programming obtained from a wider variety of sources than the customary fare available on Univisión, giving the new network appeal to Hispanics of other than Mexican origin, especially those on the East Coast. The venture was a token of mainstream capital's faith in the new discourse, and marked the emergence of Spanish-language television as an industry.

The 1990s – crisis and renewal

The 1990s saw the concentration of this industry in Miami. There are various structural reasons for this, which will be mentioned later in the paper, but it is worthwhile to note the role played by Univisión's reluctance to accommodate itself to the demands of non-Mexican Hispanics. Already in 1986, heavy-handed intervention in Univisión's news service by management from Mexico precipitated a

Chapter 9 • From Latin Americans to Latinos

Fig. 4. The logo first adopted by Telemundo around the time of its acquisition by Sony and Liberty Media in 2000, and still identifying it today, both in the US and internationally, following the network's purchase by NBC Universal in 2001. [Telemundo Inc.]

mass resignation of staff who then set up their own company in Miami to produce a news service for the competing network, *Noticiero Telemundo* (Marín, 1986). Telemundo itself had studios in Miami where it was producing original entertainment programming oriented to US Hispanics, and in 1991, moved its headquarters to that city.

Two other major developments in the industry during the 1990s were the expansion of the activities of US cable networks in providing their services in Spanish, and the institutionalization of audience measurement. CNN showed an early interest in exploiting the linkage between US Hispanic television and Latin American cable markets, first with dubbed entertainment programming, and subsequently with taking over *Noticiero Telemundo*. The sports channel ESPN began satellite transmission to cable systems in six nations of South America with a Spanish sound track in 1991, the same year in which Time-Warner launched a whole movie channel for Latin America, HBO Olé. As the 1990s progressed, these were joined by MTV Latino, Discovery, Cinemax, Fox Latin America and Spelling's TeleUno.

The other major transition was the establishment of a ratings measurement service for Spanish-language television. Prior to this, the network owners had not been able to provide the figures needed to convince potential advertisers of the nature and extent of Spanish-language television's reach. This had been a major disadvantage in their competition, not with each other, but with the mainstream networks, because many national advertisers believed, and many still do, that it was sufficient to advertise with the mainstream networks alone, particularly if the audiences for Spanish-language television were unknown.

So, in order to provide the hard data needed to sell the Hispanic audience, the commodity which they had created, to the major advertisers for whom they had made it, both the Spanish-language networks collaborated in commissioning Nielsen Media Research, the major US audience measurement company, to set up a ratings measurement service for Spanish-language television, the Nielsen Hispanic Television Index. The first national figures were produced in 1992, and documented

Univisión's commanding position, an overall 61 per cent share of the prime time audience (Sinclair, 1999: 111).

The quincentennial year of 1992 was a watershed in the development of both the major networks themselves. Given the high costs of local production and their limited access to Mexican *telenovelas*, the kind of programming perennially most popular with the majority of the Spanish-speaking audience, Telemundo's uncompetitive position resulted in bankruptcy. At the same time, there was a significant change of ownership at Univisión. Televisa had lost control of Univisión in 1986 when its level of Mexican ownership was found to be illegal, and both the stations and the network were sold to Hallmark, the greeting cards company. In 1992, Hallmark sold Univisión to a carefully-structured consortium which had a majority of its ownership in US hands, but with very significant minority shares being held by Televisa, and also by a major Venezuelan production/distribution company, Venevisión. This arrangement effectively gave both the Latin American companies a guaranteed outlet for their programming in the US, just as it secured a supply of programming for Univisión and consolidated its dominance over the industry in the US (Subervi-Vélez, Ramírez Berg, Constantakis-Valdés, Noriega, & Wilkinson, 1994).

Before the end of the decade, there was also a significant change of hands at the ailing Telemundo, this time marking the incursion of transnational capital to the industry. The deal took the form of the Sony Corporation acquiring about 40 per cent of Telemundo, and Liberty Media, about 35 per cent ('Telemundo Communications Group, Inc.', 2001). This internationalization of the players active in the industry is one of a number of contemporary trends and further developments to be considered in the next and final section of the paper.

Trends in the New Millennium

As the situation appears in early 2005, there has continued to be internationalization in the US Spanish-language television industry, other main trends being the expansion of the present networks, the diversification of the programming on offer, and the continued concentration of the industry in Miami.

There is further internationalization in the ownership of networks taking place, given that TV Azteca, the competitor to Televisa in Mexico and one-time collaborator with Telemundo in the US, has been seeking to develop a network in the US Azteca America Incorporated was first announced as a joint venture in the US of TV Azteca with Pappas Telecasting Companies, which owns stations in the key markets, and was to control 80 per cent of the company ('TV Azteca and Pappas Telecasting', 2000). However, after months of inaction, and much scepticism amongst observers, Pappas Telecasting announced it would drop its investment in favor of a much more modest affiliate relationship with Azteca. By late 2004, Azteca America was transmitting through 38 affiliates in most of the major cities with substantial populations of Latinos (Azteca America, 2004). However, it did not appear to be gaining market share. Similarly, Hispanic Television Network (HTVN), a US public company listed on Nasdaq and led by an Anglo businessman in Dallas, was launched in 2001 ('Hispanic Television Network, Inc.', 2001). In

Chapter 9 • From Latin Americans to Latinos

Fig. 5. Born in East LA: Almost half the population of Los Angeles is Latino, according to the 2000 Census, and predicted soon to be a majority. Many advertisers on Spanish-language television are selling their goods and services through shops like this in the barrio *(neighbourhood).*

2002 it filed for bankruptcy ('FCC approves merger of Spanish-language media companies', 2003). Cable-delivered HTVN had only three to four million subscribers: This compares to the 80 per cent market share held by Univisión (DiCarlo, 2001). Telemundo has most of the rest.

Yet in terms of ownership and control, the most significant development in the new century occurred in October 2001, when a completely new era was ushered in with the acquisition of Telemundo by General Electric, parent to the leading US network NBC (DiCarlo, 2001; Stern, 2001). This brought Spanish-language television fully into the corporate mainstream of US broadcasting, and poses the strongest ever challenge to Univisión's dominance of the traditional duopoly.

Both Univisión and Telemundo have been expanding themselves, the former having bought USA Networks from Barry Diller in 2001, which it has since developed as a second broadcast network, Telefutura. Univisión has a cable network as well, Galavisión, which goes back to the 1980s. Telemundo has just the one broadcast network, but even before the GE/NBC takeover, it had bought the Spanish-language channel GEMS to be relaunched as its cable network, Mun2 (a pun in Spanish for 'worlds', *mundos*). These new networks are bringing about an interesting diversification of programming through linguistic hybridity. Whereas Univisión in particular has always kept a strict policy of correct Spanish only (even advertising slogans have to be rendered in Spanish), Telefutura is aimed at younger and less Spanish-dominant audiences. In this, they are competing with Telemundo's Mun2 which has made considerable concessions to the widespread use of the bilingual vernacular of Latino youth often referred to as 'Spanglish', thus goading Telefutura in the same direction (Sutter, 2003a).

A corollary is that there is an increase in the amount of US-made programming, but there is also a trend to the use of material from elsewhere in the Spanish-speaking world, including co-produced formats and reality genres (Sutter, 2003b). This is a particular departure for Univisión, which traditionally relies heavily on programming from shareholders Televisa of Mexico and Venevisión of Venezuela, as has been noted. Indeed, there is keen competition for international sources of programming. Following the success of the unconventional *telenovela*, *Betty la Fea*, on Telemundo, Univisión moved in quickly to secure the rights to the new series by signing a program agreement with the producers, RCN Televisión of Colombia. Univisión also made a new agreement with RCTV of Venezuela – interestingly, the arch-rival to Univisión's part-owner Venevisión in its home market. Univisión is claiming that these kinds of program are attractive to the one-third of its audience that is other than Mexican, though it continues to be oriented mainly to the Mexican majority (Calvo, 2001). For its part, Telemundo has been doing co-productions for the international market with Globo of Brazil, the region's pre-eminent producer of *telenovelas* (Sutter, 2001).

Finally, for a number of reasons, the industry has become even more concentrated in Miami, which is now the base of operations for Univisión as well as Telemundo. Demographically and culturally, Miami is an Hispanic or Latino city, and no longer just for the Cubans, as it now attracts immigrants from a range of other Latin American countries, including wealthy Colombians and Brazilians. According to Kevin Baxter, Arts Editor of the *Miami Herald*, US Latino and Latin American celebrities who visit or even have homes in Miami say they like it because they never feel like second class citizens there (personal communication, July 26, 2001), suggesting that even in other cities with Hispanic majorities, like Los Angeles, the Anglo cultural hegemony still makes itself felt. Portes and Stepick have argued that Miami's origins in real estate and tourism were 'economically underdetermined', but its proximity to Cuba made it politically overdetermined in the years of the Cold War. This resulted in the rise of a Spanish-speaking elite able to assert the hegemony of their language and culture over the city in a process of 'acculturation-in-reverse', making Miami 'easily the most "internationalised" of American cities' (1993: 210). This in turn gave Miami a linguistic and cultural basis for developing links not just to the Caribbean but all of Latin America. In conjunction with its geopolitical location, these cultural advantages have enabled Miami to become a major financial and trade center, with advantageous transport and communication links between the Americas, including for Spanish-language satellite television services and other media, notably music. A clustering effect has led to related audiovisual companies basing themselves in the area. Miami has become the media capital of Latin America and its diaspora in the US (Sinclair, 2003).

Assessment and conclusion

The 2000 Census touched off an apparent boom of interest from new would-be network and cable services, and international program producers, in Spanish-

Chapter 9 • From Latin Americans to Latinos

language television in the US. This paper will now conclude with an assessment of that boom, and some consideration of the likely shape of the industry in the future, and its capacity to serve the constituency which it seeks to commercialize.

The boom occurred against a background of a widespread fashion for US-Latin American 'crossover' music and its celebrities like Ricky Martin and Jennifer Lopez. Arguably, this trend somewhat overshadowed the traditional stigma which Hispanic popular culture has had from its association with a disadvantaged group, and this has implications for Hispanic identity itself: 'Now it's cool to be Hispanic', enthuses Univisión Creative Director, Marketing and Communications, Stephen Gaymont (personal communication, 1 August 2001). More substantial has been the release of data from the 2000 Census which confirmed the long-standing prediction, now come to pass, that Hispanics would overtake African Americans as the nation's largest minority group.

Certainly, demographic trends give good reason to believe in the future of Spanish-language television. As América Rodriguez quite correctly argues, contemporary Latin American immigration to the US has characteristics which make it quite distinct from traditional European migration, with its concomitant expectations of assimilation into the mainstream after a period of adjustment (1997: 289). Univisión agrees, listing these factors about Hispanics: the majority of adults were born outside the US; their influx is ongoing; they are geographically concentrated and tend to preserve their cultural identity; and they can easily travel back to their country of origin and maintain communication with each other (2001).

The Census and social science research bear these trends out: In 2000, 51 per cent of the foreign-born population in the US was from Latin America, and 39.5 per cent of them had entered the US during the 1990s (US Census Bureau, 2001b). Thus, in addition to the rapid natural increase in the population of Hispanics in the US, their total numbers are constantly being swelled by recently-arrived adult immigrants. Their Spanish-dominance not only makes them likely members of the audience for Spanish-language television, but increases the critical mass of Spanish speakers in the population at large, particularly since they tend to be geographically concentrated. For these reasons, they can so resist assimilation, and maintain the strength of Spanish. Furthermore, studies such as that of Roger Rouse indicate that the geographical proximity of their countries of origin allows many of these migrants to come and go in a whole 'continuous circulation of people, money, goods and information' which make up today's 'transnational migrant circuit' (1991: 14). It is at this point that we begin to see the value in conceptualizing the US Hispanic population as a kind of diaspora.

However, there are limits to which a wholly commercial Spanish-language television industry is truly able to serve the interests of this diaspora as a whole. It would be apparent that the traditional economics of the industry favors the use of cheap imported programming oriented towards the most recently-arrived, Spanish-dependent, predominantly Mexican immigrant. Yet the mode in which 'the Hispanic audience' is addressed seeks to play down this bias, and interpellates Hispanic peoples universally as if they were untouched by the realities of ethno-national, socioeconomic, and other differences. In particular, many of the more affluent and established people of Latin American origin are English-dominant or totally bilingual, but the industry has a vested interest in ignoring them, and rather, defining its audience as 'othered' by its use of Spanish (Rodriguez, 1997: 290–293). This façade is necessary for the production of an Hispanic audience, and for the sale of that audience to advertisers, the industry's whole commercial rationale.

Yet even in the era of audience measurement, the industry has continued to have difficulties in convincing advertisers of the value of advertising specifically to Hispanics. Neilsen data shows that although 90 per cent of US Hispanics speak at least some Spanish at home, only 32.3 per cent speak mostly Spanish, and 20.4 per cent only Spanish. This totals a bare majority of Hispanic adults as Spanish-dominant. Thus, even in the leading network's own publicity, Univisión claims only 27.4 per cent of total viewing in Hispanic households, with 7.1 per cent going to rival network Telemundo – the remaining viewing is by far the majority, 71.5 per cent, which is of English-language mainstream network and cable television (Univisión, 2001).

Thus, even with having over 80 per cent of the primetime audience for Hispanic network television, Univisión's Gaymont can quite rightly claim that their real competition is not Telemundo, but the four mainstream networks (personal communication, 1 August 2001). Furthermore, in spite of the success of both Hispanic networks in attracting major national advertisers over the last decade, many the same as advertise on mainstream television, they have not been able to command the same rates – in fact, for Hispanic viewers, these advertisers only pay around half of what they pay to advertise on the major networks (Rodriguez, 1997: 296).

To return then, finally, to the assessment of the current boom, it would not appear that the structure of the industry is likely to change for the immediate future. Even with the advent of GE/NBC backing for Telemundo, Univisión's position within the Hispanic market seems solid, given its several competitive advantages, not the least being both access to imported programming and a capacity to generate programming of its own, in Spanish. Apart from Univisión's pre-eminence, the marginal position of Azteca America and the failure of HTVN and others would indicate that the market itself is not big enough to bear the competition of new entrants, and it has proved itself still unable to attract advertising revenue commensurate with its share of total viewing. Indeed, in a significant recent development and in spite of the protests of its competitors and Hispanic advocacy groups, Univisión merged with the largest Spanish-language radio broadcaster in the US, Hispanic Broadcasting Corporation, thus shoring up its position and making for even more concentration in the industry ('FCC approves merger of Spanish-language media companies', 2003). The Spanish-language television industry may be one US institution which has recognized the significance of, and has become engaged with, the fundamental demographic, cultural and linguistic transformation which the diasporic flow of Latin American immigration has brought to the US However, given its commercial *raison d'être*, it has done so very much on its own terms.

References

Anderson, B. (1991) *Imagined communities: Reflections on the origin and spread of nationalism*. (2nd edn). London: Verso.

Astroff, R. (1997) 'Capital's cultural study: Marketing popular ethnography of US Latino culture', in M. Nava, A. Blake, I. MacRury and B. Richards (eds) *Buy this book: Studies in advertising and consumption,* pp. 120–136. London and New York: Routledge.

Azteca America (2004, May 18) 'Azteca America unveils programming strategy at 2004 Upfront in New York City', *Hispanic Business.com*. Retrieved 8 October 2004, from http://www.hispanicbusiness.com/news/newsbyid.asp?id=16249

Bagamery, A. (1982, November 22) 'SIN, the original', *Forbes*, 97.

Burciaga, J. (1993) *Drink cultura: Chicanismo.* Santa Barbara: Joshua Odell Editions/Capra Press.

Calvo, D. (2001, June 19) 'Univision adds muscle to its original lineup', *Los Angeles Times*. Retrieved July 23, 2001, from http://www.calendarlive.com/top/1,1419,L-LATimes-Print-X!ArticleDetail-3608 5,00.html?

Cunningham, S. & Sinclair, J. (eds) (2001) *Floating lives: The media of Asian diasporas.* Boulder CO: Rowman & Littlefield.

Dávila, A. (2000) 'Mapping Latinidad: Language and culture in the Spanish TV battlefront', *Television and New Media, 1*(1), 75–94.

Davis, C., Haub, C. and Willette, J. (1983) 'US Hispanics: Changing the face of America', *Population Bulletin, 38*(3), 1–43.

Dicarlo, L. (2001) 'Will NBC-Telemundo deal spur consolidation' *Forbes.com*. Retrieved October 2, 2003, from http://www.forbes.com/2001/10/12/1012telemundo.html

'FCC approves merger of Spanish-language media companies', (2003). *Online Newshour*. Retrieved September 25, 2003, from http://www.pbs.org/newshour/media/media_watch/july-dec03/univisionmerger_09-22-03.html

Guernica, A. & Kasperuk, I. (1982) *Reaching the Hispanic market effectively: The media, the market, the methods.* New York: McGraw-Hill.

Hispanic Television Network, Inc. (2001) *Hoover's Online*. Retrieved July 25, 2001, from http://www.hoovers/com/co/capsule/9/0,2163,101289,00.html

Marín, C. (1986, October 26) 'A Zabludovsky no se le cree por considerarlo vocero del gobierno', *Proceso*, 20–25.

Portes, A. & Stepick, A. (1993) *City on the edge: The transformation of Miami.* Berkeley CA: University of California Press.

'TV Azteca and Pappas Telecasting to launch Spanish language TV network in the US' (2000). [Press Release]. Retrieved from Pappas website July 30, 2001, from http://www.pappastv.com/PressReleasesdetail.asp?ID=4

Rodriguez, A. (1997) 'Commercial ethnicity: Language, class and race in the marketing of the Hispanic audience', *Communication Review, 2*(3), 283–309.

Rouse, R. (1991) 'Mexican migration and the social space of postmodernism, *Diaspora, 1*(1), 8–23.

Sinclair, J., Jacka, E. and Cunningham, S. (eds) (1996) *New patterns in global television: Peripheral vision.* Oxford and New York: Oxford University Press.

Sinclair, J. (1999) *Latin American television: A global view.* Oxford and New York: Oxford University Press.

Sinclair, J. (2003) ' "The Hollywood of Latin America": Miami as regional center in television trade', *Television and New Media, 4*(3), 211–229.

Soruco, G. (1996) *Cubans and the mass media in South Florida.* Gainesville FA: University Press of Florida.

Sosa, L. (1998) *The Americano dream.* New York: Dutton.

Stern, C. (2001, 11 October) 'NBC to buy Spanish network Telemundo', *Washington Post*. Retrieved October 17 from http://www.washingtonpost.com/wp-dyn/articles/A46103-2001Oct11.html

Strategy Research Corporation (1986) *1987 US Hispanic market study.* Miami FA: Strategy Research Corporation.

Subervi-Vélez, F., Ramírez Berg, C., Constantakis-Valdés, P., Noriega, C., & Wilkinson, K. (1994) 'Mass communication and Hispanics', in F. Padilla (ed), *Handbook of Hispanic cultures in the United*

States: Sociology, pp. 304–357. Houston TX: Arte Público Press & Instituto de Cooperación Iberoamericana.

Sullivan, T. (2000) 'A Demographic Portrait', in P. Cafferty & D. Engstrom (eds), *Hispanics in the United States,* pp. 1–29. New Brunswick, NJ: Transaction.

Sutter, M. (2001, January 15–21) ' Telenovelas still simmer', *Variety,* 47, 52.

Sutter, M. (2003a, January 20–26) 'A savvy grab for auds', *Variety,* 32.

Sutter, M. (2003b, January 20–26) 'B'casters eye bigger share of US auds', *Variety,* 27–28.

Telemundo Communications Group, Inc. *Hoover's Online.* (2001). Retrieved July 25, 2001, from http://www.hoovers/com/co/capsule/8/0,2163,43678,00.html

Univisión. (2001) *The US Hispanic market in brief* [Promotional brochure]. Miami FA: Univisión.

US Census Bureau. (2001a) *The Hispanic population: Census 2000 brief.* Retrieved September 3, 2001, from http://www.census.gov/prod/2001pubs/c2kbr01-3.pdf

US Census Bureau. (2001b) *The foreign-born population in the United States.* Retrieved September 3, 2001, from http://www.census.gov/prod/2000pubs/p20-534.pdf

Valdez, L. (1972) 'Introduction: "La plebe"', in L. Valdez and S. Steiner (eds), *Aztlán: An Anthology of Mexican American Literature,* pp. xiii–xxxiv. New York: Vintage.

Yankelovich, Skelly and White. (1981) *Spanish USA: A study of the Hispanic market in the United States.* New York: Yankelovich Skelly and White..

Chapter 10

National cinema as cultural exchange: the international circuit of Scottish films

Duncan Petrie

Introduction

The last decade has seen a concerted move towards a process of devolution within the British cinema. Martin McLoone has argued that the ways in which films like *Trainspotting* (Danny Boyle, 1996), *Divorcing Jack* (David Caffrey, 1998) and *Human Traffic* (Justin Kerrigan, 1999) depict contemporary society in Scotland, Northern Ireland and Wales respectively serves to set them

> … firmly against the accumulated traditions of representations that underlie both the cultural term 'British' and the political entity 'United Kingdom'. Perhaps, also, it marks a significant moment in the cultural decolonisation of Britain's Celtic fringe – a process that not only begins to re-imagine the periphery but also marks the beginnings of a cultural project to re-imagine the very notion of British cinema.'
> (McLoone 2001: 186)

Within academic film studies this has generated a small but growing body of work examining the various histories of film-making on Britain's Celtic fringe. McLoone for example has examined cinematic representations of Ulster within the context of a history of Irish film-making, challenging their more usual incorporation into traditions of British cinema (McLoone 2000). While in *Screening Scotland* I explore how an identifiable and distinct 'Scottish Cinema' gradually emerged over the 1980s and 1990s, providing perhaps the most concerted challenge to the idea of a homogenous and unified concept of British cinema (Petrie 2000a, 2000b). The situation in Scotland is primarily the result of certain key institutional developments, in particular the emergence of a number of modest but highly significant funding initiatives. The most important of these has undoubtedly been the Scottish lottery fund, initially administered through the Scottish Arts Council and subsequently by Scottish Screen, the principal publicly-funded moving image agency north of the border.* Around £3 million of lottery cash per annum is currently invested in film

---

* Scottish Screen was established in 1998 through an amalgamation of existing public bodies including the Scottish Film Council, the Scottish Film Production Fund, the Scottish Film and Television Archive, Scottish Screen Locations and the Film Training Trust.

development, production and related initiatives, providing an invaluable raft of indigenous support for Scottish film-making. Moreover, since the early 1990s the nurturing of an indigenous Scottish film industry has also been supplemented by economic development schemes like the Glasgow Film Fund (which ran from 1993 to 2000) and by the support of the Scottish broadcasters, BBC Scotland, Scottish Television (STV) and Grampian.

Collectively, these funding initiatives have resulted in the production of a stream of feature films that have come to suggest that Scottish cinema has a certain tangibility. This impressive output includes *Shallow Grave* (Danny Boyle, 1995), *Small Faces* (Gillies MacKinnon, 1996), *The Near Room* (David Hayman, 1997), *Regeneration* (Gillies MacKinnon, 1997), *Mrs Brown* (John Madden, 1997), *The Winter Guest* (Alan Rickman, 1997), *Carla's Song* (Ken Loach, 1997), *My Name is Joe* (Ken Loach, 1998), *Stella Does Tricks* (Coky Giedrocyk, 1998), *Orphans* (Peter Mullan, 1999), *The Acid House* (Paul McGuigan, 1999), *Ratcatcher* (Lynne Ramsay, 1999), *Gregory's Two Girls* (Bill Forsyth, 1999), *This Year's Love* (David Kane, 1999), *The House of Mirth* (Terence Davies, 2000), *Late Night Shopping* (Saul Metzstein, 2001), *Gas Attack* (Kenny Glennan, 2001), *Sweet Sixteen* (Ken Loach, 2002), *Morvern Callar* (Lynne Ramsay, 2002), *The Magdalene Sisters* (Peter Mullan, 2002), *The Last Great Wilderness* (David Mackenzie, 2003) and, more recently, *Young Adam* (David Mackenzie, 2003), *16 Years of Alcohol* (Richard Jobson, 2003), *Solid Air* (May Miles Thomas, 2003) and *Afterlife* (Alison Peebles, 2003). Collectively these films have made an considerable critical impact both at home and abroad, with implications for how Scottish film is acknowledged. Writing in the US periodical *Film Comment* in 1996, Harlan Kennedy noted that 'Scotland is becoming the flavour of the zeitgeist' (Kennedy 1996: 29), while the high profile success of films like *Sweet Sixteen* and *The Magdalene Sisters* at the 2002 Cannes and Venice film festivals respectively suggests that the international profile of Scottish films remains buoyant. In addition to the establishment of the Scottish feature film as a distinct entity, the last decade has also witnessed a major increase in the number of short films being produced in Scotland. Again the dynamic behind this has been institutional, spearheaded by a number of high profile short film schemes administered by Scottish Screen in collaboration with the Scottish broadcasters. Taking feature and short film production together, such concerted stimulation of film-making at different levels in Scotland has contributed to the establishment of a tentative infrastructure comprising a number of new independent production and facilities companies located primarily in Glasgow and Edinburgh. While existence for these fledgling enterprises remains precarious and hand-to-mouth, they do constitute an identifiable 'sector' within the British film and television industries and their output (primarily but not exclusively) serves to both reflect and stimulate the increasingly distinctive cultural preoccupations and obsessions of a nation that has also recently regained a sense of its own political self-determination with the re-establishment of a Scottish parliament in Edinburgh in 1999.

What I want to do in this essay is to examine the international circulation of recent Scottish cinema in order to consider the wider impact of the institutional developments I have briefly described. Central to my focus here however will be the question of cultural exchange. While the policies that have facilitated the production and circulation of Scottish 'audio-visual' products have been primarily industrial and economic, the resulting films constitute a cultural phenomenon that I would like to argue is distinctively Scottish. These films engage with and project various aspects of contemporary Scotland and its specific cultural, social and geographical formations, reflecting in the process particular stories, sensibilities, experiences and world views that in turn serve to define Scottish identity as a complex, dynamic and multi-faceted phenomenon. This is not to suggest that particular film-makers ignore the internationally familiar conventions of genre-based story-telling, but their films – be they thrillers, romantic comedies, heritage dramas or indeed idiosyncratic and highly personal 'art' films – are making a distinctive Scottish contribution to their respective genres. However my main purpose here is not to ponder the cultural or aesthetic lineaments of Scottish film and TV drama, but rather how such images are located within the nexus of moving-image cultural exchange that is the primary concern of this volume.

Scotland, art cinema and the international film festival

While the new Scottish cinema may have a particular significance in a domestic cultural context, the sustainability of a distinct Scottish film industry is heavily dependent on the resulting films finding an international audience. A key element in the circulation and visibility of Scottish cinema in this respect is the international film festival circuit. In an article primarily motivated by a retrospective of Iranian cinema at the Toronto Film Festival in 1992, Bill Nichols identifies the crucial role played by film festivals in what he terms 'the discovery of new cinemas'. And while Scottish cinema is clearly a very different kind of example to the idea of 'third cinema' (Willemen, 1994) represented by a non Western cultural entity such as Iranian film, Nichols' general observations still have a clear relevance:

> Films from nations not previously regarded as prominent film-producing countries receive praise for their ability to transcend local issues and provincial tastes while simultaneously providing a window onto a different culture. We are invited to receive such films as evidence of artistic maturity – the work of directors ready to take their place within an international fraternity of auteurs – and of a distinctive national culture – work that remains distinct from Hollywood-based norms both in style and theme.
> (Nichols, 1994: 16)

In this way the international film festival plays a vital role in ensuring that in an age of increasing globalisation and the commodification of all aspects of life cinema can still be regarded as an important and vital art form. While recent Scottish cinema has benefited greatly from interest generated by the presence of bona fide stars like Ewan McGregor and Robert Carlyle, the distinctive personal style and thematic preoccupations of particular film-makers also remains a major critical focus. This is equally the case for newcomers like Lynne Ramsay, Peter Mullan and David Mackenzie as for veterans such as Bill Forsyth and Ken Loach – the fact that the latter has chosen to make four of his last five features in and around Glasgow being is a testament to the current significance of film-making in Scotland. A similar critical attitude has been taken to the collective authorship of films like *Shallow Grave* and *Trainspotting* (which effectively instigated the idea of a new Scottish cinema in the mid-1990s) by the Danny Boyle/John Hodge/Andrew MacDonald troika. As I have argued elsewhere (Petrie 2001), Scottish films have an affinity with the traditions of art or independent cinema – both European and North American – in terms of their particular stylistic, narrative and thematic concerns. Moreover the eschewal of mainstream aesthetics by these films is also frequently noted, for example in his *Sight and Sound* review of the 2002 Cannes film festival Nick James describes Ramsay's *Morvern Callar* as 'a brave piece of sumptuous-looking intuitive impressionism and about as far away from Hollywood as you can get.' (James, 2002: 13)

The major showcase for new Scottish work is undoubtedly the Edinburgh Film Festival which began in 1947 and has since earned the distinction of the longest continuously running film festival in the world. A screening at Edinburgh also acts as a hub within a wider international network: presenting the work to a wide range of audiences from the paying public, to journalists who will publicise new films beyond the audience at the festival and to other film-makers and industry types including potential distributors both domestic and international. Therefore films screened at festivals stand to gain more than critical plaudits and reviews. They may also secure invitations to other festivals around the world and much needed distribution deals that will guarantee greater exposure (to say nothing of much needed income for producers). Beyond Edinburgh, and perhaps the London Film Festival, the key festivals for Scottish films include the major high profile European events held annually in Cannes, Berlin and Venice. While in North America the Toronto and Sundance film festivals also function as important showcases for the kind of films currently coming out of Scotland, the majority of which as we have seen tend to be 'authored', low budget works supported by a combination of public finance and input from broadcasters. Consequently the circulation of these productions tends to be handled by art house and other specialist distribution and exhibition outlets in the theatrical, video and DVD and broadcast sectors.

While the notion of personal expression may plays an important role in the discussion of Art cinema, this is often situated within the broader context of national cinemas and movements such as Italian Neo Realism, French *Nouvelle Vague*, New German Cinema, Brazilian Cine Novo, Fifth Generation Chinese cinema or even American independent cinema (as a specifically national alternative to the implied internationalism of Hollywood). However transnational the concerns of particular film-makers, very few film 'auteurs' have managed to resist being categorised in specifically national terms. As Steve Neale pointed out in his 1981 essay, 'Art Cinema as Institution', the concept of European Art Cinema involves an important balance between a national and an international dimension in that while such cinema is often predicated on a strong sense of national identity or specificity, art films also tend to be produced as much for international distribution and exhibition as they are for local consumption, constituting a distinct 'niche-market' in the process. Neale notes the vital role in this process of cultural exchange played by the film festival, an arena

> ... where international distribution is sought for these films and where their status of 'Art' is confirmed and re-stated through the existence of prizes and awards 'thereby neatly balancing the criteria of artistic merit and commercial potential'. (Neale, 1981: 35)

Chapter 10 • National cinema as cultural exchange

Indeed there are various examples of particular films and film-makers that have enjoyed a far higher profile on the international film festival circuit than in their own domestic markets.

The recent high profile of Scottish films has been boosted considerably by success on the international film festival circuit with the Edinburgh Film Festival playing an increasingly important role in this context. Almost all new Scottish features and shorts receive their world premiere at Edinburgh, with some being given the added boost of being chosen to open the festival including *Ratcatcher* in 1999, *Morvern Callar* in 2002 and *Young Adam* in 2003. A number of Scottish films have also won the prestigious Michael Powell Award for best British Film at Edinburgh including *Small Faces* in 1995, *Gas Attack* in 2001 and *Young Adam* in 2003.[*] But beyond the platform of Edinburgh Scottish films have made their presence felt at the major European festivals which, in addition to functioning as important international market places, continue to play a key role in affirming the cultural and artistic status of contemporary cinema. Scottish successes at Cannes in recent years have included the best actor award for Peter Mullan in 1998 for his performance in *My Name Is Joe*, and Paul Laverty's best screenplay award for *Sweet Sixteen* in 2002.[**] Peter Mullan's debut feature as writer and director, *Orphans*, dominated the 1998 Venice Film Festival, winning four major prizes including the Golden Lion, in addition to picking up major awards in Gijon, Paris and Angers. While in 2002 Mullan repeated his Venice triumph with *The Magdalene Sisters*, a film that went on to win further awards at Toronto and Ljubjliana in addition to the Prix MEDIA 2003 given by the European MEDIA programme. Elsewhere, *Late Night Shopping*, written by Jack Lothian and directed by Saul Metzstein, was awarded the audience prize at the 2001 Berlin Film Festival. Other major festival awards for Scottish films include the 1999 Stockholm Film Festival critics prize for *The Acid House*, directed by Paul McGuigan and adapted by Irvine Welsh's from his own collection of short stories; the BFI's Sutherland Prize awarded to Lynne Ramsay for *Ratcatcher* at the 1999 London Film Festival; while Thomas Riedelsheimer's documentary about the sculptor Andy Goldsworthy, *Rivers and Tides*, won major prizes at San Francisco and Montreal in addition to picking up a Lola for best documentary at the German equivalent of the Oscars. The collective success of such films has had an important knock-on effect for the profile of Scottish cinema in general, with many other films performing well at these major events both in terms of sales and press and publicity.

The profile of Scottish film in Europe has also stimulated a move towards greater co-operation between Scottish producers and their European partners. Established film-makers like Ken Loach have consistently sought financial support for their projects from European sources. His recent film *Sweet Sixteen* is listed in *Sight and Sound* as a co-production between the United Kingdom, Germany, Spain, France and Italy – although it could be argued that the financial input from the Scottish Screen lottery fund and the Glasgow Film Office constitute an identifiably Scottish contribution distinct from the British input from BBC Films. Other interesting

---

[*] In 2003 *Sixteen Years of Alcohol* was awarded an unprecedented special commendation by the Powell Award jury, while at the same festival the digital feature *Afterlife* received the audience award.

[**] At the 2002 Cannes Festival *Morvern Callar* also won the Prix Confédération des Cinemas Art et Essai.

partnerships have also been developing based in part on a sense of cultural affinity between Scotland and other parts of northern Europe. For example Mullan's *The Magdalene Sisters*, a harrowing exposé of the Magdalene Asylums in 1960s rural Ireland, was financed by the Scottish Screen lottery, the Irish Film Board and the London-based Film Council and is listed as a United Kingdom/Irish co-production. However Mullan's own background as a Glasgow catholic is not only rooted in particular historical links between Scotland and Ireland, but all of his work as a writer/director including *Orphans* and his short films is imbued with certain thematic preoccupations that reveal his cultural heritage and that of a sizeable part of the Scottish population. The idea of Scottish-Irish co-productions has been developed further in a more straightforward business sense with *Blind Flight*, John Furse's film based on Brian Keenan's experiences as a hostage in the Lebanon during the 1980s. Meanwhile 2003 also saw the release of two co-productions with Danish companies, *Wilbur* (Lone Scherfig) and *Skagerrak* (Soren Kragh Jacobsen), a reminder of the success of Lars von Trier's innovative 1996 feature film *Breaking the Waves* which anticipated the Dogme 95 initiative. Set in a small Calvinist community in North West Scotland in the 1970s, *Breaking the Waves* was made without any significant British (or indeed Scottish) financial input but again it conveyed a powerful sense of shared cultural, religious and geographical links between Scotland and Scandinavia that could be just as significant as those with Ireland.

Stimulating a new Scottish cinema: the importance of short films

In addition to showcasing new feature films, international film festivals have also provided a major forum for the promotion of short films produced in Scotland. While Noel McLaughlin's observation that due to a combination of critical and industrial neglect short films have constituted 'the hidden history of British cinema' (McLaughlin 2001: 62) is generally true, the growth in the production of shorts has proved to be a cornerstone in the successful emergence of a Scottish film industry in the 1990s. The policy of concerted intervention in this sector by initially the Scottish Film Production Fund and subsequently by Scottish Screen has been central, echoing similar developments in Ireland where, as Martin McLoone notes, the policies of the Irish Film Board in the early 1980s 'had begun to build towards a "critical mass" in indigenous production' (2000: 151). The most visible of the recent Scottish short films tend to be those made under the auspices of the various schemes run by Scottish Screen and other key institutions. The flagship initiative in this respect is undoubtedly 'Tartan Shorts', a collaborative venture between Scottish Screen and BBC Scotland which has been running since 1993. Each year three 35mm short films are produced from an initial shortlist and while running times and budgetary levels have changed over time, 'Tartan Shorts' are currently around 10 minutes in length and made on a budget of £60,000 per film. The resulting films are showcased at the Edinburgh and London Film Festivals and then are broadcast by BBC Scotland. While some of the other schemes have had shorter lives – 'Prime Cuts' and the Gaelic language initiative 'Gear Ghearr' each lasted just three years – others have been introduced. These include 'New Found Land',

Chapter 10 • National cinema as cultural exchange

Fig. 1. Lynne Ramsay's acclaimed poetic short Gasman *(1997), with James Ramsay and Lynne Ramsay Jnr. as father and daughter. [Scottish Screen/BBC Scotland.]*

established in 2000 and run by Scottish Screen and the Scottish Media Group, resulting in the production of six 25 minute digital films budgeted at around £50,000. The success of this scheme led to the creation of 'New Found Films', an initiative to fund 90 minute low budget digital features at £200,000 a production. The first of these, *Afterlife*, directed by Alison Peebles, was premiered at the 2003 Edinburgh Film Festival where it won the audience award. Other shorts schemes worth noting include 'Tartan Smalls', an initiative introduced in 2002 by Scottish Screen for films aimed primarily at a young audience; 'Cineworks', an entry level scheme run by a partnership involving the Glasgow Media Access Centre, Edinburgh Film and Video Access Centre, Scottish Screen and BBC Scotland, which aims to produce five films a year; and the independent initiative, 'Eight and a Half' initiated in 2000 and run by the Short Film Factory.

These various schemes share a strong emphasis on professional training and talent development and involve a rigorous process of selection and the development of projects, with the result that a wider group of film-makers benefit beyond those projects that are finally produced. The opinion of Deborah Keogh, co-founder of 'Eight and a Half', that 'short films are the backbone of filmmaking careers for any writer, director or producer' (Keogh, 2001) is frequently cited as a primary justification. Consequently initiatives tend to explicitly emphasise the collaborative nature of the film-making process, with writing and production skills seen as particularly important elements in the development of a viable industry in Scotland. The irony here however is that the most conspicuously successful graduates of 'Tartan Shorts' have been highly distinctive individual writer/directors like Lynne Ramsay and Peter Mullan, who may justifiably be regarded as bona fide 'auteurs'.[*] Prior to directing their respective debut feature films, both Ramsay and Mullan had already made their

---

[*] However both have tended to work consistently with the same creative teams who have graduated with them to the realm of feature production.

mark on the Film Festival circuit. All three of Ramsay's short films won major awards: both *Small Deaths* and the 'Tartan Short', *Gasman* picked up the Prix de Jury at Cannes in 1996 and 1998 respectively, while *Kill the Day* was awarded the Jury Prize at the Clermont Ferrand short film festival in 1997. While Mullan's 'Tartan Short', *Fridge*, won the main prize at the International Festival of Documentary and Short Films in Bilbao in 1998.

But there have been several other success stories to relate. The circulation of Scottish shorts at international film festivals has increased dramatically over the last few years with Scottish Screen taking a leading role by setting up a service for the international distribution of Scottish short films. Moreover, this facility is open to films beyond those financed under the auspices of the various production schemes. Over the last five years Scottish shorts have been screened at over 100 International Film Festivals. However at the heart of Scottish Screen's distribution strategy is a target list of some thirty key festivals[*], with such proactive promotion resulting in around fifty international festival screenings of Scottish short films each year. In addition to a number of titles proving particularly popular in terms of the number of festivals which programme them, a significant number of awards have been won in the process. 'Tartan Shorts' has proved to be particularly successful in this respect, indeed one of the first films made under the scheme, *Franz Kafka's It's a Wonderful Life*, written and directed by Peter Capaldi won the Oscar for best live action short in 1994. Since then, and in addition to the triumphs of *Fridge* and *Gasman*, films like *Marcie's Dowry*, directed by David Mackenzie, has picked up awards at Essonne, Brest and Palm Springs, Brian Kirk's *Billy and Zorba* has been awarded the best international short drama at the Brooklyn Film Festival and David Cairn's *Cry For Bobo* has won more than a dozen awards from such places as Athens in Georgia, Naples, Milan, Sitges, Brussels and Darwin. The most successful 'New Found Land' film has been *Leonard*, directed by Brian Kelly, which picked up the audience prize at Clermont Ferrand in 2002. Scottish prize winners made outside the major schemes include Jim Stark's three minute film, *Desserts*, which won the best film at the Winterthur Short Film Festival in Switzerland; Morag Mackinnon's Channel Four funded short, *Home*, which in addition to winning best short at BAFTA, picked up awards in Chicago, Palm Springs and Hamburg; and *Daddy's Girl*, directed by Irvine Allan for the BBC's '10x10' slot, which has been screened at over twenty five international film festivals and won awards in Budapest, Naples, Florence and the Special Jury Prize at Cannes in 2001.

---

[*] These include the following festivals: Edinburgh International Film Festival, Scotland; Palm Springs International Short Film Festival, USA; Atlantic Film Festival, Halifax Nova Scotia, Canada; New York Film Festival, USA; Mill Valley Film Festival, California, USA; Chicago International Film Festival, USA; Murphy's Cork International Film Festival, Ireland; London International Film Festival, England; Sundance Film Festival, USA; Goteborg Film Festival, Sweden; Clermont Ferrand Short Film Festival, France; Berlin Film Festival, Germany; Tampere International Short Film Festival, Finland; Minimalen Short Film Festival, Trondheim, Norway; San Diego International Film Festival, USA; Cannes Film Festival, France; Canadian Film Centre Worldwide Short Film Festival; Hong Kong International Film and TV Market; Hamburg Short Film Festival, Germany; Sydney Film Festival, Australia; Melbourne International Film Festival, Australia; Celtic Film and TV Festival; Brest Short Film Festival, France; Aspen Short Film Festival, USA; Message to Man Film Festival, St Petersburg, Russia; Barcelona Film Festival, Spain; Vendome Film Festival, France; Stuttgart Film Festival, Germany; Capalbio Film Festival, Rome, Italy; Vallodolid Film Festival, Spain.

Chapter 10 • National cinema as cultural exchange

Fig. 2. A poster for Peter Mullan's award winning Tartan Short Fridge *(1995), featuring Gary Lewis and Vicki Masson as a couple of down and outs. [Scottish Screen/BBC Scotland.]*

This remarkable performance of Scottish short films in the international arena has also been confirmed and consolidated by a number of special programmes including a showcase of Scottish shorts at the Flickerfest in Australia in 1999 and major retrospectives in Pescara in the same year, and at the Capalbio Short Film Festival in Tuscany in 2000. These have also helped sales of Scottish shorts – primarily to broadcasters like PBS in the States, and important European television companies like ARTE and Canal+. In addition, distribution possibilities for shorts have also increased in recent years through internet companies such as Atom Films. While a major factor in the success of particular short films has undoubtedly been down to the talent and imagination of the film-makers concerned, the organisation of Scottish shorts in terms of identifiable production schemes has also played an important role in marketing terms. An established schemes like 'Tartan Shorts', which at the time of writing has seen some thirty three films being produced over an eleven year period, has come to function as a particular brand in the international market place. And despite being in only its third year, 'New Found Land' is already gaining a similar kind of identity on the festival circuit. In terms of the nurturing of an indigenous film industry in Scotland, such developments are clearly to be welcomed however distant such overt 'market-speak' might seem from the creation of cinematic art.

Conclusion

In a consideration of the emergence of a new Irish Cinema in the 1980s and 1990s, Martin McLoone identifies a tension around the phenomena of the short film. On one hand shorts constitute an important and distinct cultural and aesthetic entity, 'an "institutional space" carved out from the cut and thrust of the commercial world of feature film-making and the tyranny of the television schedules' (2000: 155). On the other hand their value in relation to training and talent development suggests a pressure towards complying with the dominant form of the feature film. The implications of the latter being precisely to undermine the very potential of short films as somehow an alternative 'institutional space', informed by a greater degree of creative freedom and experimentation. Allied to this is a concern shared by other commentators including Colin McArthur (McArthur 1994) and Noel McLaughlin (2001) that the establishment of short film schemes in Scotland, Ireland and elsewhere aimed at developing a national industry has entailed an inevitable tendency towards a conservatism in form and content governed by traditional Hollywood narrative norms. While one may have a certain sympathy with this argument in the sense that it is almost impossible to find examples of (institutionally funded) short films that employ avant garde techniques or radically challenge the boundaries of traditional film form, this has certainly not eclipsed all aesthetic possibilities other than the dominant Hollywood model. Films like *Fridge, Gasman* and *Home* invoke a range of (primarily) European cinematic references from Robert Bresson and Bill Douglas to Luis Buñuel and Emir Kusturica. In all three cases the film-makers have found different ways to use the medium of cinema to depict and analyse the moral and emotional complexities of human interaction, often against a backdrop of material or psychic poverty. While the cultural and geographical specificity is urban Scotland (Glasgow in the case of all three films), the issues tackled are universal and deal in different ways with the complex substance of human relationships. Moreover they also suggest a common thread uniting 'arthouse' film-makers from Europe with practitioners in the third world and with some of the less cynical exponents of American independent cinema in terms of the necessity of retaining alternative cinematic traditions to the increasingly banal and regressive product of a mainstream Hollywood defined by blockbusters and sequels.

The recent success of Scottish cinema on the international film festival circuit has helped to mark out a cultural space that serves to validate the aesthetic achievements of Scottish film-makers. This applies to both feature films and shorts, vindicating in the process the institutional policies that have attempted to stimulate the latter sector as a training ground or workshop for new talent. Consequently it should come as no surprise that those Scottish film-makers whose short films have been acclaimed at film festivals – such as Ramsay, Mullan, David Mackenzie, Saul Metzstein and Kenny Glennan – should continue to achieve success after graduating to feature films. Such a consideration of the international circulation of Scottish cinema also raises the perennial question of the relationship between culture and economics in the context of a aspiring national cinema. One of the primary goals of Scottish Screen has been articulated in relation to the nurturing of 'vibrant and sustainable Scottish screen industries' (*Scottish Screen Annual Review 2002*, p. 7). This has involved placing an emphasis on encouraging the growth of production companies in Scotland in order to achieve some kind of meaningful critical mass and to ensure the on-going nurturing of new talent. The results to date have been clearly mixed in that while a significant number of new producers have been encouraged to take their first steps by the various schemes and opportunities created by Scottish

Screen, very few have subsequently achieved the levels of sustainability that a successful indigenous industry requires. While the new Scottish cinema may be primarily associated with talented directors, it is also important to recognise the contribution made by hard working Scottish-based producers like Angus Lamont, David Muir, Gillian Berrie, Eddie Dick, Catherine Aitken and their struggle to establish viable independent companies. It is the producer who often brings together a creative team in the first place and it is he or she who has the onerous responsibility of raising production finance. If a project fails to be funded it is often the producer who will shoulder the responsibility, but if the film is made and proves to be a success the producer will rarely receive the kind of critical acclaim that a director does.

And yet in the context of cinema as an art form the figure of the auteur as the main driving force of a national cinema remains impossible to dispel. Consequently the successful circulation of Scottish film in recent years has owed a great deal to an emerging international recognition of the creative talents of a small number of distinctive film-makers. While undeniably a key element in the global economy of moving images, the international film festival cannot simply be reduced to yet another sales mechanism for commercial product. Rather it remains a crucial forum for critical appreciation, debate and discussion of film as art and culture, a space in which the exciting new film-makers of today will return as the critical retrospectives of tomorrow. Some of the most intelligently programmed festivals continue to make explicit this essential dialogue between aesthetic traditions and current trends. For example, the Robert Bresson retrospective at Edinburgh in 1999 incorporated an intense public discussion of the French film-maker's achievements and legacy by Scottish directors Bill Forsyth and Lynne Ramsay, both of whom had their latest films screening in the same festival. Such an event functioned as a reminder of the passionate cinephilia that continues to inspire film-makers and which has undoubtedly informed the most interesting films to come out of Scotland in recent years. Their increasing international circulation and profile has served to confirm the sense of a distinctive, a vibrant and an increasingly visible Scottish national cinema distinct from an increasingly redundant all-encompassing notion of British cinema.*

References

James, N. (2002), 'Cannes 2002: Rich and Strange', *Sight and Sound*, July.
Kennedy, H. (1996), 'Kiltspotting: Highland Reels', *Film Comment*, July/August.
Keogh, D. (2001), 'Shorts Success', *Roughcuts*, September.
McArthur, C. (1994), 'Tartan Shorts and the Taming of First Reels', *Scottish Film*, Issue 9. Summer.
McLaughlin, N. (2001), 'Short Sighted: Short Filmmaking in Britain', *Cineaste*, Vol xiii, No. 4.
McLoone, M. (2000) *Irish Film: The Emergence of a National Cinema*, London: British Film Institute.

---

*   The other alternative domain is that of the music video and it is interesting to note that Scottish film-makers have benefited from the new 4-minute wonders scheme – also run in Wales and the Midlands. In Scotland this involves a competition resulting in the production of eight music videos budgeted at £5,000 each. These are very low budgets and like Cineworks, this is primarily an entry level scheme but affording a very different set of aesthetic and formal possibilities to the other production schemes. It also addresses Noel McLaughlin's argument that music video production not only offers a different route for film-makers to the subsidised short film schemes like Tartan Shorts, 10x10 and others but that it also creates the possibility of more diverse, plural and hybrid forms of aesthetic experimentation.

McLoone, M. (2001), 'Internal Colonialisation: British Cinema in the Celtic Fringe' in R. Murphy (ed), *The British Cinema Book, Second Edition*, London: British Film Institute.

Neale, S. (1991) 'Art Cinema as Institution', *Screen*, Vol. 22, No. 1.

Nichols, B. (1994) 'Discovering Form, Inferring Meaning: New Cinemas and the Film Festival Circuit', *Film Quarterly*, 47 (3), Spring.

Petrie, D. (2000a), *Screening Scotland*, London: British Film Institute.

Petrie, D. (2000b), 'The New Scottish Cinema' in M. Hjort & S. MacKenzie (eds), *Cinema & Nation*, London: Routledge.

Petrie, D. (2001), 'Devolving British Cinema: the New Scottish Cinema and the European Art Film', *Cineaste*, Vol xiii, No. 4.

Willemen, P. (1994), *Looks and Frictions: Essays in Cultural Studies and Film Theory*, London: British Film Institute.

SECTION III:
National Cultures in a Transatlantic Context

Introduction

The research presented in this section has a focus upon selected economic and cultural transactions conducted 'across' the North Atlantic over a period of some seventy years.

Sarah Street examines the 'special relationship' between the United States and the United Kingdom as this might be considered to play out in the realm of fiction film. Street selects two key films- *The Ghost Goes West* (1935) and *A Matter of Life and Death* (1946) – from the period around the Second World. The entry of the US into the war against Hitler – giving support to a previously isolated and beleaguered Britain – saw an intensification in the always complex and contradictory relations between the two countries. Cinema romance is here seen to be a key locus for the representation of these relations.

Tom Ryall and Steve Neale explore, respectively, the role of American capital in the British film industry and the considerable contribution to early television made by some blacklisted and effectively exiled American scriptwriters working in the UK in the 1950s and early 1960s. An acrimonious trade war in 1948–9, involving a Hollywood boycott of the British market, was followed by a formal 'Anglo-American' agreement, setting the stage for decades of future tense and intense collaboration as well as for what came to be called 'runaway production'. But, within this context, the sphere of representation is seen to have some considerable independence from the sphere of finance even where there is evidence of extensive investment by American companies within the British industry.

Tino Balio outlines the early successes of foreign 'art films' shown in hundreds of theatres throughout the US in the period immediately after the Second World War, and goes on the trace the process whereby – by the 1960s – the small independent distributors of these films had been taken over by the Hollywood majors. In this period of growing uncertainty for cinema, along with the growth of a 'counter-culture', the majors sought to diversify their home market with a judicious admixture of the 'adult themes' that foreign directors appeared to promise. However, Balio's research indicates that by the 1970s the major studios had moved away from a policy of investment in indigenous European production, re-directing resources to the youth oriented blockbuster, effectively designed to play in worldwide markets.

This story of the complex interactions between Europe and the US is taken up for the period of the 1990s and early 2000s in Andrew Higson's chapter on the exporting of 'indigenous heritage' movies to the US. Higson offers some critical reflections on the proposition that films embodying strongly local characteristics will find themselves in the category of the inexportable. He suggests that, on the contrary, the English (not British) heritage movies of the end of millennium period have enjoyed some international success. Taking as his case study recent cinematic representations of the novels of Jane Austen, he identifies the mix of cultural specificity and astute narrative construction that has allowed producers to raise finance and to reach international audiences.

Chapter 11

Special relationships: Anglo-American screen romance and nationality

Sarah Street

In several British films of the 1930s and 1940s romance was used as a textual strategy to explore the possibilities, problems and conflicts of transatlantic collaboration.* The key examples analysed in this chapter are *The Ghost Goes West* (1935) and *A Matter of Life and Death* (1946), films which through the fates of their Anglo-American central couples played out the aspirations, hesitancies and contradictions that pervaded Anglo-American relations during a period when co-operation between Britain and the USA was desirable for political and economic stability. The primary contexts are the inter-war movement against isolationism – the encouragement of greater American involvement in European economic and political affairs, particularly in opposition to Fascism – and the need to maintain a solid Anglo-American alliance after the Second World War, particularly with reference to the European Recovery Programme which depended on American economic aid. Although the 'special relationship' between Britain and the USA usually refers to the wartime alliance, it has origins in Winston Churchill's idea of cultural commonality between 'English-speaking peoples', most frequently advocated in the 1930s when Churchill was seeking to enlist American support against Fascism. As Reynolds has argued, the evolution of the 'special relationship' was however neither inevitable nor without conflict. In particular, economic competition between the two countries resulted in an undercurrent of transatlantic rivalry which persisted well into the post-war years and beyond. Divergent assumptions about 'Englishness' and 'Americanization' also threatened transatlantic collaboration, as American politicians saw Britain as a class-ridden country which was clinging to a fading Empire, and many British diplomats viewed America as 'a land of "eternal superficiality", bereft of civilization and integrity. Its people were either brash and vulgar or else coated in a self-conscious veneer of culture' (Reynolds, 1984: 11).

---

* There are both British and American films which fall into this category, including *A Yank at Oxford* (1937), *Foreign Correspondent* (1940), *One Night in Lisbon* (1941), *This Above All* (1942), *Eagle Squadron* (1942), *I Live in Grosvenor Square* (1945) and *The Way to the Stars* (1945). The two films I have selected in this essay are however linked by similar 'liminal' narratives which make them particularly good candidates for comparison.

The 'special relationship' has been analysed primarily in terms of its political development and consequences. This chapter will explore its cultural expression through an investigation of 'special relationship' films. It will demonstrate how the concept of the 'special relationship' exceeded political discourse, permitting ambivalent feelings about Anglo-American co-operation to surface in the popular medium of cinema. An analysis of the extent to which the cross-cultural couple operated as a site of interrogation of these wider issues of Anglo-American economic, diplomatic and cultural relations reveals how films relate to their contemporary contexts. The two films suggest that while forging the 'special relationship' was a laudable goal, it could never be achieved without anxiety, sacrifice and conflict.

The period 1935–46 was not only important for securing greater US commitment to European affairs, but also signalled a distinctive phase in Anglo-American film relations. Boosted by state protectionism and vertical-integration, the British film industry was in a strong position to suggest trading arrangements with Hollywood. The 'special relationship' can be said therefore to have extended to optimism about star trading policies, reciprocal agreements between British and American film companies, and regarding British films as exportable commodities. Both *The Ghost Goes West* and *A Matter of Life and Death* were intended for overseas distribution and were released at critical moments in the history of British cinema: in their subject-matter and economic trajectories they are therefore 'indigenous' texts with 'exportable' ambitions.

As 'romance' narratives, the films deploy classic structural devices. As Pearce and Stacey have outlined, these accord with a quest for love which is frustrated by conflicts and barriers which constitute the major focus for the spectator: 'Pleasure in the "progress of romance" lies in the solution to the narrative problems, and the affirmation of the desire to see "love conquering all", thus confirming its transcendental power' (Pearce and Stacey, 1995: 12). In the films I have selected for analysis the cross-cultural couple is a 'special' one. The 'special' couple is a concept elaborated in terms of American film comedies by Stanley Cavell (1981). Cavell demarked a sub-genre of romantic comedy (sometimes referred to as 'screwball comedy') of films involving volatile relationships, often featuring separated couples who reunite by the end of the narrative (his list includes *His Girl Friday* [1940], *The Lady Eve* [1941] and *The Awful Truth* [1937]). What is important about his analysis for my concerns is the identification of the 'special' couple, which, assisted by a variety of textual strategies, removes obstacles to union by narrative closure. In the context of screwball comedies we recognize their 'special' status in a number of ways: their sparkling, vivacious conversation, which is wittier and more exciting than conversation with rivals for their affection. They are also favoured by formal strategies, including their positioning in the frame. In these ways the couple is presented as a desirable unit, despite narrative information which points to the contrary or which on closer analysis gives cause for doubt.

Similarly, in the British films the 'special' couple is made clear to us despite national differences. While they may not be as witty as their screwball relations, they are nevertheless signalled as compatible and are rendered compelling by a series of narrative and textual strategies which grant them a privileged status. In *The Ghost Goes West*, for example, the central couple's courtship struggles against deeply ingrained assumptions about cultural incompatibility and difference, extending the obstacle to union from personal to national differences. As such, Donald (Robert Donat) and Peggy (Jean Parker) are symbolic of a desired, utopian symbiosis between Britain and the USA which, by the end of the film, appears to triumph against the odds. Much as with Cavell's 'special couples', the Anglo-American couple in *The Ghost Goes West* depends on a particular strategy of comparative preference that presents the couple as different in a generational sense from others in the film. As such the couple represents a future of Anglo-American collaboration, promising a culture of transatlantic exchange that overcomes long-held prejudices.

Extending this belief further, and with arguably even greater conviction informed by the experience of Anglo-American co-operation during the Second World War, *A Matter of Life and Death* elevates the cross-cultural couple to such an extent that an American jury in heaven permits a defiance of the laws of life and death by granting a young British pilot's wish to live out his life with an American woman. The film thus posits a successful cross-cultural romance, with its attendant symbolism of more extensive Anglo-American political and economic collaboration, as a desirable goal which triumphs against extraordinary odds. In both films the 'special couple' is therefore rebellious, acting as a site of interrogation of long-held assumptions about Britain and the USA as nations which although sharing a common language are nevertheless quite distinct and incompatible. As with more conventional romance narratives the goal of union therefore overrides evidence presented in the narrative of contradictions: in this context irreconcilable differences between two cultures.

The two films resemble each other in terms of theme since both romances involve the male characters being suspended in a 'liminal' state. This is another variation on the 'classic' romance narrative in which a 'liminal' phase of enigma precedes closure and union. While this 'space' reveals conflicts and confusion, it is also a site of possibility where nothing is fixed, offering a potential challenge to the status quo. It reveals discourses which might qualify the idea that union is unproblematic, for example, and most crucially in the arena of romantic fiction, it suggests a contradiction between the desire for union and the knowledge that this may well be based on irreconcilable differences. The particular emphasis of the 'liminal' phase in connection with the male characters invests these two films however with a progressive discourse: in comparison with their partners, it is the male characters who have to undergo the greater degree of transformation. This is perhaps ironic in the sense that both films and their key male protagonists are British, implying that in Anglo-American relations it is the British who have to change the most to achieve a satisfactory rapport with the USA.* In *The Ghost Goes West* Donald is caught between his 'real', modern self, and that of his ghostly ancestor, Murdoch, who haunts his castle and who is mistaken for Donald when he appears to Peggy. This both facilitates romance and frustrates it since Peggy becomes confused by what she experiences as Donald's inconsistent and frustrating behaviour. In many ways Murdoch is a romanticised 'other' against whom Donald is compared as a less

---

* Although in *A Matter of Life and Death* the case for the prosecution in heaven is argued by a sceptical American. He too undergoes a change of heart when persuaded by the evidence of love and compatibility between Peter and June.

TRADING CULTURE

Fig. 1. Montage of production stills from The Ghost Goes West *(Rene Clair, 1935) starring Robert Donat, Jean Parker and Eugene Pallette.*

romantic and more conservative man. As I shall argue, the romance with Peggy and consequent removal of the castle to Florida forces Donald to become directly involved in the ghost's quest for 'wholeness': Murdoch cannot escape from his existence between heaven and earth unless he avenges the family name. Similarly in *A Matter of Life and Death* Peter is caught in a liminal state between heaven and earth. He is arguably more attractive to June because of his dilemma, his vulnerability and removal from 'normal' masculine pursuits. The state of liminality is interesting in this respect because it is associated with change, transgression and transformation. These facets will be explored in more detail in the following analyses which demonstrate how through the prism of romance, in very particular 'liminal' ways, these two films present and investigate Anglo-American relations.

The Ghost Goes West

The Ghost Goes West was made by London Film Productions with the American market in mind. It was part of an explicit strategy to produce films that would do well at the box office at home and abroad. In this sense it is a film with 'exportable' aspirations whose cross-cultural narrative concerns reflect its desired economic trajectory. Tracing its progress in *Variety*'s box-office reports, it did excellent business at some US theatres and was held over by many for several weeks, inviting comments from exhibitors such as: 'Donat acquiring quite a following here' (Kansas City); 'best seven-day opener house ever had' (Los Angeles); 'bucking some strong competition' (St. Louis).* American distributor United Artists's head office also received reports of good business from Los Angeles, Ohio and New York.** It was in the top ten best films of 1936 nominated by critics from the *New York Times*. A

---

*   *Variety*, 5 Feb 1936: 10; 12 Feb 1936: 3; 19 Feb 1936: 10. *The Ghost Goes West* featured regularly in *Variety* box-office reports throughout its first run.

** See Telegram from Harry Gold to LA exchange, 5 Feb 1936; Gold to Libson, 11 Feb 1936; Telegram from Arthur Kelly, 1 Nov 1936. United Artists archive, State Historical Society, Madison, 99AN 1E, B3, F6. Karol Kulik (1975: 140) contends that the film was 'immensely successful at home and overseas'; Rachael Low (1985: 171) describes it as 'tailored for the American market', and Tino Balio (1976: 144) refers to it as a 'success'.

circular to all domestic exchanges urged salesmen to promote the film as suitable for 'mixed class right down to low-brow … we have in *The Ghost Goes West* a picture that definitely appeals to everybody. It is not a costume picture; it is not a so-called British picture. It is made strictly to appeal to an American audience'.* The film had a French director, René Clair, and was publicized as an 'international' production, featuring several American actors including Jean Parker who was signed by MGM after appearing as a swimwear model on posters for the Olympic Games and Ralph Bunker who was familiar to millions of Americans as a radio personality. Its major star, the half-Polish Robert Donat, was already known to US audiences in *The Count of Monte Cristo* (1934) and *The 39 Steps* (1935). As an indication of his international reputation Alexander Korda, the film's producer, had to increase Donat's salary in order to secure his services which were being courted by Hollywood.**

A Scottish-American theme also gave the film transatlantic appeal, resulting in a gentle comedy based on a story by Eric Keown published in *Punch*. Donat plays Donald, a descendant of the Glourie clan whose castle is haunted by the ghost of Murdoch Glourie (also played by Donat) who was killed in the eighteenth century as a result of rivalry with the McLaggan clan. In the twentieth century the castle is in a state of disrepair and Donald needs to sell it in order to satisfy his creditors. When Peggy Martin, a young American woman, passes by she is enchanted by the castle and persuades her father, a rich American food magnate, to buy it. Donald is shocked when Peggy's father, Joe Martin (Eugene Pallette), tells him that he intends to dismantle the castle and rebuild it in Florida. He finally agrees because of his increasing affection for Peggy and because he will supervise the castle's reconstruction in America. An extremely unlikely event therefore occurs because Donald is attracted to Peggy, romance inducing uncharacteristic behaviour.

When the castle's haunted status is known its market value is enhanced, and Peggy's father ends up having to pay more than his original offer when a rival grocery magnate, who has purchased a French chateau to help advertise his products, also bids for the Glourie castle. Like the Scottish clans, the Americans are shown to be consumed by rivalries – in this case based on money. The film makes several satirical references to American importation and commercial exploitation of European culture. The ghost is treated similarly as news of its existence reaches the newspapers and a series of sensational reports of sightings of the ghost are published. The arrival of the castle in America is greeted with enthusiasm, illustrated by actuality footage of exuberant crowds, taken out of its original context and inserted in this fictional story for comic effect. There is a key scene when we see images of the American Senate and the House of Lords overlaid with juxtaposed aural extracts from debates in both arenas, including a British discussion of the 'heritage' issue about the export of British culture to America. While the American senators complain about the importation of a ghost 'into our progressive country … a relic of medieval superstition … which might be acceptable in the effete atmosphere of the British House of Lords', members of the House of Lords are concerned about the uprooting of 'the

---

*   Circular letter no. 3410, 14 Jan 1936: UA archive 99AN 1E, B3, F6.

** At the 10th meeting of the Moyne Committee Korda claimed that LFP had to increase Donat's salary from £6,000 to £25,000 to appear in *The Ghost Goes West* in response to an American offer of $35,000. National Archives, London: Board of Trade files, BT 64/92/6757/38.

flowers of Scottish architecture … to please the fancy of a millionaire who apparently has no ancestors of his own'. This controversial event which, ironically, has occurred because of a cross-cultural relationship, therefore exposes deep-seated assumptions about cultural difference in the public arena.

Once in Florida Donald is upset by the 'Americanization' of the castle, complete with the addition of modern technology and gimmicks such as suits of armour with in-built radios. Again, we have an example of an American appropriation of Scottish culture being satirized as jarring jazz music is heard; the castle is brightly illuminated and set amongst palm-trees, a fake moat and gondolas. These images invite a direct comparison with earlier scenes of the castle in Scotland, minimally decorated and located in a spectacular Scottish landscape. Yet confrontation of the incompatibility between tradition and modernity is avoided, especially when it threatens the romance between Donald and Peggy.

Numerous devices are used to illustrate the couple's romantic difficulties, including physical obstacles which frustrate their communication. Once in Florida with the castle, for example, Donald is shocked to see the results of Joe Martin's 'modern improvements', particularly the transformation of an ancient suit of armour into a jazz-blasting radio. When Joe regards it proudly and remarks to Donald, 'Kinda cute, eh Donald?', Donald replies: 'I don't know the meaning of the word "cute"', emphasizing cultural difference within a 'shared' language. An exchange between Donald and Peggy, in which he explains why he has to leave, occurs through a closed window which prevents her from hearing him voice his discontent. He says, knowing that she cannot hear him, 'You were right Peggy, I should never have let them turn this castle of mine into an advertisement for groceries. I've made a fool of myself, Peggy, and all because I love you'. When she manages to open the window he tells her that he must leave the next day, without giving the full explanation. In this way the film temporarily postpones confrontation of the difficult questions that would, realistically, threaten the path of the romance, although it is clear that unlike her father Peggy foresaw Donald's reaction.* This scene illustrates the privileging of romance since visual communication (Peggy is animated and charming as she catches sight of Donald through the glass) takes precedence over oral.

Peggy's mistaken impression that Donald and the ghost Murdoch Glourie are the same person is another obstacle which suggests an interesting convergence between the romantic tradition represented by Murdoch and the more reserved behaviour of Donald, his impoverished descendant. The ghost accompanies the castle to Florida but refuses to appear after being shocked by an encounter with gangsters, representing the juxtaposition of Scottish heritage with Hollywood-style imagery. Donald has to masquerade as the ghost when Peggy's father has arranged a showing at the castle to entertain his friends. The ghost is eventually freed from haunting the castle when one of the visitors turns out to be a descendant of the rival McLaggan clan which caused Murdoch's death, thus enabling him to honour his father's wish to obtain an apology for McLaggan wrongdoings to the Glourie clan. In his encounters with Peggy the ghost Murdoch is charming, so charming that Donald appears to be lacking in comparison. Believing them to be the same person, Peggy

---

* Peggy also objects to her father wearing a Glengarry, indicating that she is sensitive to cultural difference.

is disturbed by what she perceives to be Donald's changes of mood. Also, when she hears Murdoch wooing another woman on the ship she assumes that Donald is a philanderer. The closure of this narrative strand is significant because once Murdoch is laid to rest Donald can put the past behind him and be less bound by tradition. Also, importantly, Peggy's phantom 'other' lover is no longer Donald's rival, leaving the path clear for the emergence of the modern, cross-cultural couple, the irony being that the move to America, prompted by the attraction of a modern, American woman, has facilitated this major change in the Glourie clan's family history.

The film is therefore 'transatlantic' in its themes and the satire of the American characters is always gentle and sophisticated. As Peggy Martin is being shown around the castle, for example, she says 'You don't know what it means to us to see something that's not new', implying a self-knowingness about caricatured images of Americans as crass and uncultured. Similarly, Donald's love for Peggy outweighs his disturbance about the castle's 'Americanisation', investing the film with an over-arching discourse about love breaking down prejudice. The film ends rather abruptly with the implication that Donald will marry Peggy but without an indication about the fate of the uprooted castle. Donald's objections to its removal to Florida are not therefore addressed, nor are his qualms about commercialism. The film's ambiguous ending makes us unsure as to what might have followed: will Donald insist that the castle is returned to Scotland or will he begin a new life with Peggy in America? While the latter is more likely, it is not entirely unproblematic.

On another level, the film can be seen to make unconscious reference to the many transatlantic crossings which were taking place in the 1930s as producers encouraged British film stars such as Robert Donat to visit and work in America so that they would be more familiar to American audiences.* The film's view of Americans suggests a 'special relationship', a fond familiarity rather than a suspicious antagonism. It is these elements in particular which influenced the lavish and light-hearted marketing of *The Ghost Goes West* as a film that would appeal to Americans even though, as we have seen, they were the object of considerable satire in the film. In this sense Korda was seeking to 'woo' US audiences on the basis of Donat's appeal as a romantic hero.

A comparison of the British and American press books for *The Ghost Goes West* shows that it was marketed in a very specific way in the USA. The British press book highlights Donat as a 'matinée idol of the world'; René Clair's directorial credentials and publicity stunts involving shop window displays of Scottish costumes.** While the American material features these elements it places far more emphasis on Donat as a romantic hero/dare-devil lover, implying that the film contains risqué subject matter. Posters contained captions such as: 'A dashing ghost who made love to every

---

*   In fact Robert Donat was largely resistant to offers to star in Hollywood films. While he appeared in *The Count of Monte Cristo* (1934) he turned down many subsequent opportunities, preferring instead to star in British films and on the stage.

** Donat did not approve of this kind of merchandising. In a letter to Alexander Korda he wrote: 'Did you know that the Ghost's costume was exhibited in the window of an Edinburgh store(s) [sic]? This seems to me to be not only poor publicity, but damn silly! Why stress the material properties of the Ghost, anyway?' RD1, file 1/239: Donat to Korda, 21 Feb 1936 in Robert Donat Collection, John Rylands Library, Manchester.

pretty girl he met!'; 'No passion greater than the violence of thwarted love!'; 'A girl with two identical lovers ... one human ... the other a ghost!' and 'Shocking, sensational, stirring!'. Korda's involvement is signalled when he is described as 'The man who gave you *Henry VIII*', seeking to establish a link between that successful film and the comedic liveliness of *The Ghost Goes West*. Fashion tie-ins were encouraged, particularly with Jean Parker's costumes that the press book declared were typical of fashions worn by 'the average young girl'. Theatres were advised to stage ingenious publicity stunts including placing luminous cut-outs of the ghost outside cinemas. These instructions were followed by exhibitors, for example the Keith Memorial theatre in Boston reported that their 'excellent' business for the film was assisted by elaborate stunts, described as 'an inanimate "ghost" answering questions via a p.a. set drew plenty of attention; a truck tie-up, and a play for Scotch population, in addition to an impressive lay out of newspaper publicity' (*Variety*, 5 February 1936: 10).

The American press book also contained examples of reviews, highlighting one from *New York American* which made the point that everyone in the film is satirized: the Scots, the British, the Americans and ancient institutions. In other publications the film was praised very highly. The *New York Times* heralded it as 'the first important film of the new year, and a joyous one' (11 January 1936: 9). Although appreciative of the film *Variety* was concerned that its humour might be too sophisticated and ironic for the mass audience. The satiric tone and elements of what might be construed as anti-Americanism were not taken seriously and even used to suggest that the American sense of humour was tolerant of parody. The *Variety* reviewer declared, for example, that 'the American people as a whole are amazingly good-natured about themselves. Had Americans made this film for instance, about the British, or the Scotch, or the French, or any other nation, the screams would have risen to the skies' (15 January 1936). It would appear therefore that *The Ghost Goes West* attracted attention for its relaxed attitude towards Anglo-American differences, its irreverent, comic sensibilities and quality of the cast. Many of these elements had been present in *The Private Life of Henry VIII* (1933), and with a brief appearance by Elsa Lanchester in *The Ghost Goes West*, Korda's desire to distinguish his productions with the mark of transatlantic success was demonstrated once again (See Street, 2002: 43–69). The film's marketing therefore reflects its textual concern to 're-write' the special relationship, to break down cultural barriers by interrogating national difference through a similarly inclined romantic narrative.

A Matter of Life and Death

Just over ten years later Powell and Pressburger's *A Matter of Life and Death* was similarly preoccupied with using romance as a means of commenting on contemporary Anglo-American relations. The imperative was informed by the experience of American involvement in the Second World War, the intensification of the 'special relationship' united against Fascism, and optimism about its continuation after 1945 even though it was clear that collaboration between the two countries had become strained. This film was made with explicit instruction from Jack Beddington of the film division of the Ministry of Information that it should have the propagandist aim of easing fraught Anglo-American relations (Christie, 2000: 12). As with

Chapter 11 • Special relationships

Fig. 2. The 'special relationship' of Kim Hunter and David Niven in A Matter of Life and Death *(Powell and Pressburger, 1946).*

The Ghost Goes West, *A Matter of Life and Death* was therefore born of an anti-isolationist imperative. While the film's production was delayed by the temporary unavailability of the Technicolor stock considered essential for its making by Powell and Pressburger, it was released just after the Second World War ended and was therefore pertinent to the international situation.

Its story of Peter (David Niven), a British pilot caught between life and death due to a mistake by heavenly Conductor 71 (Marius Goring), when his plane was shot down in the fog, uses romance as the crucial factor which gives him the right to appeal against heaven's decision to claim him from earth. His romance with June (Kim Hunter), an American WAC working on an American air base in Britain, begins from the very start of the film, as Peter's blazing plane makes a rapid descent and they establish radio contact. The pair forge an emotional bond as Peter recites poetry and asks June to send messages to his mother and sisters. He imparts his last words to an American stranger who has become his intimate confidante in just a few minutes. He also jokes that he will see her for the first time when he visits her as a ghost. Peter awakens on a seashore near to June's airbase. They meet and continue where their radio conversation left off as they puzzle over his miraculous survival and further establish their mutual affection. Their transatlantic rapport is developed in scenes which allude to the idea of bonds between 'English-speaking peoples' when both remark that they are attracted by each other's voices. Peter describes his attraction to June thus: 'Her accent is foreign; it sounds sweet to me. We were born thousands of miles apart but we were made for each other'.

The romance is thus established immediately and their status as a special couple is never in doubt. Like Peggy and Donald in *The Ghost Goes West*, June and Peter are presented as models for future co-operation but who nevertheless have to overcome considerable obstacles to stay together. The threats to the pairing of Peter and June can be likened to those evident in Shakespearean romances, in particular to *A Midsummer Night's Dream*, the play being performed at the air base by an Anglo-

155

Fig. 3. UK poster for A Matter of Life and Death *(Powell and Pressburger, 1946).*

American cast. As Christie has noted, the scene when an American airman is reprimanded for playing Bottom as if he were an American gangster, introduces an intertextual reference to both the play, with its magical barriers to romance, and to the opposition between 'English' and American culture (Christie, 2000: 16–17). Peter's 'liminal' predicament is the major barrier to their union, which he learns of when Conductor 71 informs him that he must take his place in heaven. Time is suspended when Conductor 71 visits Peter as all those around them are 'frozen', oblivious to their conversation. The rest of the plot, conveyed in a satirical manner, concern's Peter's struggle to remain on earth, assisted in his quest by June and Reeves (Roger Livesey), a doctor who realizes that Peter's symptoms of concussion and hallucinations can only be cured by a brain operation. Acknowledging that Peter's predicament is his fault, Conductor 71 tells him that he can appeal to the High Court in heaven at a trial which coincides with Peter's operation at the climax of the film.

The trial scene juxtaposes Peter and June's relationship with past instances of Anglo-American incompatibility and conflict. Peter's American prosecutor, Abraham Farlan (Raymond Massey), a Boston patriot who was the first American to be shot by an English soldier in the American War of Independence, argues that Peter and June's love is purely 'of the moment', forged in the extraordinary circumstances of war and therefore condemned to be ephemeral. Reeves asks for the first jury, which consisted of people with grounds to resent British imperialism, to be replaced by one consisting entirely of Americans. Against Farlan's claim of cultural incompatibility based on past political conflicts between Britain and the USA, Reeves however suggests a common cultural heritage. When Farlan plays an extract from a cricket match to illustrate British inwardness and particularism, Reeves responds by playing a radio extract from an American big band concert which they both find incomprehensible. The point of the juxtaposition of contrasting evidence serves to place greater value on Peter and June's relationship, since it has been formed in the face of these apparently insurmountable obstacles. The most convincing evidence presented to the jury is a tear stolen from June and placed on a rose petal during one of the 'suspended' time-events when she watches Peter undergoing his operation. Finally the American jury and Farlan are persuaded that this special couple must live their lives together when June demonstrates her love further by agreeing to take Peter's place in heaven. Peter and June's union is symbolic of Anglo-American co-operation since it is made clear that they stand for the future and that their love has the potential to erase past prejudices. The film explicitly states that Peter and June represent love, truth and friendship, qualities 'to build a better world today and tomorrow'. Their union therefore represents heightened aspirations for the continuation of the 'special relationship' in peacetime.

These aspects were enhanced in the US marketing campaign for the film. The romance angle featured extensively, described in one poster as 'the love story that won the year's greatest acclaim. It soars to thrilling new heights of wondrous romance and breath-taking spectacle!' It received the highest accolades from New York critics, particularly Anglophile Bosley Crowther who described the film as 'wonderful'. *Variety* predicted a good chance for the film in the USA provided it received the selective, special handling associated with the most successful British releases. This opinion was echoed by the *Motion Picture Herald* critic who wrote that 'it's one of those films in which Britain lately has specialised which will attract the discriminating who never normally frequent the motion picture'.* The satirical treatment of issues of national identity was also appreciated, even though for some this was far from subtle: *Variety*'s critic commented that 'even American audiences will find [Powell and Pressburger's] usual anti-British barbs too obvious'.

A Matter of Life and Death was released at a time when Anglo-American relations were extremely delicate since European recovery depended on American economic assistance. From an American perspective, continued alliance with Britain was necessary in the fight against Communism.** On the film front however, the situation was far from being conducive to co-operation. The US release was in November 1947, when Anglo-American film relations were bitter and volatile and any sense of a 'special relationship' was severely strained. The 'Bogart or Bacon' controversy was raging (See Street, 1997: 14–15). In August the Chancellor of the Exchequer placed a 75 per cent *ad valorem* duty on American films and Hollywood retaliated by boycotting the British market. A settlement was not reached until March 1948, so that when *A Matter of Life and Death* was released there was intense anxiety over both the Marshall Plan and the film situation. While originally conceived as wartime propaganda the film was therefore relevant to a similarly urgent post-war context. But it shared with its predecessors the concern to fictionalise international tensions by exploring them through a romantic narrative of frustration, perseverance, endurance and eventual triumph.

Conclusion: re-writing the special relationship

In their different ways, the films I have analysed deal with the complexities of Anglo-American relations in the 1930s and 1940s. While the 'special couple' is identifiable and united at narrative closure, the progress of their relationship has

---

*   *New York Times*, 26 December 1946, 28: 1; 13 November 1946 in *Variety's Film Reviews, 1943–48*, New York: Reed Publishing; *Motion Picture Herald*, 16 November 1946, 'Product Digest' section, p. 3310.

** In the Soviet Union it was interpreted as an example of anti-Communist propaganda. See Sue Harper and Vincent Porter (1989).

been far from unproblematic. *The Ghost Goes West* raises questions about commercialism versus culture and history, and posits the American woman as a modernizing, progressive influence. But as we have seen, this is not unambiguous, as Donald stifles his qualms about 'Americanization' in the name of love. While the film ends with the assumption that the couple will unite, in its delineation of national differences the film has nevertheless highlighted serious tensions within the 'special relationship'. Similarly, in *A Matter of Life and Death* it is the woman who causes the 'natural' laws of life and death to be transgressed. Despite the existence of deep-seated past prejudices the film contends that the future can transcend difference in a new generation of optimists. The extent to which Peter and June's situation is highly specific is not questioned, implying perhaps to sceptics that it would indeed take an extraordinary situation that flies in the face of realism for cultural differences to be entirely erased.

The films' engagement with the theme of modernity is linked to questions of nationality. As we have seen, *The Ghost Goes West* associates new technology with Americanization. Donald is disturbed by the transformation of his castle. In terms of national differences, the inference is that although Joe Martin is wealthy, he has no taste. In his distaste for the castle's expensive American refurbishment it is the impoverished Donald who is seen to possess greater cultural capital. Yet on another level, the film's stance on modernity is more optimistic, since Peggy is presented as a modernising influence in terms of Donald's personal and romantic development. Modernity, travel and exposure to a new environment is also responsible for the ending of the Murdoch-McLaggan feud. In this sense Donald's traumatic experience facilitates change and progression in a way that would have been impossible if he had not met Peggy. In *A Matter of Life and Death* technology is both terrifying and a force for good. Peter's plane crashes and Dr Reeves' fast motorbike contributes to his death. On the other hand, radio communication brings Peter and June together and an American surgeon successfully operates on Peter in an American-run hospital with the latest equipment and experienced staff. The films therefore present varied and at times ambivalent responses to technology and modernity, particularly as it is identified with American enterprise.

In both films the barriers preventing the union of the couple involve distances and 'other worlds' which must be conquered for the couple to proceed to happy union. In *The Ghost Goes West* the barrier is the Atlantic: it is when the castle is finally transported to Florida that Donald experiences his greatest doubts; there is also another, more ethereal barrier in the figure of the ghost who provides competition for Peggy's affections. In *A Matter of Life and Death* the barrier again involves a journey, although measured by distance of a different nature. The celebrated staircase (the American title of the film was *Stairway to Heaven*) designed by Alfred Junge symbolises the ascent to heaven which can be compared to the physical distances which feature so prominently in *The Ghost Goes West*. Peter must conquer the dictates of heaven by making a case based on earthly love, suggesting another sort of paradise that can be reached before death. In his suspended existence between life and death, Peter is similar to the ghost Murdoch Glourie. Peter is also all the more fascinating for his poetic sensitivity, his heightened imagination and contact with the world beyond the grave. In this sense both characters can be associated with the Freudian concept of 'the uncanny' in which the existence of a 'double' (in

Chapter 11 • Special relationships

Fig. 4. US poster for Stairway to Heaven/A Matter of Life and Death (Powell and Pressburger, 1946).

Donald's case the ghost and in Peter's his dual existence on earth and in heaven) preserves the ego in its struggle against death.* Murdoch assists Donald in his romantic quest, teaching him how to declare his love for Peggy, while Peter's successful fight for a long life defies death in a very literal manner.

In terms of gender relations the American women in *The Ghost Goes West* and *A Matter of Life and Death* are associated with modernity. Neither Donald nor Peter could be said to represent 'hard' masculinity: both are soft, gentle characters and, particularly in the case of Peter, are physically weak. Both are disturbed characters, much more so than their respective love-objects. Their 'liminal' narrative positioning removes them from the norms usually associated with masculinity, conferring on them both a state of 'becoming' which is similar to the romance narrative itself. In this sense the dilemmas facing both Donald and Peter can be likened to the state of emotional tension associated with romance – as an arena of hope and possibility which has not yet been contaminated by the mundanities of marital life. Donald's non-confrontational persona is inherited from Murdoch who was more interested in romance than in fighting for his clan or country. In their different ways Peggy and June are uncomplicated, modern women who inspire Donald and Peter respectively into behaving uncharacteristically. Donald allows his castle to be taken to Florida and Peter puts himself through the agonies of a trial in heaven based entirely on the strength of his love for June. His preference to remain on earth contrasts with Murdoch's quest to go to heaven; in both films heaven is characterised as a desirable place, making Peter's choice all the more remarkable.

Referring to the wider extra-textual context, the state of Anglo-American relations was similarly unequal in 1935 and 1946. Britain was on the defensive, needing to court American support. Just as the male characters in the films are required to change, Britain had to become less patriarchal in a geo-political context of greater US economic and political power, and also of decolonization. Interestingly, this gendering of the 'special relationship' contrasts with Reynolds' analysis of diplomatic discourses of the 1930s which characterized the USA as the partner most in need of education: British diplomats would use terms 'such as "educate" or "woo", which betray the belief that America was like a youthful adolescent or a skittish belle who needed the guiding hand of John Bull' (Reynolds, 1984: 12). This switch indicates that in many ways the films were more honest about the current geo-political situation in which Britain was clearly on the defensive. Both men therefore undergo transformation by association with 'the feminine', a process further

---

*   Noted in relation to *A Matter of Life and Death* by Christie (2000: 75).

emphasized by their characters which are associated with 'soft', 'feminised' masculinity. In the case of Donald this is enhanced through his knowledge of Murdoch's courtly romantic behaviour and Peter's artistic sensibilities as a poet are emphasized throughout his ordeal. The films are therefore about possibility – represented by the liminal state of romance – which can also be related in this context to utopian ideas about Anglo-American relations and to a conception of gender which is not based on rigid binary oppositions between masculine and feminine. The films' romantic pairings are thus rebellious forces in both narratives. As the films demonstrate, cultural differences are evident, but they are capable of being overcome by a belief in romance and common understanding that transcends potential conflict. The 'special relationship' is therefore an ideal which while under threat reveals contradictions and at the same time suggests a utopian possibility of convergence and union.

In their different ways these films also suggest that suffering and sacrifice are necessary for a successful cross-cultural relationship in private and public terms. Donald must surrender his castle to another country, see it degraded and 'Americanized', and Peter and June must both prove that they would die for each other in order to demonstrate that their love is genuine. The goal of collaboration is not questioned, underlining the wartime sentiment of the Allied community superseding regional and national differences. Both films were released in contexts of delicate Anglo-American relations, and in so doing demonstrated facets which can be described as both 'indigenous' and 'exportable'. Satirical humour is levelled against both British and Americans as stereotypical representations of nationality are played off against possibilities which are more progressive and nuanced. In their similar and different ways they propose that cross-cultural romance can reveal a more satisfactory, complete and dyadic state of Anglo-American co-operation than was prevalent in the past. Like all enduring romance narratives they imply that a re-scripting of the 'special relationship' is necessary. In this and in other ways, British cinema can be seen to deploy the Anglo-American couple as a means of alluding to contemporary preoccupations about what was under threat, but also what was to be gained, by transatlantic collaboration.

References and bibliography

Balio, T. (1976) *United Artists: The Company Built By the Star*. Madison, Wisconsin: University of Wisconsin Press.

Cavell, S. (1981) *Pursuits of Happiness: The Hollywood Comedy of Remarriage*. London: Harvard University Press.

Christie, I. (2000) *A Matter of Life and Death*. London: British Film Institute.

Harper, S. and Porter, V. (1989) 'A Matter of Life and Death – the view from Moscow', *Historical Journal of Film, Radio and Television*, 9 (2).

Kulik, K. (1975) *Alexander Korda: The Man Who Could Work Miracles*. London: W.H. Allen.

Low, R. (1985) *Film Making in 1930s Britain*. London: W.H. Allen.

Pearce, L. and Stacey, J., (eds) (1995) *Romance Revisited*. London: Lawrence and Wishart.

Reynolds, D. (1984) *The Creation of the Anglo-American Alliance 1937–41: A Study in Comparative Co-operation*. London: Europa

Street, S. (1997) *British National Cinema*. London: Routledge.

Street, S. (2002) *Transatlantic Crossings: British Feature Films in the USA*. New York: Continuum.

Chapter 12

American production in Britain during the 1950s: culture, economics and geography

Tom Ryall

Preamble

American film production in Britain is associated primarily with the post-Second World War period. It has been seen as a phenomenon which emerges in the wake of factors internal to Hollywood such as the repercussions of the divorcement decrees on the traditional structure of the industry, increasing labour costs in the industry, and the HUAC investigations, and external factors such as the blocking of overseas distribution earnings by national governments in Europe anxious to protect their domestic film industries. However, overseas production in Europe by Hollywood companies was not entirely new and, in Britain, can be traced back to before the First World War. Both the Independent Moving Picture Company, part of the recently formed Universal group, and Vitagraph, noted for its adaptations of classic British literature including Shakespeare, had come to Britain with a view to making films in the 1912–1913 period (Burrows, 2002: 34–35; Low, 1949: 131–132). In 1920, Paramount, the most powerful studio of time, established a studio in London which produced some eleven films during a two year period (Ryall, 2001: 28–33). The company also established a base in France in the early 1930s when it set up a studio at Joinville, near Paris, to produce films in multiple language versions (Andrew, 1995: 96–70). A number of US firms – Warner Bros., Fox – set up British units to make low budget quota pictures during the 1930s and MGM established a more ambitious British production arm in 1936 to make 'quality' films in anticipation of the 1938 quota legislation (Glancy, 1998: Ch. 3). However, such arrangements, prompted by exigencies such as foreign quota legislation and the advent of the dialogue film, were tangential to the main production activity of the American companies in the interwar period which was centred on the highly developed range of studio facilities in Hollywood – the movie-making capital of the world.

TRADING CULTURE

In the post-war period Hollywood film companies (majors, independents) increased their investment in overseas production making their films in Britain, Spain, France, Italy, mixing American stars and directors with local technical expertise, utilising Hollywood generic traditions and narrative patterns often in conjunction with non-US subject matter, indeed often with subject matter drawn from the country in which the film was made. Such inter-cultural collusion resulted in a bewildering variety of films, many of which attracted epithets such as 'mid-Atlantic', 'international' and 'runaway'. Such terms were partly descriptive but they also incorporated a criticism of the phenomenon. 'Runaway', according to *Variety*, was coined by 'the craft unions of Hollywood' which 'invented the term "runaway production" as a propaganda term' aimed at what was construed as renegade activity by the studio bosses which threatened their jobs (2 November 1960: 4). Apart from threatening the livelihood of American film workers, however, the hybrid films which resulted from the overseas activities of American film makers were frequently denigrated for failing to achieve the vigour and vitality of 'genuine' Hollywood films while also constituting a potential threat to the integrity of the host culture. The word 'runaway' itself, with its connotations of 'being out of control,' captures aspects of such films insofar as the secure cultural identity assumed in the context of traditional Hollywood-based production is jeopardised by the geographical and cultural mix represented by the new conditions of film making. 'Mid-Atlantic' suggests an unhappy merging of cultures in films remote from both their ostensible creative contexts, stranded between Hollywood and Europe. The term, 'international,' applied to films takes us into the territory of 'cultural homogenisation' (Morris, 2002: 279), the alleged erasing of cultural specificity and identity consequent upon a cultural mix invariably dominated by the American film conventions. Yet, many of the titles which emerged in the era of Anglo-US production, in the period of complex cultural interaction between national cinemas, are of considerable interest. Films such as *Night and the City* (1950), *The African Queen* (1952), *Captain Horatio Hornblower R.N.* (1951), *Ivanhoe* (1952), *Knights of the Round Table* (1953), *Moby Dick* (1956), *Bhowani Junction* (1956), *The Bridge on the River Kwai* (1957), *Night of the Demon* (1958), *Heaven Knows, Mr Allison* (1958), *Gideon's Day* (1958), *Sons and Lovers* (1960), and *Suddenly Last Summer* (1960), command a degree of attention for one reason or another. Many featured top Hollywood stars such as Elizabeth Taylor, Gregory Peck and William Holden; some were directed by top Hollywood names such as John Ford, George Cukor, Raoul Walsh and John Huston; and others are significant contributions to important Hollywood genres of the period such as the film noir, the historical epic and the horror film. At the very least such titles cannot be dismissed in the way in which the American-sponsored inexpensively-produced 'quota quickies' of the 1930s are often relegated to the dustbin of film history on the grounds of the cynical production motivations involved.

This study, focused on the role played by Hollywood companies in the British cinema of the 1950s, combines historical reflection, cultural criticism, and film analysis, to examine the phenomenon of Hollywood's overseas production and its impact upon the British film. It will incorporate an examination of the reasons for the new strategies of production adopted by Hollywood during the period, a discussion of the cultural implications of such strategies, and a survey of the films that were made in Britain with US involvement.

Chapter 12 • American production in Britain during the 1950s

Hollywood abroad

The development of Hollywood overseas production in the post-war period represented a significant internationalizing of Hollywood's production base. From the late 1940s onwards the major Hollywood firms began making films in a range of countries including Britain, France and Italy, a trend which continued to a point in 'the late 1960s, when nearly half the features made by American companies were produced abroad' (Maltby, 1995: 70). As previously noted, some of the reasons for this shift can be understood in terms of the internal structural changes in Hollywood itself. The 'divorcement' decisions of the 1940s robbed the major companies of guaranteed exhibition outlets for their films, making production a more precarious business; in addition, labour costs in America were increasing, and a number of directors, stars and writers began to base themselves overseas, some to take advantage of the beneficial tax regimes available, others fleeing from the political witch-hunt climate which beset America in the late 1940s (Harper & Porter, 2003: 115). Lower British labour costs provided an obvious incentive for shifting the production base to Britain but there were also a number of governmental moves in the late 1940s which provided additional reasons for American film makers to base themselves in the United Kingdom. The acrimonious trade war of 1947/48, during which Hollywood actually introduced a boycott of the British market, was settled by the 1948 Anglo-American agreement which stipulated that a percentage of the distribution earnings of the American majors could not be remitted to America but could be spent in Britain on a range of specified activities. One of these was film production which became an important way in which the Hollywood companies could use their 'frozen coin', *Variety*'s term for the blocked revenues. Incentives to produce in Britain were also provided by the British Film Production Fund and the Eady Levy, mechanisms for production subsidy set up by the government in the late 1940s. Though designed to help the British film industry, the subsidy system proved crucial for Hollywood. As Thomas Guback has suggested, '(w)hile blocked earnings were responsible for the first wave of runaway production, the availability of subsidization was the cause of its perpetuation and development into a second phase which cannot be attributed to unremittable revenues' (Guback, 1969: 166). Access to subsidies was relatively straightforward through the establishment of British production subsidiaries. Guback again:

> In organizing a subsidiary, an American parent can incorporate a company under British laws and appoint a majority of British subjects to the board of directors. This yields a British company whose affairs are conducted by directors predominantly British, but which is owned by, and its overall policies determined by, the American parent. The membership lists of the Federation of British Film Makers and the British Film Producers Association (prior to their merger) included such subsidiaries as Columbia (British) Productions Ltd., Paramount British Pictures Ltd., M.G.M. British Studios Ltd., Twentieth Century-Fox Productions Ltd., Walt Disney Productions Ltd., and Warner Brothers Productions Ltd (Guback, 1969: 167).

As a consequence of the various factors mentioned, major American firms became heavily involved in overseas production and *Variety* reported that more than $10,000,000 was invested in British production during the first two years of the Anglo-American agreement (28 June 1950: 4); and over a longer term, the 'American companies produced around 170 American-British films during the 1950s' (Harper and Porter, 2003: 114).

In some senses, the late 1940s saw the reinforcement of the trend discernible in MGM's 1930s strategy of making high quality films in Britain as part of their annual production schedule. Films such as *A Yank at Oxford* (1937) and *Goodbye Mr Chips* (1939) were treated as part of MGM's normal output and, before the various changes of the late 1940s, company plans were in place to resume quality quota production in Britain, including a refurbishing of its bomb-damaged Elstree studio complex for this purpose. As early as 1943, *Kine Weekly* reported meetings between Alexander Korda and top MGM figures including Louis B. Mayer which 'laid the foundations of a long-term enterprise which will make possible British-American film production on the largest scale' (20 May 1943: 3). Although Korda's links with MGM did not last, the company embarked on a programme of quality production in the late 1940s with films such as *Edward My Son* (1949) and *Conspirator* (1949) incorporating such titles into their American release lists as part of the studio's normal production schedule (see advert in *Variety*, 8 June 1948: 19). Indeed, one of the studio's most successful film strands of the early 1950s, the historical epic, rested on a number of 'runaway' titles. The American-Italian co-production *Quo Vadis* (1952) shot at Rome's Cinecittà studios was followed by a number of American-British productions including *Ivanhoe* and *Knights of the Round Table*. Such films were highly significant for MGM; *Quo Vadis* and *Ivanhoe* became the studio's most successful box-office earners of 1952, indeed they were second and third respectively on *Variety*'s annual list of top box-office performers (7 January 1953: 61); *Knights of the Round Table* was the studio's first venture in the new CinemaScope format, the only CinemaScope film made in 1953 outside of the Twentieth Century-Fox studio which developed the process, and part of a production trend of the period in which images on the screen grew bigger and wider and sounds on the soundtrack became louder and more resonant. Hollywood's traditional maxim – 'A tree is a tree. Shoot it in Griffith Park' (cited in Fadiman [1962]) – belonged to an era when films were created entirely in the Los Angeles studios or their environs; the post-war period brought a new attention to 'realism' and authenticity and an emphasis on location shooting appropriate to the subject matter of the film. It was felt that a medieval British epic required a British location – landscapes, castles, etc. – for its period authenticity. Indeed, Darryl Zanuck, the production head at Twentieth Century-Fox, suggested that the key motivation for shooting overseas was to provide authentic settings for films set in foreign parts rather than lower labour costs or access to frozen revenue, the traditional economic explanations for the 'runaways' (*Variety*, 10 January 1951, p. 20). According to the British trade press, Disney's *The Story of Robin Hood and His Merrie Men* (1952) sought geographical authenticity with producer, Perce Pearce, claiming that 'the production would be unique among Robin Hood films in that they meant to shoot at least part of it on the actual site – what little now remains of Sherwood Forest' (*Kine Weekly*, 8 February 1951: 26A). In addition, it was reported that technical staff on the film, 'have been visiting Nottingham to ensure the authenticity of local settings to be reproduced later at Denham Studios' (*Kine Weekly*, 1 March 1951: 23). As well as 'authenticity', overseas production enabled a greater and more varied exploitation of the new wide screen processes in the 1950s, providing a potentially exotic global 'shooting stage' to provide the spectacle appropriate to the physical scale of films shot in Cinerama, CinemaScope, and VistaVision.

Chapter 12 • American production in Britain during the 1950s

Majors and independents

US involvement in British production was varied. Though the large American companies had to balance the lower costs of overseas production against the expenditure required to run their expensive Hollywood studio facilities, a number of them were to contribute significantly to the Anglo-American production trend. As previously noted, MGM revived MGM-British in the late 1940s and embarked upon a relatively ambitious production programme which included *The Miniver Story* (1950), a sequel to *Mrs Miniver* (1942), their wartime hit, the adventure epics *Ivanhoe* and *Knights of the Round Table*, and a remake of their 1930s title, *The Barretts of Wimpole Street* (1957). Warner Bros. made a number of titles including Alfred Hitchcock's *Stage Fright* (1950), the historical naval epic, *Captain Horatio Hornblower R.N.*, a number of 'swashbucklers' including *The Crimson Pirate* (1952) and *His Majesty O'Keefe* (1954), and an adaptation of the Robert Louis Stevenson novel, *The Master of Ballantrae* (1953). Twentieth Century-Fox made *Night and the City*, a film noir, costume pictures such as *The Black Rose* (1950) and *The Mudlark* (1950), a number of World War Two titles including *The Man Who Never Was* (1956), and *Sink the Bismarck!* (1960), and *The Inn of the Sixth Happiness* (1958), a 'biopic' of the English missionary Gladys Aylward set in China during the 1930s. The Disney company in conjunction with RKO made a number of historical adventure films. *Treasure Island* (1950), the first solely live-action film from the studio, was followed by *The Story of Robin Hood and His Merrie Men* (1952), *The Sword and the Rose* (1953), and *Rob Roy, the Highland Rogue* (1953).

However, independent producers, with no fixed studios to maintain, stood to gain most by shifting their production from Hollywood to other parts of the world including Britain, and much of the 'runaway' activity of the 1950s came from smaller production companies though often these were to act in conjunction with major American companies. As with the explanations for the growth of runaway production itself, the explanation for the rise of the independent producer in the 1950s is a complex matter involving the divorcement decrees, taxation matters, political witch-hunting, and recalcitrant actors rejecting the 'slavish' conditions of the traditional Hollywood contract. A range of stars and directors were involved, many on a one-off basis, and Anglo-US productions include *Pandora and the Flying Dutchman* (1952), a collaboration between American director, Albert Lewin, and the British Romulus company, shot mainly on location in Spain with interiors filmed at Shepperton, *The Prince and the Showgirl* (1957), made by a company set up by its star, Marilyn Monroe, and Chaplin's *A King in New York* (1957). In other parts of Europe, the Harold Hecht–Burt Lancaster team made *Trapeze* (1956) in France, and Joseph Mankiewicz produced and directed *The Barefoot Contessa* (1954) in Italy, at Rome's Cinecittà studios and on location. The most prominent independent producer in this context was Sam Spiegel who established a substantial reputation mainly on the basis of Anglo-US productions, including *The African Queen*, *The Bridge on the River Kwai* and, in the 1960s, *Suddenly Last Summer* and *Lawrence of Arabia* (1962).

Small British companies such as Warwick Films and Coronado established links with American companies such as Columbia and RKO. Warwick Films set up in 1952 by the Americans, Irving Allen and Cubby Broccoli, produced a number of Anglo-American titles for Columbia including the Second World War films, *The*

Red Beret (1953) and *The Cockleshell Heroes* (1955), and the Arthurian costume picture *The Black Knight* (1954). Coronado, also founded by an American, David E. Rose, made *The End of the Affair* (1955), an adaptation of the Graham Greene novel, and a Second World War picture, *The Safecracker* (1958), for Columbia and MGM respectively. The Warwick and Coronado films featured prominent Hollywood stars such as Alan Ladd, José Ferrer, Van Johnson and Deborah Kerr. On a more modest level, Robert Lippert, a small-scale American B-picture producer, set up a deal with Hammer Film Productions to make low-budget films for American distribution. The Hammer films also used American stars as the selling point for US audiences, although these tended to fall into the 'minor' or 'second-rank' star category – Dane Clark in *The Gambler and the Lady* (1952), John Ireland in *The Glass Cage* (1955) – or the 'fading' star past his or her prime, such as George Brent in *The Last Page* (1952) or Paulette Goddard in *The Stranger Came Home* (1954). The American majors were abandoning B-production at this time and independents such as Lippert were stepping up their supply of such films still in demand from exhibitors (see *Variety*, 21 November 1951: 7).

Actors and directors

As indicated previously, the Anglo-US films utilised a range of Hollywood actors and directors. The policy of featuring American actors in British productions to enhance a film's international appeal had been tried previously in the interwar period by Michael Balcon, Herbert Wilcox and Alexander Korda, but the influx of American stars in the 1950s was on a much greater scale. Many of the American actors who came to work in Britain in the 1950s were top stars of the period such as Spencer Tracy in *Edward My Son*, Humphrey Bogart and Katharine Hepburn in *The African Queen*, James Stewart and Marlene Dietrich in *No Highway* (1951), Greer Garson and Walter Pidgeon in *The Miniver Story*, Gregory Peck in *Captain Horatio Hornblower R.N.* and *Moby Dick*, Robert Taylor in *Ivanhoe* and *Knights of the Round Table*, Cary Grant and Ingrid Bergman in *Indiscreet* (1958), Clark Gable in *Never Let Me Go* (1953) and James Cagney in *Shake Hands with the Devil* (1959). In fact, the list could be extended considerably and others who came to Britain for one or more films include Joan Crawford, José Ferrer, Ray Milland, Van Johnson, Dana Andrews, Joseph Cotton, Joel McCrea, George Raft, Tyrone Power, Gene Kelly, Glenn Ford, Jeffrey Hunter, Alan Ladd, Burt Lancaster, Elizabeth Taylor, Ava Gardner, Charles Coburn, Gene Tierney, Errol Flynn, Rita Hayworth, Jack Lemmon, Jennifer Jones, Victor Mature, Joan Fontaine, Marilyn Monroe, Rock Hudson, Cornell Wilde, Maureen O' Hara, Shelley Winters, Ginger Rogers, Macdonald Carey, Clifton Webb, Gloria Grahame, Donna Reed, Olivia de Haviland, Larry Parks, Paul Douglas, Ruth Roman, Richard Widmark, Victor Mature, Jayne Mansfield, and Robert Mitchum. Among these US 'imports' were a small number of British stars who had established themselves in Hollywood by the 1950s; David Niven, James Mason, Stewart Granger, Jean Simmons and Deborah Kerr returned to their native land for the occasional appearance in an Anglo-US production. As well as the major stars and featured players mentioned, a number of names associated firmly with low-budget Hollywood production also worked on the more modestly financed Anglo-American productions including John Ireland, Tom Conway, Dale Robertson, Skip Homier, and Wayne Morris.

Chapter 12 • American production in Britain during the 1950s

The directors brought over from Hollywood ranged from prominent auteurs such as John Ford and Alfred Hitchcock, to seasoned professionals such as Vincent Sherman, Tay Garnett, Sidney Franklin, and Richard Thorpe. The full list includes John Huston, Charles Chaplin, George Cukor, Edward Dmytryk, Albert Lewin, David Miller, Jean Negulesco, Jules Dassin, Raoul Walsh, Jacques Tourneur, William Kieghly, Robert Siodmak, Henry Koster, Byron Haskin, Mark Robson, George Marshall, Otto Preminger, Joseph Mankiewicz and Stanley Donen. British directors were involved as well and while Englishmen Alfred Hitchcock and Charles Chaplin may be regarded 'American imports' of sorts, other prominent British film-makers, such as Carol Reed, Herbert Wilcox, David Lean, Ronald Neame, Victor Saville, Laurence Olivier, the Boulting brothers, Muriel Box, Robert Hamer, Terence Young, John Guillermin, Ken Hughes, the Launder and Gilliat team, Terence Fisher, and Ken Annakin, directed Anglo-American productions.

The films

The Anglo-American productions came from a variety of sources – Hollywood majors such as Twentieth Century-Fox and MGM, small British companies such as Hammer, Warwick Films and Coronado, and ambitious independent producers such as Sam Spiegel. Accordingly, the resultant films were varied in quality, budget levels and ambition and drew on a variety of sources and genres. Many of the films were routine genre pictures and, in Thomas Guback's words, 'of little merit, hardly more noteworthy than the grade B pictures made in this country' (1969: 165). Yet alongside the routine there were interesting genre pieces such as the crime films, *Tiger by the Tail* (1955), *Town on Trial* (1958), John Ford's *Gideon's Day*, and *The Whole Truth* (1958), the espionage thriller, *Rough Shoot* (1953), horror films including *Night of the Demon*, a superior horror film released in 1958 in the wake of the first Hammer classics, and *Village of the Damned* (1960). A number of titles from the popular Second World War cycle of the period were Anglo-American productions including *The Hasty Heart* (1949), *The Miniver Story*, a sequel to the wartime hit which starts its narrative in the final year of the war, *Circle of Danger* (1951), *The Red Beret*, *The Cockleshell Heroes*, *The Man Who Never Was*, *The Safecracker*, *The Two-Headed Spy* (1958), and *Sink the Bismarck!*, as well as the enormously successful, *The Bridge on the River Kwai*. There were also colonial films such as *The African Queen*, *Bhowani Junction*, *Beyond Mombasa* (1956), *Safari* (1956), *Tarzan and the Lost Safari* (1957), *Harry Black* (1958), and *Killers of Kilimanjaro* (1959), and a small number of romantic pictures including *Pandora and the Flying Dutchman*, *The End of the Affair*, and *Bonjour Tristesse* (1958). There was even a British western, *The Sheriff of Fractured Jaw* (1958)! At the opposite end of the financial spectrum from the 'routine' genre pictures dismissed by Guback were a number of well-financed historical costume pictures including the lavish medieval spectaculars such as *Ivanhoe*, *The Story of Robin Hood and His Merrie Men*, *Knights of the Round Table*, *The Black Knight*, and *The Dark Avenger* (1955), the Regency-set *Beau Brummell* (1954), a 'Scottish historical adventure strand' including *The Master of Ballantrae*, *Rob Roy, the Highland Rogue*, and *Kidnapped* (1960), maritime adventure films such as *Treasure Island*, *Captain Horatio Hornblower R.N.*, *The Crimson Pirate*, and *Sea Devils* (1953), and a range of films set in the nineteenth century such as Paramount's first Anglo-American production, *So Evil*

My Love (1948), *Britannia Mews* (1949), *The Mudlark* with Hollywood star Irene Dunne as Queen Victoria, and *Footsteps in the Fog* (1955), a costume film redolent of a Gainsborough melodrama of the 1940s and featuring one of that cycle's major stars, Stewart Granger.

The films which emerged from the Anglo-American collaboration were in a variety of genres and it is difficult to discern a clear pattern in the forms taken by the cultural mix of Hollywood and British film making conventions. Some of the best-known films rooted themselves in the host culture by the traditional British method of literary and dramatic adaptation. Prestigious literary names were involved with versions of D.H. Lawrence's *Sons and Lovers*, and Graham Greene's *The End of the Affair*, and *Our Man in Havana* (1960). Theatrical sources included George Bernard Shaw represented by no less than four adaptations of his plays, *Saint Joan* (1957), *The Doctor's Dilemma* (1958), *The Devil's Disciple* (1959), and *The Millionairess* (1960), and Terence Rattigan, the prominent West End playwright, with versions of *The Deep Blue Sea* (1955) and *The Sleeping Prince* (*The Prince and the Showgirl*). The nineteenth century novels of Sir Walter Scott and Robert Louis Stevenson were adapted for historical films such as *Ivanhoe*, *The Adventures of Quentin Durward* (1954), *The Master of Ballantrae*, and *Treasure Island*, while *Knights of the Round Table* acknowledges *Le Mort D'Arthur*, Sir Thomas Mallory's fifteenth century version of the Arthurian legends, in its credits. Other British writers whose work was adapted include C. S. Forester (*The African Queen*, *Captain Horatio Hornblower R. N.*), G. K. Chesterton (*Father Brown*[1954]), John Masters (*Bhowani Junction*), M. R. James (*Night of the Demon*) and John Wyndham (*Village of the Damned*). However, the literary sources were not confined to the host country. Two important American writers were adapted for 'runaways' – Herman Melville (*Moby Dick*) and Mark Twain (*The Million Pound Note* [1953]), and although *The Bridge on the River Kwai* was the best-known adaptation from a French writer (Pierre Boulle), two other Anglo-American films, *The Man Who Watched the Trains Go By* (1952) and *Bonjour Tristesse*, were adapted from novels by Simenon and Françoise Sagan, respectively.

Predictably, one of the main features of the Anglo-American films was the use of American actors in leading roles, a strategy which British films had used intermittently since the 1920s at least. Some titles providing a clear narrative motivation for the use of American actors and centred on an American character transplanted to Britain following a pattern set by MGM-British's *A Yank at Oxford* in the late 1930s, and creating similar opportunities for depicting cultural interaction. A diversity of films featured one or more American actors playing American characters including crime films and thrillers such as *Night and the City*, *Tiger by the Tail* and *Rough Shoot*, war films such as *The Red Beret*, the naval film, *Seagulls over Sorrento* (1954), the romantic *The End of the Affair*, and the horror title, *Night of the Demon*.

Sometimes the US nationality of the central characters played a role in the narrative. For example, in the noirish B picture, *Tiger by the Tail*, the central character played by Larry Parks, in real life a refugee from the McCarthy witch-hunt, is a journalist posted to London by his American newspaper. The opening sequences of the film play upon his unfamiliarity even discomfort with his new cultural surroundings though his nationality is rendered less important as the 'plunge into nightmare' scenario of the film unfolds. In *The Red Beret*, Alan Ladd plays an American in the

Royal Air Force's parachutist section though he is masquerading as a Canadian in order to cover up his past as a US airman involving an accident in which a friend of his died. In *Seagulls Over Sorrento*, Gene Kelly plays a US Naval Officer working with a British naval team testing a new torpedo. In both cases the cultural and temperamental differences between the nationalities play a role though both films end on a harmonious note. *The Bridge on the River Kwai* presents a more complicated case with the character of Shears, a British officer in the Boulle novel, changed to an American in the screenplay to accommodate the film's Hollywood star, William Holden. As a consequence, Shears' American pragmatism is presented as a foil to the different concepts of discipline, honour and conduct in wartime, embodied by the British officers, Colonel Nicholson (Alec Guinness) and Major Warden (Jack Hawkins). *Night and the City* features Richard Widmark and Gene Tierney, both strongly identified with the film noir genre in 1940s Hollywood (*Kiss of Death* and *Laura*); in particular, Widmark's emblematic presence as small-time spiv, Harry Fabian, provided the film with a noirish authenticity prompting critics to see it as a key contribution to the genre despite its British production context. As Colin McArthur has pointed out, it 'is significant that Borde and Chaumeton chose as the cover illustration of their *Panorama du Film Noir Américain* a close up of Harry Fabian' (1972: 100). By contrast, in a number of films, Hollywood actors are used in a more neutral fashion, with the American nationality of the central character remaining peripheral to the narrative. In *The End of the Affair*, although British in the novel, Bendrix, the writer involved in the 'affair', becomes an American; he is played by Hollywood star, Van Johnson, though the US nationality of the character is barely alluded to apart from an oblique reference in the opening voice-over. Similarly, in *Night of the Demon*, the central character becomes an academic specialist in the paranormal played by Dana Andrews, though the shift in nationality is inconsequential in terms of the narrative.

More often than not, however, American stars simply played British roles such as Irene Dunne's controversial depiction of Queen Victoria in *The Mudlark*, Gregory Peck's playing of a British sea captain in *Captain Horatio Hornblower R.N.*, Mel Ferrer as King Arthur in *Knights of the Round Table*, Errol Flynn as the 'Black Prince' in *The Dark Avenger*, Jennifer Jones as the poet, Elizabeth Barrett Browning, in *The Barretts of Wimpole Street*, and Ingrid Bergman as the English missionary, Gladys Aylward, in *The Inn of the Sixth Happiness*. James Cagney and Robert Mitchum played Irish revolutionaries in *Shake Hands with the Devil* and *A Terrible Beauty* (1960) respectively, and Dean Stockwell appeared as Paul Morel (based on Lawrence himself as a youth) in *Sons and Lovers*. Robert Taylor was the most versatile though playing a British army major in *Conspirator* and an engineer in colonial Africa in *Killers of Kilimanjaro*; in MGM's medieval cycle, he played Wilfred of Ivanhoe, a Saxon nobleman, a medieval knight, Lancelot (a Breton), and the Scottish Quentin Durward in *Ivanhoe*, *Knights of the Round Table*, and *The Adventures of Quentin Durward*, respectively! In all cases, the use of Hollywood stars had an economic motivation – the selling of the film to an American audience. Yet the cultural consequences of this varied at the level of the text.

In a number of films, the British status derived in part from the fact that their location elements were filmed in British dependencies, or where locations in other

European countries were used but with studio shooting in Britain. For example, titles such as *Fire Down Below* (1957), and *Island in the Sun* (1957) were filmed in the West Indies but used MGM's Borehamwood studio for interiors. *Duel in the Jungle* (1954), *Beyond Mombasa*, *Safari* and *Tarzan and the Lost Safari* were appropriately filmed in various parts of Africa as well as in British studios; *Harry Black* was filmed in India but the Indian-set *Bhowani Junction* was filmed in Pakistan after MGM encountered problems with the Indian government. Many of the above titles had British elements – colonial themes – but some of the runaways had minimal contact with their ostensible country of origin. Despite drawing its title from Shakespeare and featuring Sean Connery in a small role, *Action of the Tiger* (1957) filmed in Spain and Greece as well as Borehamwood, was about the adventures of an American people-smuggler and was set largely in Albania. John Huston's *Heaven Knows, Mr Allison*, filmed in the West Indies with interiors shot at Borehamwood, and set during World War Two, featured Robert Mitchum as a US marine stranded on a remote South Pacific island with a nun and a battalion of Japanese soldiers for company. Mitchum's other runaway, *The Angry Hills* (1959), also set during World War Two, had Stanley Baker (playing a Nazi), Leslie Phillips, and Donald Wolfit in the cast, but was a story of an American journalist caught up in the Nazi occupation of Greece.

The Anglo-American dimension of the British film industry in the 1950s covered a variety of situations. At the top, ambitious end of a spectrum was the sustained quality production programme at the MGM-British complex at Borehamwood described by one writer as a 'Los Angeles-style studio' (Warren, 1995: 89), and Twentieth Century-Fox's comparable ambitious programme which included costume dramas such as *The Mudlark* and *The Black Rose* as well as the noir *Night and the City*. The independent producer, Sam Spiegel, raised the level of ambition with projects such as *The African Queen*, *Moby Dick* and, especially, *The Bridge on the River Kwai* which pointed the way for the lavish 'international' productions of the 1960s. On a more modest level, British companies such as Warwick and Coronado provided the American majors with a steady supply of programme films utilising prominent Hollywood stars such as Alan Ladd and Van Johnson, while, at the lower end of the spectrum, Hammer's collaboration with the American Robert Lippert produced a steady stream of low-budget films to meet the demands of the double-bill programme both in Britain and the United States.

As has been noted, the Anglo-American films had a variable relationship to British culture, some mobilising its history and literature in the interests of the spectacular costume film, some drawing on its generic strengths providing an energising American dimension to the crime film and the war picture. The primary reasons for Hollywood's overseas production lay in access to funding, both blocked earnings and government subsides such as the Eady Levy, lower labour costs, and, possibly, the authenticity and variety provided by the relevant location shooting when the subject matter was drawn from non-American sources. The Anglo-American venture undoubtedly served the interests of the American film industry yet it has been suggested that some British interests were also served as a consequence:

> While strident criticisms of the subsequent infiltration from Hollywood were raised, several positive factors had to be borne in mind. Most obviously British studios were in

use, and British technicians were given work. Also, of course, the presence of Hollywood stars and directors gained valuable publicity in America for British films. But most important of all, films like *Night and the City*, *The Mudlark*, *The Miniver Story* and *Captain Horatio Hornblower, R.N.* were recognized in the course of their wide release in America as British, thus conditioning audiences towards a more general acceptance of British films. (Perry, 1975: 143)

Whatever the cultural character of the films which emerged, Anglo-British production did create employment opportunities for British film-workers, directors, actors and technical personnel, in an industry still recovering from the problems of the late 1940s. In addition, the profiling of the British film for an American audience, suggested by Perry, may have paved the way for the more extensive American financing of British films and British subject-matter which occurred in the 1960s. In the 1950s, many of the US-financed films, with their higher production values, their top Hollywood star names, and, often, their 'international' orientation, could be distinguished from the popular domestic war films and comedies. In the 1960s, by contrast, American finance lay behind numerous British films with a relatively secure cultural identity. *The L-Shaped Room* (1962), *Tom Jones* (1963), *Zulu* (1963),*The Knack* (1965), *The Spy Who Came in from the Cold* (1965), *Alfie* (1966), *A Man for All Seasons* (1966), *Funeral in Berlin* (1966), *Far From the Madding Crowd* (1967), *If. .* (1968), *The Charge of the Light Brigade* (1968), *Women in Love* (1969), and *The Prime of Miss Jean Brodie* (1969), together with series such as the Margaret Rutherford 'Miss Marple' films, the Beatles films, *A Hard Day's Night* (1964) and *Help!* (1965), the 'Swinging London' films, *Georgy Girl* (1966) and *Joanna* (1968), constitute a convincing profile of a national cinema in the mid-1960s despite their origins in the boardrooms of the Hollywood majors.

Acknowledgements: I would like to thank Sylvia Harvey and the Arts and Humanities Research Council for funding this research through the AHRB Centre for British Film and Television Studies.

Filmography
Action of the Tiger (1957)
Adventures of Quentin Durward, The (1954)
African Queen, The (1952)
Alfie (1966)
Angry Hills, The (1959),
Barefoot Contessa, The (1954)
Barretts of Wimpole Street, The (1957)
Beau Brummell (1954),
Beyond Mombasa (1956)
Bhowani Junction (1956)
Black Knight, The (1954)
Black Rose, The (1950)
Bonjour Tristesse (1958)
Bridge on the River Kwai, The (1957)
Britannia Mews (1949),
Captain Horatio Hornblower R.N. (1951)

Charge of the Light Brigade, The (1968)
Circle of Danger (1951)
Cockleshell Heroes, The (1955)
Conspirator (1949)
Crimson Pirate, The (1952)
Dark Avenger, The (1955)
Deep Blue Sea, The (1955)
Devil's Disciple, The (1959)
Doctor's Dilemma, The (1958)
Duel in the Jungle (1954)
Edward My Son (1949)
End of the Affair, The (1955)
Far From the Madding Crowd (1967)
Father Brown (1954)
Fire Down Below (1957)
Footsteps in the Fog (1955)
Funeral in Berlin (1966)
Gambler and the Lady, The (1952)
Georgy Girl (1966)
Gideon's Day (1958)
Glass Cage, The (1955)
Goodbye Mr Chips (1939)
Hard Day's Night A (1964)
Harry Black (1958)
Hasty Heart The (1949)
Heaven Knows, Mr Allison (1958)
Help! (1965)
His Majesty O'Keefe (1954)
If . . (1968)
Indiscreet (1958)
Inn of the Sixth Happiness, The (1958)
Island in the Sun (1957)
Ivanhoe (1952)
Joanna (1968)
Kidnapped (1960)
Killers of Kilimanjaro (1959)
King in New York, A (1957)
Knack The (1965)
Knights of the Round Table (1953)
Last Page, The (1952)
Lawrence of Arabia (1962)
L-Shaped Room, The (1962)
Man for All Seasons, A (1966)
Man Who Never Was, The (1956)
Man Who Watched the Trains Go By, The (1952)
Master of Ballantrae, The (1953)
Million Pound Note, The (1953)

Chapter 12 • American production in Britain during the 1950s

Millionairess, The (1960)
Miniver Story, The (1950)
Moby Dick (1956)
Mudlark, The (1950)
Never Let Me Go (1953)
Night and the City (1950)
Night of the Demon (1958)
No Highway (1951)
Our Man in Havana (1960)
Pandora and the Flying Dutchman (1952)
Prime of Miss Jean Brodie, The (1969)
Prince and the Showgirl, The (1957)
Quo Vadis (1952)
Red Beret, The (1953)
Rob Roy, the Highland Rogue (1953)
Rough Shoot (1953)
Safari (1956)
Safecracker, The (1958)
Saint Joan (1957)
Sea Devils (1953)
Seagulls over Sorrento (1954)
Shake Hands with the Devil (1959)
Sheriff of Fractured Jaw, The (1958)
Sink the Bismarck! (1960)
So Evil My Love (1948)
Sons and Lovers (1960)
Spy Who Came in from the Cold, The (1965)
Stage Fright (1950)
Story of Robin Hood and His Merrie Men, The (1952)
Stranger Came Home, The (1954)
Suddenly Last Summer (1960)
Sword and the Rose, The (1953)
Tarzan and the Lost Safari (1957)
Terrible Beauty, A (1960)
Tiger by the Tail (1955)
Tom Jones (1963)
Town on Trial (1958)
Trapeze (1956)
Treasure Island (1950)
Two-Headed Spy, The (1958)
Village of the Damned (1960)
Whole Truth, The (1958)
Women in Love (1969)
Yank at Oxford, A (1937)
Zulu (1963)

Bibliography

Andrew, D (1995) *Mists of Regret. Culture and Sensibility in Classic French Film*. Princeton, NJ: Princeton University Press.

Burrows, J (2002) ' "England Invaded"!: The Contested Authenticity of IMP's *Ivanhoe* (1913)', in A. Burton and L. Porter (eds) *Crossing the Pond Anglo-American Film relations Before 1930*. Trowbridge, Wiltshire: Flicks Books, pp. 34–44.

Fadiman, W (1962) 'Runaways', *Films and Filming*, July, pp. 40–41.

Guback, T (1969) *The International Film Industry*. Bloomington & London: Indiana University Press.

Glancy, H. M (1998) 'Hollywood and Britain: MGM and the British "Quota" Legislation' , in J. Richards (ed) *The Unknown 1930s: An Alternative History of the British Cinema, 1929–1939*. London & New York: I. B. Tauris, pp. 57–72.

Harper, S & Porter, V (2003) *British Cinema of the 1950s*. Oxford: Oxford University Press.

Harper, S (2001) 'Bonnie Prince Charlie Revisited: British Costume Film in The 1950s', in R. Murphy (ed) *The British Cinema Book*. London: BFI Publishing.

Jarvie, I (1992) *Hollywood's Overseas Campaign. The North Atlantic Movie Trade 1920–1950*. Cambridge: Cambridge University Press.

Low, R (1949) *The History of the British Film, 1906–1914*. London: George Allen & Unwin.

McArthur, C (1972) *Underworld USA*. London: Secker & Warburg.

Maltby, R. and Craven, I. (1995) *Hollywood Cinema*. Oxford: Blackwell.

Morris, N (2002) 'The myth of unadulterated culture meets the threat of imported media', *Media, Culture and Society* 24: 278–289.

Murphy, R (1992) *Sixties British Cinema*. London: BFI Publishing.

Murphy, R (ed) (2001) *The British Cinema Book*. London: BFI Publishing.

Nowell-Smith, G. and Ricci, S. (eds) (1998) *Hollywood and Europe. Economics, Culture and National Identity: 1945–95*. London: BFI Publishing.

Perry, G (1975) *The Great British Picture Show*. London: Paladin.

Ryall, T (2001) *Britain and the American Cinema*. London: Sage.

Warren, P (1995) *British Film Studios*. London: B.T. Batsford.

Chapter 13

Adventure, exchange and identity: British, American, and Un-American involvement in costume adventure TV series and films in the postwar era

Steve Neale

Introduction

In what is so far the only book written on the export of British television programmes to the United States, Jeffrey S. Miller (2000) notes the success in the US in the mid- to late-1950s of a number of costume adventure series produced in Britain for Britain's new commercial TV channel, ITV (Independent Television). Among the series he mentions are *The Adventures of Robin Hood* (which was initially broadcast in Britain from 1955 to 1959 and on CBS in America from 1955 to 1958) and *The Adventures of Sir Lancelot* (initially broadcast in Britain and on NBC in America in 1956 and 1957). Others included *The Buccaneers* (initially broadcast in Britain and on CBS in America in 1956 and 1957), *Sword of Freedom* (initially broadcast from 1957 to the early 1960s in Britain and syndicated in America in 1958), *The Adventures of William Tell* (initially broadcast from 1957 to 1959 in Britain and syndicated in America in 1958), and *Ivanhoe* (initially broadcast in 1958 and 1959 in Britain and syndicated in America in 1958).

Miller argues that the trans-Atlantic success of these series provides a counterweight to simplistic or one-way accounts of American cultural imperialism, that they were received in America as distinctively British, and that they served in Britain to allay anxieties over the increasing Americanization of British culture (anxieties fuelled, among other things, by the advent of ITV itself). 'No matter how much influence American television may have exerted in the establishment of commercial broadcasting in Britain,' he writes, '*Robin Hood* and its fellow imports were presented to and perceived by American audiences as British. The United States did not possess medieval castles; Americans did not speak with those accents'. He goes on to suggest some of the factors governing their reception, their success and what he sees as their cultural role, arguing that they were ... contained within an American political and ideological context that presented a significant 'dialogical turn' to their reception. *Robin Hood* arrived in the United States at the moment in which the anti-Communist fervor of the McCarthy years was passing in what historians Douglas Miller and Marion Nowak would call "the era of conservative consensus." Whatever problems may have existed in American society were pushed to the back of the collective consciousness in order to celebrate a golden age of peace and prosperity ... As potentially critical reporting and commentary began to fade quietly from American prime-time television, stories of knights and maidens and Merry Men from long ago and far away Britain, especially stories connoted as superior to what was being produced in the United States, served as worthy diversions from social and political problems of the day (Miller, 2000: 23).

I myself have little sympathy for crude conceptions of cultural imperialism, especially when it comes to considering the cultural and commercial relations between first world countries like America and Britain, and particularly when one of these countries, Britain, still possessed colonies and the remnants of an empire when series like these were being made.* Like Michael Walsh (1997 and 1999), Ian Jarvie (1990, 1992 and 1998) and Jeffrey S. Miller himself, I am much less interested in reiterating the monolithic power of the American media industries, then as now, than in contributing to the provision of what Walsh calls 'more complex and detailed accounts of the multiple strategic and tactical considerations' at stake in relations between American and British media industries, companies and personnel (1997: 4), in restoring a sense of agency to the institutions and individuals involved, whatever their nationality, and in emphasizing the heterogeneous and multi-dimensional nature of national industries, identities and cultural products, including those of America itself.

I am also aware that what Miller has to say about these 1950s series is essentially a preamble to a more detailed study of the 1960s and 1970s. However, there are at least three sets of factors which complicate any straightforward designation of these series as British and Miller's reading of their political context and ideological significance. They include the extent to which generic precedents for series like these were provided by American (as well as British) film companies; the extent to which American (as well as British) TV companies were involved in their funding, distribution and production; and the extent to which many of the series themselves were pseudonymously scripted by American screenwriters branded as 'Un-American' by the House Committee on Un-American Activities (HUAC) on account of their Communist sympathies and subsequently blacklisted by the major Hollywood studios. These factors all serve to qualify rather than exemplify straightforward conceptions of cultural imperialism and national identity.

Costume adventure in cinema in the postwar era

Series like *The Adventures of Robin Hood*, *Ivanhoe* and *The Buccaneers* did not appear out of the blue. They traded on a currency in costume adventure that had been

---

* Indeed, the British film industry sought to revive the pre-war system of 'imperial preference' in its post-war export drive, to extend its theatre holdings in Commonwealth countries, and to exploit both the scenic and economic advantages of shooting overseas in Commonwealth countries in late 1940s and 1950s. See *Variety*, 27 March 1946: 21, 19 June 1946: 18, 2 February 1949: 16, 5 April 1950: 18.

Chapter 13 • Adventure, exchange and identity

initiated in Hollywood in the mid-1940s. Brian Taves (1993) has identified 1945, the year in which films such as *The Fighting Guardsman*, *Captain Kidd*, *Sudan* and *The Spanish Main* were first released in America, as the starting point for the third of four major cycles of historical adventure prior to the 1990s. As Taves shows, the cycle and its various strands were by no means confined to Hollywood. While Hollywood studios produced films such as *The Bandit of Sherwood Forest* (1946), *The Return of Monte Cristo* (1946), *The Three Musketeers* (1948), *Captain from Castille* (1949), *Prince of Foxes* (1949), *The Highwayman* (1951), *Anne of the Indies* (1951), *Scaramouche* (1952), *Ivanhoe* (1952), *Blackbeard the Pirate* (1952) and *Botany Bay* (1953) in the late 1940s and early 1950s, the production and re-release of such British films as *Bonnie Prince Charlie* (1949), *The Four Feathers* (1939), *The Elusive Pimpernel* (1950), *The Drum* (1938), *Men of Sherwood Forest* (1954) and *Storm Over the Nile* (1955) augmented the cycle as well. Along with the increasing production in Britain of costume adventure films by American companies (examples include *The Black Rose* (1949), *Treasure Island* (1950), *The Story of Robin Hood and His Merrie Men Black* (1952) and *Ivanhoe*), the cycle helped prompt the advent of costume adventure on TV in Britain in several ways. Along the way, it raised issues of policy, culture and identity pertinent to TV and the cinema alike.

As Tom Ryall (2001) has pointed out, Hollywood had for decades drawn on British and Continental European history and culture in order to provide its output with prestige, and in order to appeal not just to its overseas audiences, but to those sectors of its domestic population whose cultural traditions had their roots either in Britain or in Europe in general. Moreover,

> In addition to the cosmopolitan domestic audiences, the film-makers themselves – producers, directors, writers, stars – were recruited from the leading European film-making nations, including Britain. The fact that American films seemed to capture the public imagination in so many countries may be linked to their ability to synthesize different cultures, to devise genres for a wide range of ethnic communities, a requirement imposed by their domestic audience. In effect, Hollywood was exporting films designed to appeal to an 'American' audience constituted partly by relatively recent immigrant communities. A certain degree of the international was inscribed in the parochial, facilitating the circulation of such films on an international basis (Ryall, 2001: 146)*

International audiences were a major preoccupation of the American and British film industries alike at the end of World War II, following a period in which markets abroad had been closed to both. Both industries engaged in major export drives, aided by government agencies (Jarvie, 1992: 205–207, Schatz, 1997: 159–160, 288-289, Seagrave, 1997: 131–139, 142–144). In America, the importance of overseas markets increased as domestic cinema attendances declined and as the structural

---

* The heterogeneity of the American market and the differences in taste between the American film-going population in the mid-west, the southwest and other rural areas and in big cities and towns should not, however, be underestimated. There was a marked hostility among the former not just to foreign productions and foreign accents, but to foreign settings, stories, characters and costumes, even in Hollywood films, which regularly provoked negative reactions to Hollywood's costume adventure productions. See *Variety*, 18 June 1947: 1, 16 and the following 'What the Picture Did For Me' columns in the *Motion Picture Herald*: 7 August 1948: 41, 8 May 1948: 50, 21 January 1952: 44, 23 February 1952: 51, 1 March 1952: 48, 29 March 1952: 56, 12 April 1952: 56, 18 October 1952: 40, 13 December 1952: 44.

changes brought about by the Paramount decision began to come into force (Balio, 1985: 401–486, Schatz: 323–333). In Britain, declining attendances were a factor as well, but the efforts of Alexander Korda and J. Arthur Rank to penetrate the mainstream US market met with limited success, and although their efforts elsewhere overseas were more successful, they were further stymied by the parlous state of the British economy, by government reactions, responses and policies, and, to a degree at least, by their own extravagance (Kulik, 1990: 286–326, MacNab, 1993: 80–198, Murphy, 1983: 164–178 and 1989: 219–230, Ryall: 91–94, Tabori, 1959: 235–256).

As is well documented, a balance of payments crisis in 1947 led to the introduction of a 75 per cent tax on the estimated earnings of foreign films in Britain, an American boycott, the first in a series of annual Anglo-American agreements and, initially at least, a raising of the quota placed on the proportion of British films to be screened in Britain each year (Dickinson and Street, 1985: 179–98, Jarvie, 1992: 213–68). These events helped established parameters within which British and American film companies alike developed their policies and practices during the course of the following decade. They helped highlight some of the divisions and alliances within as well as between the British and American film industries.* And they served as well both to focus attention on issues of nationality and to expand the industrial status and mix of films in the costume adventure cycle.

One of the aims of the Anglo-American agreements from the British point of view was the stimulation of US production in Britain. The agreements placed a ceiling on the sums earned in Britain by US companies which could be returned or 'remitted' to America. However, unremitted earnings could be spent on studio facilities and on the production of films in the UK, and this was increasingly viewed as a means of providing employment for UK production personnel and as a means of augmenting the number of British films in circulation. British producers were divided, their views inflected by the extent to which they relied on US companies for overseas distribution, by the extent to which they were involved in the distribution of US films in Britain, and by the extent to which they owned cinema chains and were therefore dependent on US (or US-made) films (Dickinson and Street: 191–219, Jarvie, 1992: 232–234). Exhibitors themselves, who throughout this period had problems meetings quotas and who tended to support American interests on the grounds that US films made more money at the box-office, were more welcoming (Spraos, 1962: 41).

Faced not only declining audiences and the aftermath of the Paramount suit, but by a wave of overseas legislation similar in kind to the legislation introduced in Britain, most American companies began producing more and more films aimed at overseas markets and overseas tastes. Many companies also moved into overseas production.

---

* American interests in these matters are usually seen as homogenous, and as embodied solely in the policies adopted by the Motion Picture Association of America (MPAA) and the Motion Picture Export Association (MPEA). However, it should be pointed out that a number of independent producers, among them Walt Disney, Samuel Goldwyn and David O. Selznick, were represented by the Society of Independent Motion Picture Producers (SIMPP), and that SIMPP was involved as a separate organization with its own distinct views in dealings with Britain and other overseas countries in the late 1940s and 1950s (Aberdeen, 2000: 169–73).

Chapter 13 • Adventure, exchange and identity

Overseas production was, initially at least, cheaper than production in the US itself, frozen earnings abroad could be invested in production of this kind, and with sterling and other foreign currencies having undergone devaluation, the dollar value of US overseas earnings in the US itself had declined. These factors were coupled with a trend towards shooting films on location, a trend augmented by a growth in independent production and hence in companies unburdened by the ownership of production facilities in Hollywood. They were coupled, too, with the increasing availability of subsidies to productions in Britain and elsewhere in Europe (Guback, 1985: 474–475, Schatz: 297–303). Together these factors led to a plethora of 'runaway' productions and co-productions, and to a general increase in the international character of the film industry (Ryall: 65–71).*

They also provided both a filip for costume adventure and grounds for disputes and worries over whether productions were 'foreign' or 'native', particularly when it came to subsidies, quotas and the distribution of films in countries other than those of their origin. *Treasure Island* was among the first runaway productions in Britain. It was the first-live action Disney film, and it was made with unremittable earnings. It was so successful that it led to a spin-off, *Long John Silver* (1954), which was produced in Australia by an American, Joseph Kaufman, to the establishment of a semi-permanent Disney unit in Britain, and hence to the production of such later films as *The Story of Robin Hood and His Merrie Men*, *The Sword and the Rose* (1953), *Rob Roy, The Highland Rogue* (1954) and *Kidnapped* (1960) (Maltin, 2000: 97–117, 167–169). Disney's films were medium budget productions aimed at children and family audiences. Their producer, Perce Pearce, was American. But their casts and their production personnel were mostly British. Other medium budget productions included *The Master of Ballantrae* (1953) and *The Black Knight* (1954). *The Master of Ballantrae* was produced by Warner Bros. and partly filmed on location in Scotland. *The Black Knight*, a contribution to the medieval adventure strand, was produced by a British company, Warwick Productions. However, Warwick was run by two expatriate American producers, Cubby Broccoli and Irving Allen, and was like other Warwick productions, distributed and partly funded by Columbia, an American company (Pulleine, 1982: 23–25).

Warwick and its films were among those cited in disputes and debates around the criteria used to define companies and films at this time. The British Film Producers Association turned down a membership application from Irving Allen, its director-general, Sir Henry French, arguing that there was 'a considerable distinction between British producers and producers of films which under the Cinematograph Films Act are entitled to be described as British films.' (*Motion Picture Herald*, 24 November 1956: 22). Even on the American side, the problem of 'quota films lensed in Britain has become a headache':

> Inequality comes ... when the British quota pix, made by American companies, are exported. Several countries, such as Germany, Belgium and France, for instance, have begun to kick about the necessity of having to pay in dollars for a British quota film.

---

*   It is important to point out that this period witnessed the advent of British runaway productions and co-productions too, and for similar reasons. See *Kinematograph Weekly*, 24 February 1949: 1, 7, 15 December 1949: 39, 23 November 1950: 1, 1 September 1955: 15, 22 September 1955: 9, 3 May 1956: 18, *Kinematograph Year Book*, 1950: 54, *Variety*, 19 October 1949:13, 14 December 1955: 12, 29, 29 February 1956: 3, 18.

> Their argument is that, being British, it should earn sterling...American execs admit that having to argue for the merits of a British quota picture as being American the minute it leaves Britain puts them into an awkward position, which they find difficult to justify. (*Variety*, 22 July 1953: 7).

It should be noted here that the laws governing the national status of runaways, quota films and other productions did not distinguish between English, Welsh, Irish or Scottish films, even though the use of Scottish locations and stories was clearly marked in some of these films, and even though there were moves in Scotland at the time to use them as the springboard for a Scottish film industry (*Kinematograph Weekly*, 14 April 1955: 9, *Variety*, 15 April 1953: 18, 15 April 1953: 15, 18, 19 April 1953: 11). It should also be noted that a film like *Men of Sherwood Forest*, though produced by an indisputably British company, Hammer/Exclusive, was part-funded by Twentieth Century-Fox through another American company, Lippert Pictures (Hearn and Barnes, 1997: 10). In the meantime, films such as *Ivanhoe*, *Knights of the Round Table* (1953) and *Captain Horatio Hornblower* (1951), whether defined in law as American or British, helped launch a policy of big budget production in the costume adventure field, a policy pursued in particular by Twentieth Century-Fox, MGM and Warners. This trend did not displace the medium budget films or, for that matter, the low budget productions that had helped launch the costume adventure cycle in the first place. But it served to expand its range and to increase its profile. By the mid-1950s, the range had begun on both sides of the Atlantic to include television programmes as well. It had also begun to include television versions of runaway productions, co-productions and quota productions too.

Television

Despite its prominence in the cinema, costume adventure was conspicuous by its absence from television in America and Britain alike in the early 1950s. The BBC produced one and two-part adaptations of *The Scarlet Pimpernel* and *The Black Arrow* in 1950 and 1951 respectively. Aside from that, though, and the screening of one or two films, there was nothing at all. It could therefore be argued that costume adventure, unlike comedy and crime, was one of the genres that differentiated the cinema from television in the early 1950s. However that soon began to change. Coinciding with the move in television away from live programming and towards filmed series, the very success of costume adventure in the cinema, coupled with the fact that it appealed to children and family audiences and that it continued to flourish in medium and low budget mode, led producers on the both sides of the Atlantic to begin planning series for TV. Among them was Joseph Kaufman, who produced *The Adventures of Long John Silver* alongside his *Long John Silver* film in 1954. *The Adventures of Long John Silver* was initially syndicated in America in 1955 and first broadcast on ITV in Britain in 1957. It was followed in America by a serialization *The Three Musketeers* (which, like *Long John Silver*, was a 'combo feature and tv package' (*Variety*, 12 May 1954: 37) and which was filmed as a co-production in Italy in 1954), and by two contributions to the empire adventure trend, *Captain Gallant of the Foreign Legion* (initially broadcast on NBC between 1955 and 1957) and *Tales of the 77th Bengal Lancers* (initially broadcast on NBC between 1956 and 1957). It was preceeded on ITV in Britain by *The Adventures of the Scarlet Pimpernel* (first broadcast

Chapter 13 • Adventure, exchange and identity

in 1955 and 1956), *The Adventures of Robin Hood*, *The Adventures of Sir Lancelot*, *The Buccaneers* and *The Count of Monte Cristo* (first broadcast in 1956 and 1957), and on the BBC by a serialization of *Robin Hood* (1953) and *The Three Musketeers* (1954).*

As is well documented, most of the ITV and BBC series were shown in America. *The Count of Monte Cristo* was initially syndicated in America in 1955 and *The Three Musketeers* in 1956. Of these and subsequent series, *The Gay Cavalier*, first broadcast on ITV in 1957, and *Richard the Lionheart*, first broadcast on ITV in 1961 and 1962, appear to have been the only exceptions. It is at this point, though, that a number of existing accounts tend to go astray, underestimating the degree of American involvement not just in the showing of these series, but in their production and distribution as well.

Jeffrey S. Miller is by no means alone in thinking that *The Adventures of Robin Hood* and ITV's other series were purely British. James Chapman argues that 'the most significant thing about *The Adventures of Robin Hood* was that it was sold to American television where it was successfully shown in syndication for many years'. In addition to suggesting that *Robin Hood* went straight into syndication, he implies that it was also a British export. He notes that *Robin Hood* was produced by Sapphire Films for Associated Television (ATV), that ATV was an ITV franchisee, and that ATV possessed 'a subsidiary,' the 'Independent Television Corporation' (ITC). He notes as well that 'ATV became the first British television company to set up its own international distribution arm' (Chapman, 2002: 7). But this by no means tells the whole story. Another recent account, by Bill Osgerby, Anna Gough-Yates and Marianne Wells, is significantly different. It, too, is inaccurate, though in a less misleading way. Like Chapman, Osgerby, Gough-Yates and Wells highlight the importance of ATV and ITC. They too suggest that *Robin Hood* was 'an international breakthrough'. But they differ from Chapman in arguing that *Robin Hood* was 'an early instance of transatlantic economic co-operation' and that 'the series was made in conjunction with the American company, Sapphire Films, and purchased in America by the CBS network' (Osgerby et al., 2001: 19).

Osgerby, Gough-Yates and Wells are right to describe *Robin Hood* as an early example of transatlantic economic cooperation. They are right, too, to imply that it was produced in conjunction with an American company. That company, however, was not Sapphire Films. Sapphire Films made *Robin Hood*. It went on to make *Sir Lancelot*, *The Buccaneers* and *Sword of Freedom*. Its executive producer was indeed an American, as we shall see. But Sapphire Films itself was a British company. Its head office was in London and its board of directors were predominantly British. ITC, meanwhile, initially stood for 'Independent Television Corporation' (or to give it its full title, 'Independent Television Programme Corporation'). It was formed in 1954 to bid for a programming franchise from the Independent Television Authority (ITA). The ITA turned down ITC's bid, but suggested it merge with ATV (or the Associated Broadcasting Development Company as it was then called) to bid for the programming of weekends in London and weekdays in the Midlands. The

---

* The BBC's role in costume adventure has been somewhat neglected, its production of *Robin Hood* almost totally ignored. What is clear is that the BBC preceeded ITV in the costume adventure field and that ITV's *Robin Hood* built on precedents not just in the cinema, but on British TV as well.

181

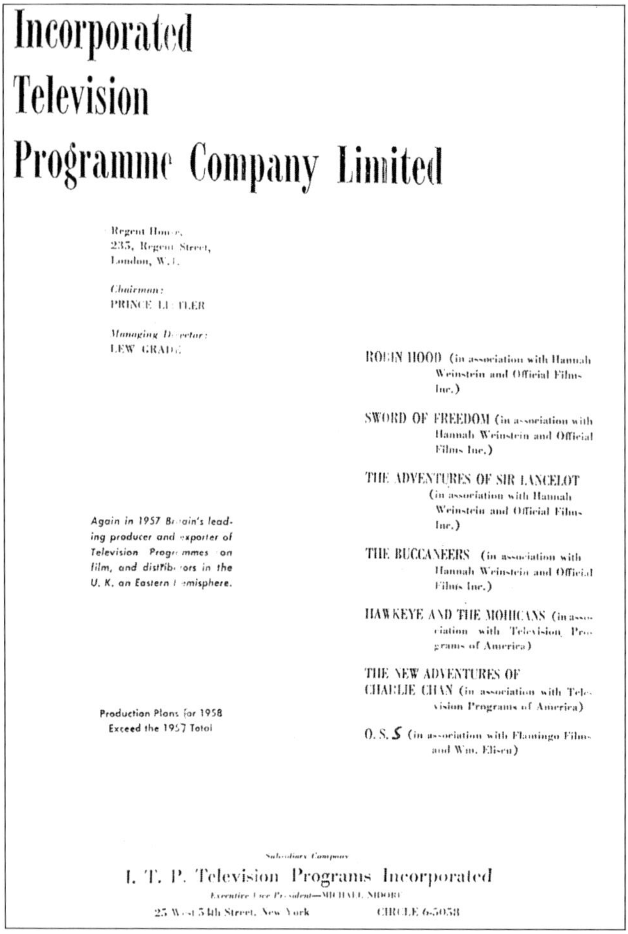

> **Incorporated Television Programme Company Limited**
>
> Regent House,
> 235, Regent Street,
> London, W.1.
>
> *Chairman:*
> PRINCE LITTLER
>
> *Managing Director:*
> LEW GRADE
>
> ROBIN HOOD (in association with Hannah Weinstein and Official Films Inc.)
>
> SWORD OF FREEDOM (in association with Hannah Weinstein and Official Films Inc.)
>
> THE ADVENTURES OF SIR LANCELOT (in association with Hannah Weinstein and Official Films Inc.)
>
> Again in 1957 Britain's leading producer and exporter of Television Programmes on film, and distributors in the U.K. an Eastern Hemisphere.
>
> THE BUCCANEERS (in association with Hannah Weinstein and Official Films Inc.)
>
> HAWKEYE AND THE MOHICANS (in association with Television Programs of America)
>
> THE NEW ADVENTURES OF CHARLIE CHAN (in association with Television Programs of America)
>
> Production Plans for 1958 Exceed the 1957 Total
>
> O.S.S (in association with Flamingo Films and Wm. Eliscu)
>
> *Subsidiary Company*
> I. T. P. Television Programs Incorporated
> *Executive Vice President* — MICHAEL MOORE
> 25 West 54th Street, New York   CIRCLE 6-5058

Advertisements from Variety *highlighting the various companies involved in the production and distribution of* The Adventures of Robin Hood *and other costume adventure series.*

Fig. 1. Variety, 8 January 1958, page 191.

merger took place and the bid was successful. The new company was called the Associated Broadcasting Company before finally becoming ATV. ITC, meanwhile, became the Incorporated Television Programme Company (ITP). This was the subsidiary that initially produced and subcontracted programmes for ATV. It was only in 1958, three years into the production of *Robin Hood*, that ITP set up a partnership with a newly-formed American group, the Independent Television Corporation, thus reviving ITC as an acronym. ITP was then bought out by ATV, which went on to acquire the new ITC in 1960 (Emmerson, Marcus and Hulse, Sendall 1982: 66–79, 118–119, *Variety*, 22 October 1958: 39, 10 February 1960: 31).

Among the directors of ATV and ITP were Lew Grade, Val Parnell and Harry Towers. Towers ran a television production and distribution company called Towers of London. Towers of London played a key role in the making of *The Adventures of the Scarlet Pimpernel* and *The Count of Monte Cristo*. Like Sapphire Films, though, and like ITP and ATV too, it neither produced nor funded nor distributed these series on its own. American companies played key roles as well.

Chapter 13 • Adventure, exchange and identity

Fig. 2. Variety, *31 July 1957, page 69.*

American involvement

Four American companies were involved in ITV's costume adventure series: Official Films, Television Programmes of America (TPA), Screen Gems (a subsidiary of Columbia Pictures) and National Telefilm Associates (NTA). These companies bought, produced and sold programmes, series and films to advertisers and sponsors, to local TV stations, and sometimes to the networks in the US in the 1950s. They also distributed programmes and series abroad. Among a relatively large group of companies specializing in syndication at this time (others included Ziv and Guild), they were in some ways analogous to those studios in the film industry who not only picked up completed product for distribution, but who also provided funding for projects brought to them by independent producers and who sometimes helped initiate projects themselves. Most of these companies were founded in the late 1940s and early 1950s. But they came into their own with the decision by the Federal Communications Commission in 1952 to lift its three-year freeze on the licensing of new television stations, when they found themselves in a position to supply a rapidly expanding domestic market at a point at which the networks alone were unable to meet the demand for syndicated programmes (Erickson, 1989: 6–10, Kompare, 2005: 47–57). They also helped feed a rapidly expanding market for TV programmes abroad, especially in English-speaking countries (*Variety*, 15 April 1953: 27, 10 February 1954: 27 and 42). The advent of ITV, in the year in which syndication became 'a $150 million a year business' (Erickson: 9), helped both cement their position and extend their activities and profits.

183

The degree of involvement of these companies in ITV's series tended to vary. Official Films, by far the most prolific, distributed *The Adventures of Robin Hood*, *The Adventures of Sir Lancelot*, *The Buccaneers*, *Sword of Freedom* and *The Adventures of the Scarlet Pimpernel* in America and, like the American distributors of British films at this time, elsewhere in the Western Hemisphere. It provided end-money for production in the form of pre-paid guarantees (*Variety*, 14 December 1955: 39). And it owned a controlling stake in Nettlefold Studios, where interiors for *Robin Hood*, *Sir Lancelot* and the first three episodes of *The Buccaneers* were filmed (*Variety*, 3 August 1955: 31). It is hardly surprising, then, that Harold Myers, writing in *Variety*, described series like these as 'co-productions', or that Hal Hackett, president of Official Films, claimed them as Official's own in the self-same issue (9 January 1957: 99, 103).

The Count of Monte Cristo, meanwhile, originated both as a project and a series in America. It was initiated by TPA. Its stars were American. Its executive producers, Hal Roach Jr. then Leon Fromkess, were American, as were Sidney Marshall, its initial producer, Budd Boeticher and Charles Bennett, its initial directors, and a number of its writers as well. Its first twelve episodes were shot at the Hal Roach studios in Hollywood. However, the remaining 27 episodes were filmed in Britain through Towers of London. Producer credits were shared by Sidney Marshall and Dennis Vance, then by Dennis Vance, who was British, alone. British directors like Don Chaffey and David MacDonald directed all the remaining episodes (http://angelfire.com/retro/CountOfMonteCristo.html). *The Count of Monte Cristo* thus began as an American series, distributed in Britain by ATV, but became a runaway British co-production, similar in status to a number of contemporary films.*

Parallels with the film industry do not end there. Worried by the increasing number of American shows on British television, a quota of foreign programming was agreed with ITV in 1955 (Sendall, 1982: 106–109). Runaway productions and co-productions provided American companies like TPA (and Official) with a means of circumventing the quota as well as a building-in an appeal to Commonwealth markets. Co-production with the likes of Towers of London, Sapphire Films and ITP meant higher budgets. This was also an important factor for British companies, who could not recoup high production costs in Britain alone (*Daily Variety*, 29 December 1955: 11). This way, they were assured not only of high production values, but of access to markets in America and elsewhere abroad and a share in any ensuing profits.

Ivanhoe provides a more straightforward example of runaway production. *Ivanhoe* was produced and shot in Britain by Screen Gems, which also distributed the series in America and elsewhere abroad. It was screened by ATV in Britain. It used British locations, British actors (notably Roger Moore and Peter Brown), British directors, a British producer (Sydney Box) and number of British writers. It thus qualified for quota purposes as a British series (and was as such partly financed by the National Film Finance Corporation, an organisation set up in the early 1950s to fund the

---

* It is worth pointing out here that in noting the appearance of new seasons of *The Count of Monte Cristo*, *Robin Hood* and *The Buccaneers* on ITV's schedules, *Variety* described them all as 'American imports ... lensed in Britain' (21 August 1957: 28).

Chapter 13 • Adventure, exchange and identity

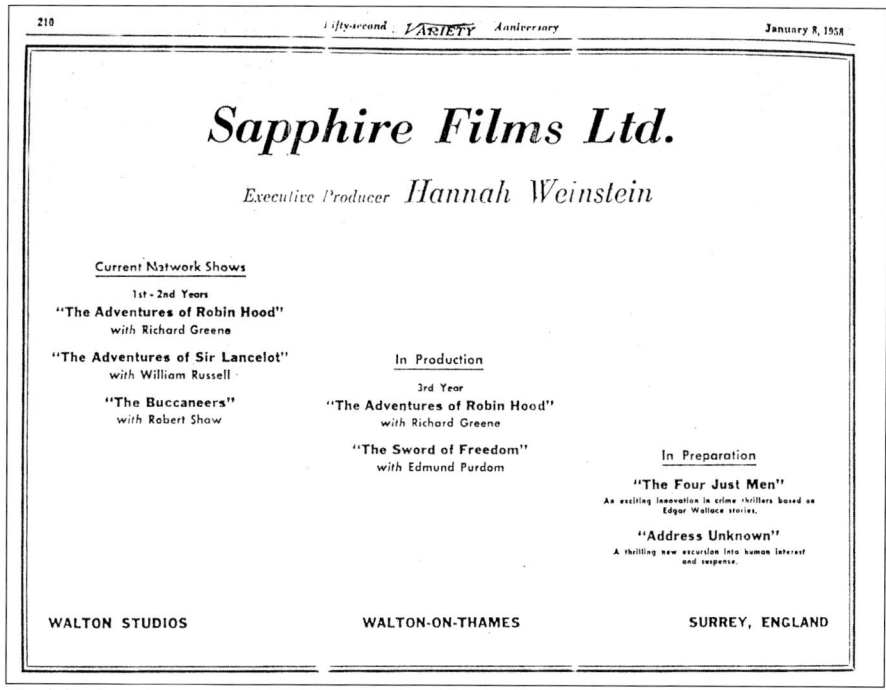

Fig. 3. Variety, 8 January 1958, page 210.

production of British films) (*Variety*, 23 July 1958: 26). But America was regarded as its principal market (*Kinematograph Weekly*, 2 August 1956: 1). In all these respects it was similar to the runaway costume adventure films produced by MGM, Disney and Warners.*

National Telefilm Associates, finally, co-financed and distributed *The Adventures of William Tell*, which was initially planned in 1956 as a British-German co-production (*Variety*, 3 October 1956: 14). The film was eventually made at a point at which the vogue for costume adventure on TV was reaching its peak. However, mention should also be made here of *Richard the Lionheart*. Like *The Adventures of Sir Francis Drake*, another late entry, *Richard the Lionheart* was initially mooted as a series in 1955 (*Variety*, 7 December 1955: 46). It was eventually produced by Danziger Productions in 1961. Danziger Productions (like Warwick Productions) had been set up in

---

* Runaway production of TV programmes by American companies dates back to the early 1950s. At this point, these companies were making programmes solely for the American market and were using British facilities largely for reasons of cost (*Kinematograph Weekly*, 3 April 1952: 22, *Variety*, 3 August 1949: 13, *Variety*, 9 May 1951: 31, 8 October 1952: 7, 31 December 1952: 19). Later on, with the growth in syndication and in overseas outlets, runaway production in numerous countries increased (*Variety*, 9 December 1953: 29, 46, 9 June 1954: 35–36, 1 December 1954: 48, 50, 4 July 1956: 27). The traffic in programmes and films was, however, by no means one-way. British feature films found a market on US TV in the late 1940s and 1950s, as did films and programmes produced by British companies for the theatrical market in Britain and for television in the US, or else for the latter alone (Wilinsky 1997, *Kinematograph Weekly*, 17 November 1949: 15, 5 April 1951: 1, *Variety*, 29 August 1951: 5, 7 July 1954: 40).

185

Britain in the early 1950s by two Americans, Edward J. and Harry Lee Danziger. Specializing initially in low-budget film productions and TV programmes for the US market, the Danzigers later produced series for ITV as well. (The best known include *Mark Saber*, otherwise known as *The Vise* and *Saber of London*, and *The Man from Interpol*.) Thus while neither an American runaway nor an American syndication company, Danziger Productions was nevertheless marked by American involvement. The same could be said of Sapphire Films. Sapphire Films, though, unlike Danziger Productions, was marked by 'Un-American' involvement as well.

Un-American involvement

As is now well documented, at least in outline, blacklisted American writers like Ring Lardner Jr., Ian McClellan Hunter, Norma Barzman, Adrian Scott, Robert Lees and Waldo Salt wrote scripts for *The Adventures of Robin Hood*, and in some cases for *The Adventures of Sir Lancelot*, *The Buccaneers* and *Sword of Freedom* as well (Neale, 2003). These series were all produced by Sapphire Films. Sapphire Films, as noted above, was a British company. But it was set up and run by an American, Hannah Weinstein, who had worked as a journalist and as a campaigner for radical causes in the US in the 1930s and 1940s. By the early 1950s, she was in self-imposed exile, firstly in France, then in Britain. In France, she had renewed contact with a number of blacklisted writers and discussed plans with Boris Karloff for a TV series, *Colonel March of Scotland Yard*. Three pilot episodes of *Colonel March* were filmed in 1952 and released as a feature film. A series was commissioned and first shown in the US through Official Films in 1954 and on ITV in Britain in 1956 and 1957. Blacklisted writers, among them Walter Bernstein and Abraham Polonsky wrote episodes for *Colonel March* and Cy Endfield, who was blacklisted in the early 1950s, directed the three pilot episodes. With the advent of ITV now imminent, Weinstein built on the precedents established by *Colonel March*. She set up Sapphire Films in 1954 and began planning the production of *The Adventures of Robin Hood* not just with ATV, ITP and Official Films, but with Ian McClellan Hunter and Ring Lardner Jr. as well. The success of *Robin Hood* led to *Sir Lancelot*, *The Buccaneers* and *Sword of Freedom*; Lardner and Hunter paved the way for Barzman, Lees, Salt, Scott and other blacklisted writers. Salt, at least, wrote scripts for *Ivanhoe* and Screen Gems as well.

Salt was no stranger to *Ivanhoe*, having written a draft of the script for what became MGM's 1952 film when the project was at RKO in the late 1940s (Lenihan, 1992: 45–47). He had also written the script for *The Flame and the Arrow* and the initial version of the script for *The Crimson Pirate* (Buford, 2000: 103–107, 115). He thus provides another example of the traffic between film and television as well as of the Un-American contribution to the costume adventure trend in the postwar era.* In this as in other respects, the programmes and films on which Salt and others worked seem to me problematise the notions of national identity and cultural imperialism upon which so much recent work on the media has traded.

---

* Melvyn Levy co-scripted *The Bandit of Sherwood Forest*, Michael Blankfort co-scripted *Lydia Bailey* (1952), and as has now been established, Henry Blankfort co-scripted *The Highwayman* and Ben Barzman wrote the script for *El Cid* (1961).

Imperialism and identity

Although some of the most vociferous proponents of national identity as a means of discussing national cinemas and media industries have recently backtracked (see, for instance, Higson, 1995 and 2000), it is still a common topic in articles and books; and although some of the problems with the concept of cultural imperialism have been brought to the fore, it remains a common means of conceptualising the influence and power of the American media industries. At least some of the series and films I have discussed here expose flaws in both of these concepts. If runaway series and films like *Ivanhoe* contained Un-American ingredients yet at the same time were financed and produced by American companies, do they constitute examples of American cultural imperialism, Un-American cultural imperialism, Un-American subversions of cultural imperialism, or something else besides? If ostensibly British productions like *Robin Hood*, *The Buccaneers* and *Sword of Freedom* involved Americans and Un-Americans on both sides of the Atlantic, what is or was their national identity?

It seems to me that there is no way of answering these questions because the terms employed do not allow them to be asked in an answerable way. For all the appeals to 'hybridity' and 'difference' in recent writing on national identity, these terms tend to homogenise plural phenomena. In the postwar era, in the era of co-productions, runaways, joint distribution deals and Un-American Americans, this is all the more notable.* As Michael Newman (2001) has recently argued, it should be possible to talk about national media industries, their components, characteristics and traditions without employing a term like national identity. Individual national labels are often, though by no means always, attached to programmes and films; programmes and films and the industries that produce them often become caught up in national, or even nationalist, cultural agendas; but that does not mean that they embody, construct or even necessarily 'imagine' a nation's identity.

Cultural imperialism, meanwhile, tends as a concept to assume a nationally-based ideological homogeneity among products which, in the case of costume adventure films and TV programmes in the postwar era, simply did not exist. As we have seen, Jeffrey S. Miller argues that Sapphire's TV series were perceived in America as distinctively British (rather than as British-American) and that they served to divert attention away from the 'social and political problems of the day' by being set in the distant past. Knowledge of the Un-American involvement in these series places them in a different ideological light. Ring Lardner Jr. argued that *The Adventures of Robin Hood* gave his fellow writers and himself 'plenty of opportunities for oblique social comment on the issues and institutions of Eisenhower-era America'. He went on to propose that *Robin Hood* and the other series for which he wrote helped to set

---

* It should be noted in this context that Thomas Guback, who is often regarded as an historian of American cultural imperialism in the cinema in the era of co-productions and runaways in the 1950s and 1960s, in fact argued that 'If one claims that British or Italian films are Americanized, then the reverse must also be acknowledged – that American films are Anglicized and Italianized' (Guback, 1969: 176). For him this resulted not in a vibrant hybridization, but in a bland internationalism lacking any sense of identity, American or otherwise. The very existence of the term 'Un-American', meanwhile, is a sign of the extent to which the nature of American identity became a site of contestation, struggle and debate in the post-war era. See Fousek (2000).

the stage 'in some small way ... for the 1960s by subverting a whole new generation of Americans' (Lardner, Jr., 2000: 141). He at least did not see them as instances of American (or British) cultural imperialism. The point here is not that he was right, or that Miller is wrong, or that there is some other correct contextual interpretation of *Robin Hood*. (It is more than likely that *Robin Hood* was subversive for some, escapist for others, and something else besides for others still). The point is that the deployment of cultural imperialism and national identity as concepts tend to curtail the range of ideological meanings and effects cultural products can be said to produce.

Acknowledgements: I would like to thank Sylvia Harvey and the Arts and Humanities Research Board Centre for British Film and Television Studies for funding this research, the British Academy for a travel grant, and Norma Barzman, Derek Kompare, Peggy Phillips, Jeffrey Richards and Al Ruben for answering my queries.

References

Aberdeen, J. A. (2000) *Hollywood Renegades: The Society of Independent Motion Picture Producers*. Los Angeles: Cobblestone.

Balio, Tino (ed) (1985) *The American Film Industry*. Madison: University of Wisconsin Press.

Buford, Kate (2000) *Burt Lancaster: An American Life*. London: Aurum Press.

Chapman, James (2002) *Saints and Avengers: British Adventure Series of the 1960s*. London: I.B. Tauris.

Dickinson, Margaret and Street, Sarah (1985) *Cinema and State: The Film Industry and the British Government 1927–84*. London: British Film Institute.

Emmerson, Andrew, 'A Quick Guide to ITC, Mainstay of ITV Programming for Thirty Years', http://www.sigtel.com/tv_info_itc.html

Erickson, Hal (1989) *Syndicated Television: The First Forty Years, 1947–1987*. Jefferson: McFarland.

Fousek, John (2000) *To Lead the Free World: American Nationalism and the Roots of the Cold War*. Chapel Hill: University of North Carolina Press.

Guback, Thomas (1985) 'Hollywood's International Market', pp. 463–86 in Balio (1985).

Guback, Thomas (1969) *The International Film Industry: Western Europe and America Since 1945*. Bloomington: Indiana University Press.

Hearn, Marcus and Barnes, Alan (1997) *The Hammer Story*. London: Titan.

Higson, Andrew (1995) *Waving the Flag: Constructing a National Cinema in Britain*. Oxford: Clarendon Press.

Higson, Andrew (2000) 'The Limiting Imagination of National Cinema', pp. 63–73 in Mette Hjort and Scott Mackenzie, *Cinema and Nation*. London: Routledge.

Jarvie, Ian (1990) 'The Postwar Economic Policy of the American Film Industry: Europe 1945–1950', *Film History* 4 (4): 277–88.

Jarvie, Ian (1992) *Hollywood's Overseas Campaign: The North American Movie Trade, 1920–1950*. Cambridge: Cambridge University Press.

Jarvie, Ian (1998) 'Free Trade as Cultural Threat: American Film and TV Exports in the Post-War Period', pp. 34–46 in Geoffrey Nowell-Smith and Steven Ricci (eds) *Hollywood and Europe: Economics, Culture, National Identity: 1945–95*. London: BFI.

Kompare, Derek (2005) *Rerun Nation: How Repeats Invented American Television*. New York: Routledge.

Kulik, Karol (1990) *Alexander Korda: The Man Who Could Work Miracles*. London: W.H. Allen.

Lardner Jr, Ring (2000) *I'd Hate Myself in the Morning: A Memoir*. New York: Nation Books.

Lenihan, John (1992) 'English Classics for Cold War America: MGM's *Kim* (1950), *Ivanhoe* (1952), *Julius Caesar* (1953)', *Journal of Popular Film and Television* 20 (3): 42–51.

MacNab, Geoffrey (1993) *J. Arthur Rank and the British Film Industry*. London: Routledge.

Maltin, Leonard (2000) *The Disney Films*. New York: Disney Editions.

Marcus, Lawrence and Hulse, Stephen R. 'The ITC Story (The Early Years)', http://freespace.virgin.net/steve.hulse/itc.html

Miller, Jeffrey S. (2000) *Something Completely Different: British Television and American Culture*. Minneapolis: Minneapolis University Press.

Murphy, Robert (1983) 'Rank's Attempt on the American Market', pp. 164–78 in James Curran and Vincent Porter (eds) *British Cinema History*. London: Weidenfeld and Nicholson.

Murphy, Robert (1989) *Realism and Tinsel: Cinema and Society in Britain 1939–1949*. London: Routledge.

Neale, Steve (2003) 'Pseudonyms, Sapphire and Salt: 'Un-American' Contributions to Television Costume Adventure Series in the 1950s', *Historical Journal of Film, Radio and Television* 23 (3): 245–57.

Newman, Michael (2001) 'Review of *Cinema and Nation*', *The Velvet Light Trap* 48: 81–83.

Osgerby, Bill, Gough-Yates, Anna and Wells, Marianne (2001) 'The Business of Action: Television History and the Development of the Action TV Series', pp. 13–31 in Bill Osgerby, Anna Gough-Yates (eds) *Action TV: Tough Guys, Smooth Operators and Foxy Chicks*. London: Routledge.

Pulleine, Tim (1982) 'Hollywood's Baby Brother? British Films of the Fifties', *Films and Filming* 339 (December): 19–25.

Ryall, Tom (2001) *Britain and the American Cinema*. London: Sage.

Schatz, Thomas (1997) *Boom and Bust: American Cinema in the 1940s*. New York: Scribners.

Seagrave, Kerry (1997) *American Films Abroad: Hollywood's Domination of the World's Movie Screens from the 1890s to the Present*. Jefferson: McFarland.

Sendall, Bernard (1982) *Independent Television in Britain* (Vol. 1). London: Macmillan.

Spraos, John (1962) *The Decline of Cinema: An Economist's Report*. London: Allen & Unwin.

Tabori, Paul (1959) *Alexander Korda*. London: Oldbourne.

Taves, Brian (1993) *The Romance of Adventure: The Genre of Historical Adventure Movies*. Jackson: University of Mississippi Press.

Walsh, Michael (1997) 'Fighting the American Invasion with Cricket, Roses, and Marmalade for Breakfast', *The Velvet Light Trap* 40: 3–17.

Walsh, Michael (1999) 'Options for American Foreign Distribution: United Artists in Europe, 1919–1920', pp. 132–56 in Andrew Higson and Richard Maltby (eds) *'Film Europe' and 'Film America': Cinema, Commerce and Cultural Exchange 1920–1939*. Exeter: Exeter University Press.

Wilinsky, Barbara (1997) 'First and Finest: British Film on US Television in the Late 1940s', *The Velvet Light Trap* 40: 18–31.

Chapter 14

Brigitte Bardot and Hollywood's takeover of the US art film market in the 1960s

Tino Balio

Of all the trends in American movie going after World War II, the one that made the largest cultural impact was foreign films. Before the war, foreign films played mostly in New York City and in a few theaters around the country. After the war, foreign films from Italy, Great Britain, Japan, France, and Scandinavia played in hundreds of theaters in larger cities and university communities nationwide and were regularly discussed in feature stories and reviews in the *New York Times*, mass circulation-magazines, highbrow periodicals, and the trade press (Gomery, 1992; Mayer, 1965; Wilinsky, 2001). Foreign films were also being shown by museums, film festivals, and university film societies. The discourse about art films attacked motion picture censorship, championed the director-as-auteur, created a set of narrative conventions radically different from Hollywood cinema, and helped establish film as a worthy object of study in American universities (Neale, 1981).

The art film market, which was devoted originally to the acquisition, distribution, and exhibition of foreign-language and English-language films produced abroad without Hollywood financial support, paled in comparison to mainstream commercial cinema and was originally controlled by dozens of small independent distributors such as Joseph Burstyn, Kingsley-International, Janus Films, and Lopert Films. Operating out of New York with small staffs and little money to promote their films, these companies led precarious lives. To reach audiences, they had to contend with the capriciousness of state and municipal censorship, the strictures of the Production Code, and threats from pressure groups such as the Catholic Legion of Decency and the American Legion (Randall, 1968).

By the 1960s, the art film market had been taken over by Hollywood. *Variety* (Canby, 1964) reported that as of 1963, 'distribution of offshore product in the US is now dominated by the major companies to the detriment of the independent distributors'. Of the total US box office gross from foreign films that year, the majors collected $50 million, more than three times the amount collected by independents. The majors eventually absorbed nearly the entire Pantheon of European auteurs with deals that offered total production financing, directorial freedom, and entrée into the lucrative US market. These auteurs included Michelangelo Antonioni, Luchino Visconti, and Federico Fellini of Italy; Tony Richardson, Joseph Losey, and Karel Reisz of Britain; François Truffaut, Jean-Luc Godard, Louis Malle, and Eric Rohmer of France; and Ingmar Bergman of Sweden (Canby, 1966).

Hollywood's motives for entering the art film market were transparent. Foreign films, especially those that depicted sex in ways forbidden by the Production Code, were attracting customers and the majors wanted a part of the business. The majors also wanted to exploit the European pop culture scene, particularly Swinging London fashions and music, as a way to reach the younger audience (Levy, 2002; Walker, 1970). As obvious as the motives appear, the takeover of the art film market was basically a conservative move that enabled the majors to cover all the bases in a period of rapid cultural, political, and social change. To bring people back to the movies during the 1960s, Hollywood adopted the policy, 'Make Them Big, Show Them Big, and Sell Them Big'. The biggest hits like *Ben-Hur* (1959), *My Fair Lady* (1964), and *The Sound of Music* (1965) were family pictures targeted at the mass audience. But the 1960s saw the rise of political activism and social upheaval that spawned a counter-culture composed mainly of the sons and daughters of the American middle-class. Where this counter-culture was heading no one knew, but foreign films offered the majors a means to tap this rapidly growing and affluent group. The core audience for foreign films during the 1960s consisted mainly of America's 'cinephile' generation, university students born during the late-1930s and the 1940s. *Variety* (Landry, 1966) described them as 'partly sophisticated, partly idealistic, somewhat dreamy about professional careers in some aspect of the film industry. Almost to a man or girl, they are more influenced by Paris and Rome than by Hollywood'. These were the students who flocked to an estimated 4,000 college film societies by 1968.

Less obvious is a clear chronology of the takeover, the companies that led the charge, and the relative commercial success of the venture. This survey will begin to fill in some of the details. To begin, we need to know how companies acquired foreign films and why. A company had two choices: it could pick up prize-winning films at international film festivals like Cannes or Venice, or it could put up financing to secure new films from promising directors. Picking up films at festivals leaves the acquisition process to chance, it can open up bidding wars, and it sometimes means going home empty handed. Putting up financing stabilizes the acquisition process and enables companies to obtain films in line with their needs.

In either case, the majors followed standard distribution practice. A new art film would be given a New York premiere in a classy art house in the hope of getting a rave review from Bosley Crowther, the influential film critic of the *New York Times*. Next, it might play in a few other art market hubs, Boston and San Francisco, for example, to build up publicity. Afterwards, it would be released to the art-house circuit, which consisted of around 450 theaters located mostly in the greater New York area, the Boston-Washington, D.C. corridor, and in college towns around the country (Mayer, 1965). Foreign-language films were released with English subtitles. If a film showed signs of crossing over to the mainstream market – the desire of every distributor – it might also be released in a dubbed version for general release.

Chapter 14 • Brigitte Bardot and Hollywood's takeover of the US art film market

In supplying the financing, Hollywood did not give auteurs *carte blanche*. A studio safeguarded its investments by evaluating the proposed budget for each new project in relation to its expected return in the art film market. The aim was to minimize risk and hope that a sleeper paid back a company's foreign film development costs and generated some profits. For example, Columbia's deal with Jean-Luc Godard in 1963 provided him with small budgets of between $100,000 and $120,000 per film with no strings attached (Canby, 1966). Columbia undoubtedly realized that Godard's chances of producing a crossover hit were slim, but it could hope for another *Breathless,* which had been a favorite with the college crowd.

Columbia might also have had another incentive to sign an auteur like Godard. It had to do with distribution overhead. The majors spent millions of dollars a year to operate their distribution arms. To recoup this fixed cost, companies levied distribution fees ranging from 30–45 per cent on the rentals of every film they handled, depending on the market. Once a company reached breakeven in any year, everything else it collected from film rentals was profit, including the returns from low-grossing pictures. Stated another way, a studio like Columbia operated on a 'tonnage' basis, meaning that 'distribution overhead is essentially fixed and that incremental product put through above break-even carries a disproportionately high profit contribution' (Londoner, 1985: 618).

Turning now to the chronology of the takeover, the film that marked Hollywood's entry into the art film market was the Brigitte Bardot hit, *And God Created Woman* (*Et Dieu créa la femme*, 1957)*. When her film opened at the Paris Theatre in New York in October 1957 with the promotional tagline, '…but the devil gave shape to Bardot!', the house manager expected it to play a fast two weeks; instead, the film lasted almost a year. Produced in CinemaScope and in color by Raoul Lévy for $400,000 and directed by Roger Vadim, Bardot's new husband, *God Created Woman* gained entry where 'foreign films have never seen the light of the screen', said *Variety* (Hift, 1958). It did this lacking a seal of approval from the Production Code Administration and with a 'Condemned' rating from the Roman Catholic Legion of Decency.

As Juliette Hardy, a sexually-liberated eighteen-year-old orphan who is the talk of Saint-Tropez, Brigitte Bardot scandalized the censors, but *God Created Woman* grossed over $4 million *in rentals* in the US to set a new record for foreign film in the US (*Variety*, 1958).

The first thing to note about *God Created Woman* is that Kingsley-International, a subsidiary of Columbia Pictures, distributed the picture. As a member of the Motion Picture Association of America, the industry trade association, Columbia was forbidden to distribute any picture that was denied a seal from the PCA or received a 'C' rating by the Legion. Independent distributors had earlier rejected the picture, presumably because it was too controversial to handle. But Columbia was unafraid of the risk, and took advantage of a loophole in the MPAA's rules by forming a subsidiary in 1956 to distribute the picture. It did this simply by acquiring Kingsley-International, a prominent independent foreign film distributor (*Variety*, 1959).

---

* The year place within parenthesis after a foreign film title is the US release date and not necessarily the production date.

The next thing to note is the impact of 'C' rating on the release. Affiliated theaters everywhere and art houses in many parts of the country did not want to antagonize local Catholics or suffer the wrath of censors by playing a C-rated film. But when Kingsley placed a dubbed version of *God Created Woman* into general release after the New York premiere, the film was spot booked by 'virtually every major circuit in the States' and played exceptionally long runs in art theaters everywhere (Hift, 1958). Where the normal run for an art film hit had been two to three weeks, *God Created Woman* ran for twelve weeks or longer in most places, creating 'one of the biggest jams in history on the "art" circuit', said *Variety* (Hift, 1958). And surprisingly, only a few censorship boards tried to stop the film. Kingsley's decision to distribute *God Created Woman* not only weakened the Legion of Decency's perceived hold on mainstream exhibitors; it also demonstrated that a 'C' rating could be exploited for its publicity value. Commenting on the impact of the rating, a Columba spokesman said that *God Created Women* would have received twice as many bookings with a less restrictive 'B' rating from the Legion, but would have done half the business (Hift, 1958).

The last thing to note is how sex was used in the marketing. Foreign films were considered sexier and more mature than Hollywood fare. During the heyday of Italian neorealism, for example, mass market magazines like *Life*, *Holiday*, and *Cosmopolitan* featured Anna Magnani, Gina Lollobrigida, Silvana Mangano, Rossana Podestà, and Sophia Loren on their covers with banner lines like 'Italy's anatomic bombs'(*Cosmopolitan*, 1954) or 'sultry *signorine*' (*Life*, 1951) and compared their 'natural' sexuality to the overtly manufactured glamour of Hollywood stars like Marilyn Monroe (Hine, 1954). Despite such coverage, only a few art films caught on in any year. Distributors, therefore, sometimes resorted to a sure way of capturing attention – they borrowed techniques from the exploitation market and 'sexed up' their advertising. For example, an ad for Roberto Rossellini's *Open City* contained a banner that proclaimed it, 'Sexier than Hollywood ever dared to be' and showed a picture of two girls in rapt embrace. Another ad, 'designed to tap the sadist trade', according to Arthur Mayer the distributor, 'showed a man being flogged' (Gallagher, 1998: 175). Distributors also dreamt up provocative new titles for their films. Thus, Luis Buñuel's *Los Olividados* became *The Young and the Damned*; Max Ophüls's *Le Plaisir* became *House of Pleasure*; and Ingmar Bergman's *Summaren Med Monika* became *Monika, the Story of a Bad Girl* (Hollinger, 1954). And lastly, showmen relied on censorship controversy to generate publicity. The practice began during the New York run of the *Miracle* in 1950. Speaking from the pulpit of St. Patrick's Cathedral, Francis Cardinal Spellman denounced the picture as blasphemous and called on every Roman Catholic in the United States to boycott it wherever it played. Contrary to expectations, his edict did not deter customers from lining up at the Paris Theater box office (Westin, 1961).

Following these trends, Kingsley's ad campaign for *God Created Woman* contained a pen-and-ink nude drawing of a reclining Brigitte Bardot from behind over a blurb that read, 'A frolic in sensuality'. Below that, a quote from a newspaper review stated, 'A study in rounded surfaces to delight anyone who likes to study rounded surfaces' (Heffernan, 1993). So what was special about the film? According to Kingsley (Hift, 1958), the campaign 'gave people what they were led to expect. They weren't

Chapter 14 • Brigitte Bardot and Hollywood's takeover of the US art film market

promised one thing in the ads and given something else on the screen'. Bosley Crowther (1957) in his *New York Times* review agreed: 'This round and voluptuous little French miss', he said, 'is put on spectacular display and is rather brazenly ogled from every allowable point of view. She is looked at in slacks and sweaters, in shorts and Bikini bathing suits. She wears a bed sheet on two or three occasions, and, once, she shows behind a thin screen in the nude. What's more, she moves herself in a fashion that fully accentuates her charms. She is undeniably a creation of superlative craftsmanship'.

Bardot's sex appeal certainly attracted crowds, especially college students. For example, *Variety* reported that *God Created Woman* broke attendance records at the University of Texas in Austin and started a Bardot craze with simultaneous showings of *Woman* and *Mam'zelle Pigalle* (*Cette sacrée gamine*), a recent Bardot film, at separate campus theaters. *Variety* quoted one of the theater managers as saying, '*And God Created Woman* is a sex film. It's called art because it's foreign' (16 July 1958: 35). Movie critics Arthur Knight and Hollis Alpert in an article for *Playboy* gave another reason for Bardot's appeal: 'Brigitte Bardot virtually personified the youth of the Fifties. And in many of her films, the plots were so contrived as to emphasize the ambivalent reactions of an older generation to her unconventional behavior. American audiences professed to be shocked by Bardot, but they were also intrigued by – and perhaps secretly envied – her emancipated attitudes toward love and life. Certainly, by the end of the Fifties her name had become as potent a box-office lure as that of any home bred Hollywood star' (1966: 24).

Observing these results, United Artists followed Columbia's lead in 1958 by acquiring Lopert Films, another prominent indie art film distributor; within a decade, all the majors had formed art film subsidiaries (Canby, 1961). As might be expected, the art film market was soon flooded with Bardot films, both old and new. *God Created Woman* was Bardot's sixteenth film, and as Knight and Alpert reported, 'Distributors dipped back into the grab bag of previous Bardot pictures, hoping to cash in on the phenomenon....Although the films were far from distinguished, by early 1958 all New York was a Bardot festival: her pictures, duly dubbed and scrubbed, were playing not only in the art houses but in exploitation grind houses and in respectable neighborhood theaters as well'(1966: 244).

Having started the Bardot craze, Columbia capitalized on its lead by teaming up with Raoul Lévy to acquire more Bardot pictures for its art film subsidiary. Lévy delivered Roger Vadim's *The Night Heaven Fell* (*Les Bijoutiers du clair de lune*, 1958), Claude Autant-Lara's *Love Is My Profession* (*En cas de malheur*, 1959), Christian-Jaque's *Babette Goes to War* (*Babette s'en va-t-en guerre*, 1960), and Henri-Georges Clouzot's *The Truth* (*La Vérité*, 1960). Although the directors were members of mainstream French cinema–the Tradition of Quality – Bardot can be regarded as the 'author' of these films, 'from both an industry and a theoretical point of view', according to Vincendeau, who noted that the 'films were marketed on her name' and 'built their narratives entirely around her'. Vincendeau also noted that *The Truth*, like *Very Private Affair* (*Vie privée*, 1962) and *Contempt* (*Le Mépris*, 1964) that followed, were devised as 'commentaries on her stardom' (2000: 114).

The critics were sure to comment on the extent of Bardot's dress or undress and on the quality of her acting. Concerning the former, *Variety* said, 'There is plenty of bare B.B. in this picture [*The Night Heaven Fell*]. Contains some ruggedly exploitable scenes with B.B. giving her all for love' (7 May 1958). Concerning her acting, Bosley Crowther said, 'Her acting [in *Love Is My Profession*] is a matter of opinion. If flirting in a few crucial scenes, pouting when she is supposed to be unhappy and throwing her chest out when she is supposed to be aroused may be calculated as acting, that is the word for what she does' (27 October 1959). Regardless of the critical commentary, Bardot became the highest-paid actress in France by 1959, and her pictures continued to do well in the US, even when *Babette Goes to War* showed 'not a single suggestive inch of Bardot's skin' (Grenier, 1959).

Since Columbia took the lead in ordering up more Bardot pictures to distribute, the Columbia-Raoul Lévy venture has to be seen within the larger context of the internationalization of the American film industry after the war. Internationalization was characterized in part by the phenomenon of runaway production. American companies started shooting on location overseas to complement the new Cinema-Scope and other widescreen processes of the 1950s and to take advantage of lower labor costs, particularly in Spain and Italy. Companies also wanted to shift production overseas to retrieve blocked funds and to conform to European quota restrictions. In meeting their quota requirements, American companies operating through their foreign subsidiaries, found it expedient to produce films suitable for regular distribution in the US. A natural next step in this evolution was to finance films overseas to exploit in the American art film market.

The question now is, which Hollywood companies were responsible for the takeover? Production rosters reveal that companies previously consigned to the lower rungs of the industry led the charge; Columbia, United Artists, and Universal–the former Little Three–and Allied Artists, a former Poverty Row studio once known as Monogram. After the Bardot craze subsided, Columbia concentrated mostly on the French New Wave. Its pack with Jean-Luc Godard yielded three films--*The Married Woman* (*Une Femme Mariée*, 1965), *Band of Outsiders* (*Bande à Part*, 1966), and *Masculine/Feminine* (*Masculin, Féminin*, 1966). Columbia went on to finance Jacques Demy's first American film, *Model Shop* (1969) and to release Truffaut's *Bed and Board* (*Domicile Conjugal*, 1971) and Eric Rohmer's *Claire's Knee* (*Le Genou de Claire*, 1971). Its biggest art film hits came from Britain–Roman Polanski's *Repulsion* (1965), a psychological thriller starring Catherine Deneuve, and Silvio Narizzano's *Georgy Girl* (1966), a Swinging London film starring Lynn Redgrave and Alan Bates that became one of the high-grossing British films in the US (Walker, 1974).

United Artists launched its new art film subsidiary, Lopert Films by picking up a recent Bardot vehicle in 1958, Michel Boisrond's *La Parisienne* (*Une Parisienne*). It then acquired Marcel Camus's *Black Orpheus* (*Orfeu Negro*, 1959), the Grand Prix winner at the 1959 Cannes Film Festival. Its third release, Jules Dassin's *Never on Sunday* (*Pote tin Kyriaki*, 1960), was a Greek-American co-production financed by Lopert that starred Melina Mercouri as a carefree, big-hearted prostitute. Produced for $150,000, the picture grossed over $4 million in rentals to rank along side *God Created Woman* (Balio, 1987). Since Lopert released *Never on Sunday* without a seal from the PCA and with a 'C' rating from the Legion of Decency, the company served the same function for UA as Kingsley-International had for Columbia.

After financing Jules Dassin's *Phaedra* (1962), another Melina Mercouri vehicle, UA sought out French New Wave directors with commercial potential. The effort yielded Phillipe DeBroca's *That Man from Rio* (*L'Homme de Rio,* 1964), Louis Malle's *Viva Maria!* (1966), and Francois Truffaut's *Stolen Kisses* (*Baisers Volées,* 1969) and *The Wild Child* (*L'Enfant sauvage*, 1970). Forming similar alliances in Italy, United Artists financed two crossover hits, *Fellini's Satyricon*, (1970) and Bertolucci's *Last Tango in Paris* (*Ultimo tango a Parigi*, 1972). The X-rated *Last Tango*, which starred Marlon Brando, broke box office records everywhere, grossing close to $40 million in the US and $60 million overseas (Balio, 1987). UA meanwhile released four Ingmar Bergman films from Sweden, including *Persona* (1967) and was the first company to capitalize on the British pop culture scene by financing Tony Richardson's *Tom Jones* (1963) and Richard Lester's *The Knack* (1965), to say nothing about financing such commercial hits as Richard Lester's *A Hard Day's Night* (1964) starring the Beatles and the James Bond series. *Tom Jones* grossed $16 million in rentals, to set new record for British films in the US and won four Academy Awards including best picture and best direction (Balio, 1987).

Universal Pictures had a brief fling with art films after the war and released a series of prestige British films from J. Arthur Rank, which included David Lean's *Great Expectations* (1947), Laurence Olivier's *Hamlet* (1948), and the Alec Guinness comedy, *The Lavender Hill Mob* (1951). After Rank's motion picture empire collapsed in the 1950s, Universal avoided art films until 1966, when it invested over $30 million in an ambitious program of British films to attract the youth market in Britain and the US (Walker, 1974). Produced in all price ranges, the films were typically based on off-beat literary properties by popular or critically acclaimed British writers and directed by a group of auteurs with international reputations, the likes of Charlie Chaplin, François Truffaut, Karel Reisz, and Joseph Losey. To give the pictures even greater box office appeal, they starred Liz Taylor, Richard Burton, Marlon Brando, Sophia Loren, Albert Finney, and Vanessa Redgrave, among others. The dozen or so films financed by the studio included Charlie Chaplin's *A Countess from Hong Kong* (1967), François Truffaut's *Fahrenheit 451* (1967), Peter Watkins' *Privilege* (1967), Joseph Losey's *Boom!* (1968) and *Secret Ceremony* (1968), and Karel Reisz's *Isadora* (1969).

Allied Artists's foreign films roster was small, but contained several noteworthy pictures, among them, Claude Lelouch's *A Man and a Woman* (*Un Homme et une Femme*, 1966), and Luis Buñuel's *Belle de Jour* (1968) Lelouch's romantic drama starring Anouk Aimée and Jean-Louis Trintignant won the Grand Prix at Cannes in 1966 and became the first big commercial success to come out of the French New Wave. It grossed $14 million at the box office to set a new art film record in the US and won Academy Awards for best foreign language film and best original screenplay (*Variety*, 2000). Buñuel's Surrealist fantasy received mixed reviews abroad, but became his biggest commercial success, due in no small measure to its scandalous story of a sexually-repressed housewife, played by Catherine Deneuve.

What motivated these companies? The United Artists that dominated the art film market of the 1960s was a far cry from the company once run by Charlie Chaplin and Mary Pickford. UA remained solely as distribution company, but the new management team that rescued UA from near bankruptcy in 1951 transformed it into an industry leader by doing what UA had never been able to do before–devise a plan to attract top producers, directors, and stars to the company as independent producers with offers of complete financing. The plan required UA to distribute a full roster of films each year, which would generate enough revenue from distribution fees to cover its overhead costs and to create a cushion to offset any production losses. United Artists, therefore, relied on volume to succeed and catered to all segments of the audience, including the art film audience (Balio, 1987).

Columbia and Universal pursued similar goals, but were motivated by different causes. As former producers mostly of 'B' films, both companies found themselves in a precarious position after the war as demand for second-tier product declined. Lacking the finances to move into 'A' films exclusively, Columbia took the offensive by opening its doors to independent producers, by venturing early into television production, and by going into foreign film distribution (Gomery, 1986). To bolster its roster, Universal Pictures merged with the small independent producer International Pictures in 1946 to become Universal-International. Universal's plight did not improve until 1952, when Decca Records purchased a controlling interest in the studio and brought in a fresh lineup of producers, directors, and stars, often as not as independent producers. Universal's full recovery occurred only when MCA, the powerful talent agency, acquired the company in 1962. At the time, MCA was the most powerful talent agency in the business and the leading producer of network television programming. A threat of a federal antitrust investigation led MCA to jettison its talent agency in 1962 and concentrate on film and television production (McDougal, 1998). British popular culture showed great promise for commercial exploitation in1966 when Universal decided to set up shop in London.

Formed in 1946 as a subsidiary of Monogram Pictures, Allied Artists was designed to be Monogram's ticket out of Poverty Row by producing quality films. Films such as William Wyler's *Friendly Persuasion* (1956) and Billy Wilder's *Love in the Afternoon* (1957) were praised by the critics but failed to earn back their costs. Continued losses in the 1960s forced Allied to cease production completely. In 1967, Allied Artists was taken over by Kalvex, Inc., a drug distributor, which sold off the old Monogram studio and 'stepped up the importing and co-production of foreign films' as an interim measure until regular production could be resumed (Sloane, 1968). As a result of the new policy, Allied put up partial financing for Lelouch's *A Man and a Woman* to acquire the US distribution rights and took on a film by Buñuel, whose previous efforts had not made much of a dent in the art film market outside New York.

The former members of the Big Five moved into art films more cautiously. No doubt they were initially more concerned than the struggling Little Three about 'tarnishing their reputations by becoming affiliated with Code-less and Legion of Decency-condemned films in the domestic market', as *Variety* (1968) observed. By 1968, however, they too had capitulated. Being more conservative, they released fewer foreign films and concentrated mainly on Swinging London and 'Euro-American' films. Alexander Walker (1974) has analyzed Hollywood's investment in British pop culture, so there no need to go over this familiar ground here. Describing the inherently conservative nature of the Euro-American art film, Peter Lev says that such films attempt 'a synthesis of the European art film and the American entertainment film' with the goal of crossing over into the mainstream exhibition market. The films are directed by European filmmakers and contain American stars, who speak English or perform in foreign-language films that are dubbed into English. Also, they utilize 'specific qualities of the European art film' while blending somehow European and American cultures (1993: 30–31). Examples of the trend include Luchino Visconti's *The Leopard* (*Il Gattopardo*, 1963) and Michael Cacoyannis's *Zorba the Greek* (1964)–Twentieth Century-Fox; Michelangelo Antonioni's *Blow-Up* (1966) and *Zabriske Point* (1970)–MGM; Luchino Visconti's *The Damned* (*La Caduta degli dei*, 1969) and *Death in Venice* (*Morte a Venezia*, 1971)–Warner Bros.; and Franco Zeffirelli's *Romeo and Juliet* (1968)–Paramount. Dassin's *Never On Sunday* and Bertolucci's *Last Tango in Paris*, released by United Artists, are also examples of the trend.

Two issues remain, the impact of the Bardot craze on independent distributors and the relative commercial success of Hollywood's venture into the art film market. Although independents snared some of Bardot's older films, they watched as the majors outbid them with production offers for her new ones. For example, MGM financed Louis Malle's *A Very Private Affair* and United Artists put up over $2 million for Louis Malle's *Viva Maria!*, Bardot's most expensive film which paired her with Jeanne Moreau. Meanwhile independent distributors found it increasingly difficult to conduct regular business. For one thing, European producers, overestimating the potential of the US art market, began demanding unrealistically high guarantees for their films. For another, art house managers began rejecting small films like Carl Dryer's *Ordet*, Robert Bresson's *A Man Escaped*, and Satyajit Ray's *Pather Panchali* in favor of more exploitable fare. Cy Harvey of Janus Films, the distributor of Ingmar Bergman's pictures, lamented, 'if the trend continues, not only will the Europeans make fewer films of artistic quality, but there'll be little incentive to import such fine pictures since the arties pass them up for the potentially more interesting sexy items' (*Variety*, 29 October 1958). Independent distributors therefore had to devise new business strategies. Janus Films, for example, began concentrating on the 16mm non-theatrical college market. Other companies turned to the so-called peripheral markets – Scandinavia and Eastern Europe, for example–in search of films. But as *Variety* (1965) noted, 'as new filmmakers were discovered, the majors seduced them as well with a host of benefits such as financial remuneration and the promise of production continuance if they clicked'.

How profitable was Hollywood's foray into foreign films? Universal's British venture failed totally both critically and commercially. A few Swinging London films financed by other companies made money, among them UA's *Tom Jones*, Paramount's *Alfie*, Columbia's *Georgy Girl*, and MGM's *Blow-Up*. And so did a few Euro-American hybrids, such Fox's, *Zorba the Greek* and UA's *Satyricon* and *Last Tango*. Surprisingly, the box office record for foreign-language films set by Lelouch's *A Man and a Woman* in 1966 was surpassed by two independent releases – Vilgot Sjöman's *I Am Curious (Yellow)* (1967) and Costa-Gavras's *Z* (1969), which were distributed by Grove Press and Cinema 5 and grossed $20 million and $16 million at the box office, respectively *(Variety, 2000)*. Scenes of nudity and simulated sex and a sensational censorship battle waged by Grove Press had much to do with the record set by *I Am Curious (Yellow)*, which would stand for twenty years. The tallies prove only that there was a limited demand for foreign films of any type in the US during the 1960s and not necessarily that independents were more astute than the Hollywood majors in evaluating the market.

At best, Hollywood's investment in foreign films broke even. In any event, the returns on their investments did not prevent the majors from disbanding their art film subsidiaries and withdrawing from European production after the art film market collapsed in 1969. Interest in Britain popular culture had run its course by then and American films targeted at college students such as *In the Heat of the Night* (1967), *The Graduate* (1967), and *Bonnie and Clyde* (1967) were capturing the spotlight. No longer constrained by the Production Code after 1968, Hollywood films were beginning to rival anything from abroad in theme and content.

This survey reveals a facet of the trans-Atlantic trade in motion pictures during the demise of the studio system. Although the vertically-integrated structure of the American film industry may have foreclosed the home market to foreign films before World War II, all the Hollywood majors invested in indigenous production in Europe during the 1960s with the aim of bolstering the US art film market. Brigitte Bardot undoubtedly triggered the move, but it should now be clear that Hollywood supported more than sexploitation fare or films with distinct crossover potential; companies like Columbia and United Artists, for example, either financed and/or distributed some of the most intellectually demanding films to come out of Europe. Conditions seemed right for European auteurs, working in partnership with Hollywood or on their own, to significantly broaden the audience for foreign films in the United States. But many critically acclaimed films that reached America during the 1960s could not find a way out of the art house ghetto. This may reflect the putative provincialism of the average American moviegoer or the misguided ideas of foreign filmmakers about what is exportable. Or it simply may be seen as part of Hollywood's learning curve to discover just what the evolving American motion picture audience of the 1960s preferred. By the 1970s, the majors discovered a formula for success that remains in effect to this day – blockbusters aimed at the young that are capable of being exploited in all the major markets worldwide, on television, and in so-called leisure-time 'profit centers'.

References

Balio, T. (1987) *United Artists: The Company that Changed the Film Industry*. Madison: University of Wisconsin Press.

Billard, G. (1964) 'An Interview with Georges Beauregard', *Film Culture* Spring: 20–23.

Canby, V. (1961) 'Shock Therapy for N.Y. Execs' *Variety* 16 August: 3.

Canby, V. (1964) 'Foreign Rentals in the US', *Variety* 29 April: 30.

Canby, V. (1966) 'Hollywood Woos Foreign Talent,' *New York Times* 26 November: 41.

Cosmopolitan (1954) 'Italian Movie Stars: Sex Without Glamour' February: 45.

Crowther, B. (1957) Review of *And God Created Woman*, *New York Times* 27 October.

Crowther, B. (1959) Review of *Love Is My Profession*, *New York Times* 28 April.

Gallagher, T. (1998) *The Adventures of Roberto Rossellini: His Life and Films*. New York: Da Capo.

Gomery, D. (1986) *The Hollywood Studio System*. New York: St. Martin's Press.

Gomery, D. (1992) *Shared Pleasures: A History of Movie Presentation in the United States*. Madison: University of Wisconsin Press.

Grenier, C. (1959) 'Gallic Screen Scene', *New York Times* 5 April: 7.

Heffernan, K. (1993) 'Censorship and the Art Film: The Production Code, Market Conditions, and Strategies for Distribution, 1951–1960', Unpublished paper, University of Wisconsin-Madison, 22 February.

Hift, F. (1958) 'Brigitte's Boxoffice Revel', *Variety* 16 April: 7.

Hine, A. (1954) 'Italian Movies', *Holiday* February: 11.

Hollinger, H. (1954) 'Foreign Pix Gain by Racy Tags', *Variety* 30 June: 12.

Knight, A and H. Alpert (1966) 'The History of Sex in Cinema, Part XIII', *Playboy* December: 244–245.

Landry, R. J. (1966) 'Who's Minding the Pantheon?' *Variety* 26 January: 7.

Landry, R. J. (1968) 'Foreign Showmen Ask for More Facts on US Market', *Variety* 8 May: 39.

Lev, P. (1993) *The Euro-American Cinema.* Austin: University of Texas Press.

Levy, S. (2002) *Ready, Steady, Go!* New York: Doubleday.

Life (1951) 'Sexy Signore' 3 September: 62.

Londoner, D. (1985) 'The Changing Economics of Entertainment', pp. 603–630 in Tino Balio (ed) *The American Film Industry*. Madison: University of Wisconsin Press.

McDougal, D. (1998) *The Last Mogul: Lew Wasserman, MCA, and the Hidden History of Hollywood*. New York: Da Capo.

Mayer, A. F. (1965) *Foreign Films on American Screens*. New York: Arco.

Neale, S. (1981) 'Art Cinema as Institution', *Screen*, 22(1): 11–39.

Pryor, T. (1949) 'The Personal History of Roberto Rossellini', *New York Times* 23 January: 5.

Randall, R. (1968) *Censorship of the Movies*. Madison, University of Wisconsin Press.

Sloane, L. (1968) 'Allied Artists Seeking a New Day in the Sun', *New York Times* 11 November: 77.

Variety (1958) Review of *Les Bijoutiers du clair de lune*, 7 May.

Variety (1958) 'BB vs.C' 16 July: 35.

Variety (1958) 'Sex-Kitten Unravels Film "Art"' 29 October: 1, 19.

Variety (1959) 'Lopert Does what UA Cannot' 15 April: 5, 11.

Variety (1962) 'Edward Kingsley: A Respected Importer' 7 February: 6.

Variety (1965) 'US Market for Foreigns', 12 May.

Variety (1968) 'All Majors Have Subsids' 13 March: 7.

Variety (2000) 'All Time Foreign-Language Films in North America', 21 – 7 February: 16.

Vincendeau, G. (2000) 'Brigitte Bardot,' pp. 112–116 in J. Hill and P. Church Gibson (eds) *World Cinema: Critical Approaches*. Oxford: Oxford University Press

Walker, A. (1974) *Hollywood UK: The British Film Industry in the Sixties*. New York: Stein & Day.

Westin, A. F. (1961) 'The *Miracle* Case: The Supreme Court and the Movies', *Inter-University Case Program #64*. Indianapolis, Bobbs-Merrill.

Wilinsky, B. (2001) *Sure Seaters: The Emergence of Art House Cinema*. Minneapolis: University of Minnesota Press.

Chapter 15

Crossing over: exporting indigenous heritage to the USA

Andrew Higson

English history, England's national heroes and the English literary canon have long been staples of the English cinema, as historical films, as costume dramas, as period literary adaptations. This is hardly surprising: a national cinema becomes such in part by recycling the national heritage. And that heritage is necessarily highly specific, local, and home-grown. The English heritage is in this sense an indigenous cultural formation, despite the long history of invasion, immigration, ethnic intermixing and cultural hybridisation. What happens when this indigenous culture is exported? What happens, for instance, to stories about very specific English identities, cultural milieux and historical periods when they are re-presented in films intended for international circulation? These are by no means abstract questions, since there is of course also a long history of international trade in the cinematic representation of English history and the English literary heritage. On the one hand, English-made films about the English national past have often found some sort of market in the USA and elsewhere; and on the other hand, Hollywood has frequently made its own versions of the English past. This chapter is in part an examination of the terms of this cultural trade in the 1990s and 2000s.

One of the things that happens to the familiar, indigenous story when it moves into an export market is that it becomes an exotic cultural good. But we should also recognise that the representation of, say, the English upper middle classes in the early nineteenth century may be just as exotic to contemporary audiences in England as it is to modern American audiences, given the elements of pastness, the class specificity and the cultural extravagance on display in the films. At the same time, cultural representations designed for a consumer market must never be allowed to become too unfamiliar, too exotic, for fear of what media economists and others call 'cultural discount' – that is, the diminished appeal that products rooted in a particular culture might have for foreign audiences who 'find it difficult to identify with the styles, values, beliefs, institutions and behaviour patterns being portrayed' (Hoskins and McFadyen, 1991: online).

What interests me here is that the cultural trade in representations of the English past depends on films that do in fact seem to retain a high degree of indigenous cultural references, and yet still achieve a certain success in export markets. Of course, period films that have been lavished with attention to authentic historical detail still bear the marks of their modern-day conceptualisation. And there is plenty of evidence that cultural products intended for export markets are shaped by expectations as to what will work in those markets. Is this an unacceptable loss of cultural integrity, a threat to the representation of local cultural identities and stories, a dilution of the indigenous in order to overcome the problem of cultural discount? Or is it a way of ensuring a certain cultural diversity, a way of ensuring that a range of different types of film, representing different tastes and sensibilities, can be effectively produced, circulated and consumed? One view of the globalisation of the media and entertainment industries is that it progressively squeezes out local cultures, not least because the cultural specificity of the local is thought of as inexportable. But the growth of 'world music' and 'world cinema' as marketable cultural categories, albeit specialised, niche categories, suggests that globalisation does leave room for the local. At the same time, as a local culture is commoditised for global consumption, we must consider the extent to which the local is modified, reconfigured and translated for its new global-niche audiences.

In order to explore these issues in more detail, I will look at the performance in the American market of several film adaptations of the 1990s and 2000s of one of English literature's most canonical authors, Jane Austen. Austen deals in her novels with a highly specific cultural milieu, one which is both historically and geographically precise, and which focuses on a very limited social formation. Some of the recent adaptations of her novels radically re-work the stories, the settings and the characters in order to produce films that might appeal more readily to contemporary multiplex audiences in the USA and the UK, as in *Clueless* (1995), Amy Heckerling's high school romantic comedy based on *Emma*, and *Bride and Prejudice* (2005), Gurinder Chadha's modern-day Bollywood re-working of *Pride and Prejudice*. But other adaptations were promoted very much in terms of their historical accuracy, their cultural specificity – their *authenticity*. Yet they have still managed to achieve a certain success internationally, with audiences for whom such representations are not indigenous but exotic. These 'authentic' Austen adaptations include *Persuasion* (1995), *Sense and Sensibility* (1995), *Emma* (1996), *Mansfield Park* (1999) and *Pride and Prejudice* (2005; released as this book was going to press).

As genteel, refined costume dramas operating at the quality end of the market, these films belong to the cycle of English heritage cinema that can be traced back to *Chariots of Fire* (1981) and the beginning of the 1980s. The heritage film was of course one of the most visible production trends of the British – or perhaps more accurately, the Anglo-Hollywood – cinema of the 1980s, 1990s and early 2000s, embracing movies as diverse as *Gandhi* (1982), *Orlando* (1992), *Mrs Brown* (1997), *Elizabeth* (1998) and *Ladies in Lavender* (2004). Perhaps the most prominent instances of the trend are Merchant Ivory's English films, especially their Forster adaptations, *A Room with a View* (1986), *Maurice* (1987) and *Howards End* (1992). Other canonical authors besides Forster and Austen whose work has been adapted include Henry James (*The Wings of the Dove*, 1997) and Thomas Hardy (*Jude*, 1996), while there are also several literary bio-pics, such as *Carrington* (1995), *Wilde* (1997), *Shakespeare in Love* (1998) and *Finding Neverland* (2004). Another favourite theme is the English upper classes and upper middle classes abroad, in films that include *A Passage to India*

Chapter 15 • Crossing over: exporting indigenous heritage to the USA

(1984), *White Mischief* (1987), *Where Angels Fear to Tread* (1991) and *Enchanted April* (1991).

Drawing on the research I undertook for my book *English Heritage, English Cinema* (Higson, 2003),* I want to identify some of the conditions that enabled this production trend – and especially the Austen films – to become as successful as it did in the American market. What I'm interested in here is the terms under which such films were sold, the development of a specialised market for such films in the USA, and the implications of American interest in English heritage. I will then return to some of the more general questions this case study raises about how 'indigenous' cultural products are traded in the international arena.

Such films draw variously on the conventions of the literary adaptation, the biopic, the woman's film and the romantic comedy. They are pre-eminently middlebrow cultural products, celebrated for, amongst other things, the way that they present 'indigenous' characters and stories and reproduce the decor, costumes, properties and landscapes of heritage England. Thus while these films are very much designed for and clearly achieve international distribution, they are also films with a strong local or indigenous flavour, with their decidedly English characters, stories and settings. Despite their cultural specificity, the commercial viability of the production trend as a whole and the Austen adaptations in particular depended crucially on the ability of producers to secure adequate exhibition in the lucrative US market, and therefore to attract the interest of American distributors.

Many of the films were produced and/or marketed as crossover films – that is, films that might move between a niche market and a 'mass' market. Such films are driven by both the commercialism and the market imperatives of the mainstream studio film and the cultural imperatives and artistic values of the specialised art-house film. Their budgets fall between the two stools too, and they frequently draw on funding sources associated with both sectors. They will also tend to be distributed on both the art-house circuit and the mainstream, multiplex circuits, and marketed so that they might appeal to the different audiences of each circuit. As I have documented elsewhere, the strategy has been very successful, with many 'English' costume dramas achieving significant commercial success relative to their production costs (Higson, 2003: chs. 3 and 4). *Chariots of Fire*, for instance, was made for less than £4m but grossed over $62m in the USA, *A Room with a View* was made for just over £2m but grossed over $25m in the USA, *A Passage to India, Sense and Sensibility, Elizabeth* and *Shakespeare in Love* were all made for between £8m and £13m and all grossed more than $20m in the USA – sometimes considerably more. *Shakespeare in Love*, for instance, grossed over $100m (Higson, 2003: 92–95). Given these sorts of profit margins, for what are in Hollywood terms modest to low-budget productions, both British and American producers and distributors have been keen to secure a slice of the action.

The companies that handled such films in the USA in the 1980s and early 1990s were typically independent distributors, such as Cinecom, who had an enormous success with *A Room with a View* in the mid-1980s, or the Samuel Goldwyn Company, which was involved with *Much Ado About Nothing* (1993), *Angels and Insects*

---

* Parts of this chapter have also appeared in Higson, 2004.

205

(1995), and *The Madness of King George* (1995). As one company executive put it, 'our task is not to read the audience with a capital A, but specific audiences', with another adding that there was plenty of scope for such activity because 'Hollywood is so homogenous that they've left the door wide open for something a little different' (quoted in Grimes, 1991: C13). What happened in the 1990s was that the Hollywood majors developed ways of going through that door themselves.

Another of the key companies at the start of the 1990s was Miramax, which in 1992 became part of the Disney Corporation, a deal that was indicative of a wider trend of the 1990s, with the major American companies increasingly moving into this particular niche, in the hope of being involved with the next *Chariots of Fire* or *Room with a View*, or the next *Crying Game* (1992) or *Full Monty* (1997) or *My Big Fat Greek Wedding* (2002). Miramax in its Disney phase handled several English heritage films, including *The English Patient* (1996), *Emma*, *The Wings of the Dove*, *Mrs Brown*, *Shakespeare in Love*, *The Ideal Husband* (1999), *Mansfield Park*, *Love's Labour's Lost* (2000), *The Golden Bowl* (2000), *The Importance of Being Earnest* (2002) and *Finding Neverland*. Several of the other majors also established their own in-house boutique outlets or designer labels, such as Sony Classics, which exploited *Howards End*, *Orlando*, *Hamlet* (1996), *Persuasion*, and *Wilde*, or Universal's Gramercy, which handled *Elizabeth*. Just occasionally, one of the major studios would take full control of such films, as Columbia, Sony's mainstream distribution division, did with *Sense and Sensibility* and *The Remains of the Day* (1993). In moving into this arena, the majors in effect created a new category of film: not the chance success that happens to cross over from the specialised or art-house sector to the mainstream multiplex market, but the film that is deliberately engineered from the outset as a cultural artefact with a dual identity and dual market appeal.

Of the period-set Austen adaptations of the 1990s, *Emma*, *Sense and Sensibility* and *Mansfield Park* were all produced by a Hollywood fascinated by the potential of on the one hand the international co-production and on the other hand the relatively low budget quality film that might cross over from the specialised, art-house cinemas to the multiplexes. A particular distribution pattern had been established for crossover films in the 1980s and early 1990s, and English costume dramas such as *Chariots of Fire*, *A Room with a View* and *Howards End* had played a key role in establishing this pattern and showing how profitable it could be. In this period, the mainstream studio film was increasingly given a nation-wide saturation release on its opening weekend, with massive amounts of expensive advertising, on television and elsewhere, and a limited theatrical window, so that it could be brought out on video as soon as possible. The crossover production, however, would typically be given some sort of expansion release, starting off on just one or two screens and gradually building up over a much longer period. When films were given this sort of release, their largest exposure was often during the awards season, building up to the Oscars in the spring. In the case of *Howards End*, for instance, this was some 9 months after the film had initially been premiered on a single screen. The Oscar tie-in could prove particularly lucrative, with *Sense and Sensibility* taking $14.7 million dollars between the announcement of the Oscar nominations and the awards ceremony itself (Anon., 1999a: 30).

In effect, where the saturation release is an attempt to create and exploit a mass market, the typically much slower rollout of the heritage film was more about exclusivity. The latter release strategy was however characteristically two-pronged. The film would tend to open in the most prestigious art-houses and continue to play throughout its run on the specialised circuit. But at selected points, once it had proved itself critically and built up enough marketing momentum, it would cross over into the mainstream cinemas. For such a release pattern, much less was spent on direct advertising, and the distributors kept costs low by building up local and/or carefully targeted publicity and by relying on newspaper reviews and word-of-mouth. The goal was to exploit those markets traditionally ignored by the majors, and to emphasise the difference of the specialised film from the mainstream release. On the other hand, if the film was to become a crossover success, then the strategy had to be twofold. Initially, its difference from the mainstream would be stressed, but as the release widened, so its similarity to the mainstream would be acknowledged.

Distribution and promotion were understood very much as specialised activities, the films requiring careful handling and dedicated personal attention. As Tom Rothman, an executive at Goldwyn, suggested of such promotional strategies, 'It's the difference between a mass production factory and a crafts cottage where things are made by hand' (quoted in Natale, 1992: 7). The task was to reach the film's perceived target audience. As a Hollywood journalist put it, 'there are only so many people in each market who are potential customers for a film with literary pretensions. They are not the people who rush out to see any movie on opening weekend' (Mathews, 1997: 5).

Persuasion, *Emma*, *Sense and Sensibility* and *Mansfield Park* all enjoyed some form of American financial and/or production involvement, and are perhaps best classed as Anglo-Hollywood rather than strictly British productions. And of course they were all distributed in the USA as well, with *Persuasion* released by Sony Classics simply as an art-house film, while the other three were carefully milked for their crossover potential by targeting two distinct audiences. Thus *Emma* and *Sense and Sensibility* led double lives as both art-house releases and mainstream films, with both going on to become major successes at the box-office. *Mansfield Park* on the other hand was given a mainstream-style multiplex release in the UK, but, having performed very poorly there, was given the sort of limited release usually reserved for art-house films in the USA.

Central to the production and marketing of all these films was the effort to create products that could work both as mainstream romantic dramas and as tasteful and 'authentic' Austen adaptations. *Persuasion* was actually made as a one-off television drama by the BBC, and only picked up for theatrical release in the USA. One can see why it appealed to Sony Classics, given its credentials as both a piece of middlebrow art cinema and an adaptation of a literary classic. Its Bergmanesque intensity, its self-consciously de-glamorised and austere mise-en-scene, its constantly moving camera, and its familiar heritage iconography and slow-moving, character-based narrative all pitched it to what was by now a well-established market. Film reviewers writing for upmarket publications were generally impressed with what they saw as its restraint, subtlety and authenticity: as one critic put it, 'Jane Austen would have approved' (Pearson, 1995: 20). The American trade paper *Variety*

Fig. 1. Widening the appeal of Roger Michell's Persuasion *(UK, France, USA, 1995): the video sleeve used for the US rental market (neither the actors nor the action depicted here appear in the actual film).*

too felt that the 'charming' film would be 'sure to appeal to dedicated Jane-ites' (Austen's fans and self-appointed protectors of her legacy) (Elley, 1995: unpaginated).

But even this tasteful quality drama was promoted in part as a conventional romantic period piece in the USA. Thus the American poster for the film showed the central couple, Anne and Wentworth, kissing – a kiss which caused some consternation to Jane-ites, since no such kiss is indicated in the novel; in an attempt to give the film wider appeal, however, the American TV co-production company insisted that one be added (Davies, 1995: 12). That attempt to widen the appeal of the film was taken a step further when the film was released for video rental. Now the video sleeve showed two entirely different actors, who have no part in the production, involved in a much more passionate and revealing pose and suggesting a much racier drama (Fig. 1).

Such strategies are very much about trying to make a culturally specific niche product into one that can succeed in a variety of markets.

Central to the crossover strategy as it developed through the 1990s was the provision of larger production budgets, the devising of increasingly costly ways of marketing the films, and a speeding up of the previously long, slow release schedule, with more attention paid to the opening weekend and the first few weeks of release. Thus as audience figures seemed to confirm the potential profitability of the 'English' costume drama, so production and marketing budgets went up. Fewer low-budget costume dramas were made as the 1990s progressed – and of the medium-budget films that were made, the American connection became more and more important (Higson, 2003: 127ff.).

Columbia, for example, handled *Sense and Sensibility*, opening it on 70 screens, which took it to eleventh place in that week's box-office charts. The number of screens on which it was showing was increased at regular intervals, until it was eventually showing on more than 1000. After reaching this peak, the number of screens gradually decreased again, although the release was widened briefly once more for

Chapter 15 • Crossing over: exporting indigenous heritage to the USA

Fig. 2. Star attractions: marketing Ang Lee's Sense and Sensibility *(USA/UK, 1995).*

the Oscar season. By the end of its run, this release strategy garnered $43 million for *Sense and Sensibility* in the USA, against production costs reported as £9.4m.[*] *Emma*, on the other hand, was handled in the American market by Miramax, who started the film off on just 9 screens – a typical art-house type opening – but built it up over the next 7 weeks to 848 screens, enabling it to earn $22m at the American box-office, against production costs reported as £6.3m.[**] It was of course this sort of box-office success that attracted American companies to invest in such 'English' productions in the first place.

Both *Emma* and *Sense and Sensibility* were designed to attract a core American

---

[*] See weekly box-office charts in *Variety*, December 1995 to April 1996; and Dyja, 1996: 27.

[**] See weekly box-office charts in *Variety*, August-December 1996; and Dyja, 1996: 27.

Fig. 3. 'Cupid is armed and dangerous': marketing Austen for the 1990s (the American video sleeve for Emma) (Douglas McGrath, UK and USA, 1996).

audience for tasteful English costume dramas – more female-oriented and more middle-brow, middle-class and middle-aged than the mainstream – but also the more youthful and downmarket general audience to whom a romantic drama might appeal. So if on the one hand both films enjoyed modest star casting (Emma Thompson, Kate Winslet, Hugh Grant and Alan Rickman in *Sense and Sensibility* (Fig. 2), and Gwyneth Paltrow in *Emma*), at the same time the core audience, the Jane-ites and the fans of English period films, were not to be frightened away.

Reviewers commenting on *Emma* were not slow to note its mainstream aspirations, remarking that the director 'keeps things moving at a delirious trot' (Eisner, 1996: unpaginated), producing an 'anachronistic snap bordering on irreverence', and 'grasping the screwball possibilities' (Maslin, 1996: C1) of the plot. The film is certainly much faster moving and less precious, less self-consciously exclusive and refined, than, say, the Merchant-Ivory films that had done so much to establish the potential of this production trend. The tagline – 'this season, Cupid is armed and dangerous' – and poster images used in publicity hardly stressed that this was either a Jane Austen adaptation or an upmarket niche product, selling *Emma* in part on star image and in part on romance (Fig. 3). In some places, it was even marketed as 'based on the story that inspired the hit movie *Clueless*!'*

But if on the one hand this was a Hollywood romantic comedy, on the other hand it was a film from what the trade paper *Variety* referred to as Miramax's 'traditional stronghold of upscale, specialised pics' (Roman, 1997: online). Other reviewers also felt the film had the hallmarks of a quality product that did justice to its highly respectable Austen source. As one put it, the 'speedy pacing' of the film was achieved 'without sacrificing period manners or the precision of the original language' (Eisner, 1996: unpaginated). The conclusion was that *Emma* 'has enough satirical edge to amuse audiences weary of big-screen explosions and computer wizardry' (Maslin, 1996: C1), so that, while there was plenty to keep the multiplex audiences happy, it should still 'have no problems moving in any of your better circles' (Eisner, 1996: unpaginated).

---

* Publicity for the video in the USA – see Buena Vista's website (www.video.movies.go.com).

Chapter 15 • Crossing over: exporting indigenous heritage to the USA

Fig. 4. Eroticising Jane Austen: Patricia Rozema's Mansfield Park *(UK, 1999).*

Mansfield Park, appearing a few years later, was in many ways symptomatic of how the crossover and heritage film production trends were developed in the late 1990s. Like *Emma*, it was a co-production between Miramax and a British company, with a comparable production budget. And like other costume dramas of the period, such as *Elizabeth*, *Plunkett and Macleane*, *Shakespeare in Love* and *The Wings of the Dove*, it was an attempt to update and open up the period film, to make it more appealing to contemporary, youthful multiplex audiences, while again not ignoring the niche art-house audience. Thus, while retaining the veneer of the authentic period adaptation, it attempts to incorporate more recent readings of Austen's work, and more modern representations of desire. It incorporates touches of the grotesque, the gothic and the expressionist, blatantly eroticises its themes and characters, and in various ways tarnishes the charms of the English national past (Fig. 4). Advance publicity also made much of the fact that the actor who played Austen's hero had previously played Sick Boy in *Trainspotting*. As the British trade paper *Screen International* commented, this film is 'anything but true to the novel – an audacious move that will prove as popular with some audiences as [it is] abhorrent to others' (Anon., 1999b: 32).

In fact, as I've already noted, the film was not a great success with multiplex audiences. In the USA, it opened on just 8 screens, moving up to 30 in week two, and 148 in week seven, from when it gradually tailed off, a release strategy that yielded only $4.8 million.* Interestingly, initial publicity for the film stressed its difference, its cutting edge qualities (the promotional tagline, 'Jane Austen's wicked comedy', sounded most un-Austenish, as did the sex scenes in the film itself). By the time it appeared on video, however, it was being promoted primarily to the core

---

* See weekly box-office charts in *Variety*, November 1999 to March 2000.

Jane-ite audience – 'will delight Austen fans everywhere'* – as another 'faithful' adaptation, rather than the radical, audience-grabbing film Miramax had evidently been hoping for, and the 'bodice-ripping shagfest' some of the initial publicity seemed to suggest (CW, 2000: 126).

What was it about the American market in the 1990s, or at least certain segments of the American market, that made it receptive to relatively indigenous English heritage products? What was it about the broader cultural context in the USA that meant such films might have the impact they did at the American box-office? Partly, we should see them as pre-sold commodities, with an established 'fan' base. Thus Masterpiece Theatre on the PBS television channel had over the years established a niche audience for quality English drama and adaptations of the literary canon, just as the success of earlier films in the cycle ensured that there was an audience for later films with similar attractions. Fashion designers and outlets such as Laura Ashley and Ralph Lauren Polo tapped into the same tasteful, conservative sensibility, while Jane Austen's literature had a long-established and very firm footing within American literary culture, not least through the highly active Jane Austen Society of North America (JASNA). Around such cultural products had emerged a discourse of quality and refinement that tied in with a particular strain of Anglophilia, a very specific understanding of Englishness. This was in many senses a nostalgic and class-bound discourse, an attempt to return to 'old world' values and lifestyles.

Films like the period Jane Austen adaptations thus in effect served an established niche market, but the crossover strategy widened that market by addressing more populist audience sensibilities through discourses of romance and celebrity, and the pleasures of costume, strong female characters, and images of female friendship and female desire. By inserting themselves into these sorts of contexts, what might be thought of as films with a high degree of local or indigenous cultural specificity were able to find a place in the busy international – and especially American – film markets of the 1990s. The design of the films, and the ways in which they were marketed were intended precisely to exploit the commercial potential of those particular contexts and audience sensibilities.

But these films and others like them are in several senses compromise products, deliberately tapping into quite distinct and diverse cultural and economic formations. As middlebrow films, they work with the cultural aspirations and identities of both the mass market and elite culture. As crossover films, they attempt to bridge the gap between the multiplex and the art-house. And as 'English' films produced with more than an eye on the American market, they foreground the complex hybridity of 'indigenous' culture – but also its exportability. This sense of both cultural and commercial compromise is crucial to how the films were conceived and sold. But even if these were compromise products, the industry and the trade press in the USA still perceived them very much as niche products for a niche market. The key point to make here is that the exploitation of that niche should be understood as a vital component in the globalisation of the media industry.

---

* Sleeve for British retail video of *Mansfield Park* (Miramax Home Entertainment/Buena Vista Home Entertainment, D611251).

Chapter 15 • Crossing over: exporting indigenous heritage to the USA

Indeed, we should see the involvement of major American companies in the funding and exploitation of these films as symptomatic of how those companies have developed over the last few years (Balio, 1998). Thus rather than focus solely on the most profitable parts of the mainstream market, those companies have bought into what are usually considered niche markets or specialised markets. Perhaps the most remarkable development in this respect was the way Disney brought both Miramax and Merchant Ivory Productions into their fold in the early 1990s. What the majors recognised was that, in the globalised multi-media market, audiences were increasingly fragmented, and there was a profit to be made by addressing specialised niches and attending to local sensibilities. It might not be the sort of profit to be made with a successful blockbuster film, but it was a profit worth exploiting all the same.

The trading of English heritage films in the American market thus plays out in very interesting ways the relationship between the local or niche product and the global aspirations of the major players in the media economy. It also raises important questions about the relationship between indigeneity and exportability. Culture is always being traded and cross-bred. In this sense, there is no such thing as a pure cultural identity. But if the 'indigenous' is thus always in some way hybrid, too often when commentators describe the trading of culture on the international stage, they adopt misleadingly homogeneous notions of national culture. Hence the familiar complaint that 'English' culture is threatened by the global forces of 'American' consumer capitalism. On the one hand, this is a very problematic view of English culture, which does not of course have a singular, distinctive and pure identity. On the other hand, this is exactly how indigenous culture is required to operate on the international stage: for the purposes of trade, 'national' cultures become brand images, which can then be exported as known quantities, as signifiers of cultural difference, or at least of an acceptable and marketable cultural variety.

The Unique Selling Point of these brand images in international niche markets is precisely their exoticism, their foreignness – so long as the sense of cultural difference is not too great. The indigenous and the exotic, strictly polar opposites, thus blur into one another. It is perhaps significant, in this context, that so many English heritage films have been directed by 'outsiders', foreign commentators on the English past. Among the Austen adaptations, *Sense and Sensibility* was made by the Taiwanese director Ang Lee, *Emma* was directed by an American, Douglas McGrath, and *Mansfield Park* by a Canadian, Patricia Rozema.

Casting American actors has been one vital way of selling English heritage films to American audiences – hence the casting of Gwyneth Paltrow to play the eponymous gentlewoman in *Emma*. On the one hand, the character of Emma contributes to the film's upmarket exoticism, its cultural difference; on the other hand, the actor anchors the film firmly within contemporary American cultural experience, both limiting the threat of cultural discount and expanding the appeal of an otherwise local product. The extent to which such films draw on the familiar generic conventions of romance fiction and romantic comedy is another way in which these 'indigenous' products are re-presented as potentially exportable and as capable of emerging from their particular niche. At one level, the product must retain the necessary shimmer of the exotic – that difference is part of its appeal in export markets. At another level, there must be a sufficient degree of cultural familiarity.

Fig. 5. Jane Austen as High School comedy: the video sleeve for Amy Heckerling's Clueless (USA, 1995).

It is of course strategies such as these that cause anxiety for those fearful that English culture is being eroded by American consumer capitalism.

One might also note in this context those other re-workings of Austen's novels that have gone much further out of their way to appeal to diverse contemporary audiences, and especially the younger multiplex audience. Thus Amy Heckerling makes no attempt to present an authentic English cultural identity or history in *Clueless*, her loose adaptation of Austen's *Emma*, in which the story and the sensibility have been entirely transposed to modern-day California, and re-presented as a high school romantic comedy (Fig. 5). This is a much more radical strategy for ensuring the exportability of an indigenous source text, stripping it of all those aspects that might seem exotic to the mainstream American youth audience. Gurinder Chadha does something similar with *Bride and Prejudice*, her Bollywood adaptation of *Pride and Prejudice*, in which the Bennets of eighteenth century Hertfordshire have become the Bakshis of twenty-first century Amritsar in India, and Darcy has become an American businessman (Fig. 6). Moving us between India, the British-Asian community in and around London, and Los Angeles, Chadha uses Austen's plot and characters to confront us with a narrative about diasporic and hybrid cultural identities in a globalised cultural space. Thus rather than presenting us with an 'authentic' version of Austen, Chadha uses Austen to challenge conventional ideas of cultural identity and to raise questions about the relationship between the local and the global.

For all these efforts to limit the experience of cultural discount, for all their crossover appeal, it's important to remember that, with the exception of *Clueless*, the Austen films remain relatively specialised products for a core niche market. The fact that they don't have a wider appeal, or receive larger budgets, is a recognition that they remain culturally quite specific and that, for many audiences, the degree of cultural discount is too great. Even so, these 'local', 'indigenous' representations do enjoy a certain form of global distribution, thereby challenging that view of globalisation that sees it as a culturally homogenising force that obliterates heterogeneity, cultural diversity, local identity and difference. Rather than the global and the local being

Chapter 15 • Crossing over: exporting indigenous heritage to the USA

Fig. 6. Jane Austen, Bollywood style: a scene from Gurinder Chadha's Bride and Prejudice *(UK and USA, 2004).*

positioned as polar opposites, they are, in instances such as these, interdependent. Globalization, from this perspective, as Roland Robertson argues, involves 'the creation and incorporation of locality' (1995: 40). What we find in the Anglo-Hollywood heritage film is in many ways typical of that global capitalism which addresses itself to and through specific local identities, adapting a global business to local conditions: 'the tailoring and advertising of goods and services on a global or near-global basis to increasingly differentiated local and particular markets' – for, 'to put it very simply, diversity sells' (1995: 28, 29).

Global capitalism, from this perspective, thus depends upon the production and reproduction of difference: the global is 'the generative frame of unity within which diversity can take place' (Featherstone, 1990: 2). Global capitalism, from this perspective, must embrace variety, it must acknowledge and attend to the indigenous and the local, and it must address niche markets. But can it do so only by imagining the local through the lens of the global? Can it do so only by creating and reproducing a standardised version of the local, a global version of the local, recognised and appreciated by a range of consumers, regardless of their location and sense of belonging? Once again, it might be argued that Englishness in the Anglo-Hollywood heritage film has been reduced to a familiar brand, a series of stock images and generic stereotypes. The problem with such a view is that it hardly does justice to the cultural richness of, say, the Austen adaptations. One might read these films as assertions of tradition, as celebrations of the family, home and the sense of a homeland, and as affirmations of cultural rootedness. One might also read them as simple manifestations of a well-established ideology of Englishness, and one that is not so much local as hegemonic. Yet each of the films is in some sense about dislocation as much as rootedness, each problematises the image of the family, and each challenges settled ideas of national identity from the perspectives of feminism, class politics or (post-) colonialism. This hardly suggests a series of ready-made stock images with no critical purchase.

These films then need to be understood both from the bottom up as resisting the drift towards global homogenisation – but also as products of global commoditisation, designed from the top down. The version of the local and the indigenous in the Austen films is neither entirely invented by the global forces of Hollywood, nor entirely authentic, whatever that might mean. Of course to some extent these films are exotic fantasies; of course to some extent they are Americanised versions of Jane Austen and of the English national past; of course they have been adapted to the conditions of the global-niche market. At the same time, they remain culturally distinctive films, they retain a sense of difference – and that difference is crucial to their perception at home and abroad and a key reason for their commercial viability.

To this extent, their very presence as films is indicative of a certain cultural diversity, a certain attention to the local within an increasingly globalised film culture. Paradoxically, this attention to the local and the indigenous is only possible because of international funding – and crucially American funding. In other words, it was the support of the Hollywood majors, as much as anything else, which enabled such films to be made. Hollywood's interest in relatively small-scale, specialist films thus suggests that the monolithic machine that some see in Hollywood may actually allow – even encourage – the production of difference. Hollywood in fact developed a business structure and a way of operating that allowed it to cater for different audiences, different tastes, and different markets. This development needs to be seen as part of a wider trend, one that is a key feature in the evolution of the global media industry. As one journalist put it, 'international financing is sophisticated enough nowadays to support … fiercely localised work' (Pulver, 1999: 19) Or as academic David Harvey has argued at length, the methods of global capitalism have shifted from mass production to flexible accumulation – wherein one of the flexibilities has been to exploit smaller markets with more specialised tastes (1990).

The international film trade in representations of heritage England clearly to some extent shapes those apparently indigenous representations – but it would be foolish to think that the indigenous was ever in fact 'pure', or that change is always a bad thing. In any case, it seems clear that the very reproduction of such representations depends in no small part upon American commercial involvement. Paradoxically it would seem that the globalisation of the film industry has actually made it possible to continue to produce a range of local cultural products. From the top down, this may be because the strategy is capable of generating income; from the bottom up, it is equally a means of ensuring a certain sort of cultural diversity. And if to some it would appear that the local can now only ever be glimpsed through the imaginative lens of the global, we should not forget the richness of the reception process, and the propensity of different (local) audiences to make sense of the same cultural product in a variety of distinctive ways. The international trade in an apparently indigenous culture in this sense opens up possibilities, rather than closes them down.

References

Anon. (1999a) 'Best Picture Nomination: What It Can Do at the Box-office', *Screen International*, 19 February: 30.

Anon. (1999b) 'Mansfield Park', *Screen International*, 1 October: 32.

Balio, T. (1998) '"A Major Presence in all the World's Important Markets": the Globalization of Hollywood in the 1990s' pp. 58–73 in S. Neale and M. Smith (eds), *Contemporary Hollywood Cinema*. London: Routledge.

CW. (2000) 'Mansfield Park', *Empire*, 136 (October): 126.

Davies, T. (1995) 'To Kiss or Not to Kiss', *Daily Telegraph*, 7 January: 12.

Dyja, E. (1996) *BFI Film and Television Handbook 1997*. London: British Film Institute.

Eisner, K. (1996) 'Emma', *Variety*, 17 June, in *Variety's Film Reviews, 1995–1996*. New York: Bowker, unpaginated.

Elley, D. (1995) 'Persuasion', *Variety*, 29 May, in *Variety's Film Reviews, 1995–1996*. New York: Bowker, unpaginated.

Featherstone, M. (1990) 'Global Culture: An Introduction', *Theory Culture and Society*, 7: 2–3.

Grimes, W. (1991) 'A Film Company's Success Story: Low Costs, Narrow Focus, Profits', *New York Times*, 2 December: C13.

Harvey, D. (1990) *The Condition of Postmodernity: An Enquiry into the Origins of Cultural Change*. Oxford: Blackwell.

Higson, A. (2004) 'English Heritage, English Literature, English Cinema: Selling Jane Austen to Movie Audiences in the 1990s', in E. Voigts-Virchow (ed) *Janespotting and Beyond: British Heritage Retrovisions Since the Mid-1990s*. Tubingen: Gunter Narr Verlag.

Higson, A. (2003) *English Heritage, English Cinema: The Costume Drama in the 1980s and 1990s*. Oxford: Oxford University Press.

Hoskins, C. and S. McFadyen (1991) 'Guest Editors' Introduction', *Canadian Journal of Communications* 16 (2): online (www.cjc-online.ca).

Maslin, J. (1996) 'Emma', *New York Times*, 2 August: C1.

Mathews, J. (1997) 'The Little Film That Could', *Los Angeles Times*, 30 March: part VI, 5.

Natale, R. (1992) 'Gramercy to the Rescue of Smaller Pix', *Variety*, 25 May: 7.

Pearson, A. (1995) 'Television: the Fine Art of Persuasion', *The Independent on Sunday*, 23 April: 'The Critics' section: 20.

Pulver, A. (1999) 'Bard to Worse at the Multiplex', *The Guardian*, 5 February: 19.

Robertson, R. (1995) 'Glocalization: Time-space and Homogeneity-heterogeneity', in M. Featherstone, S. Lash and R. Robertson (eds) *Global Modernities*. London: Sage.

Roman, M. (1997) *Variety.com*, 'Arthouse, Haunted House Buoy Miramax', 9 January: online (www.variety.com).

AFTERWORD

Chapter 16

Trading cultural commodities or promoting cultural diversity? UNESCO's new convention

Sylvia Harvey and Carole Tongue

Can film and television be thought of as commodities like any others to be traded in the world's markets? Some commentators have suggested that a country can import 100 per cent of certain goods or services without this being a problem, but that the import of a large majority of cultural commodities should be a matter of concern. This may be especially an issue in the case of film and television drama, given the impact of moving pictures on the formation of values and cultural identity. As this book has indicated, a complex international network exists, both enabling and constraining the making and sale of films and television programmes. But the trade flows across these markets and national borders are seldom equal or reciprocal; thus some countries export more of these cultural commodities or services while others import more. And those countries and companies that 'buy in' more, have become deeply dependent upon the supply of films and television programmes that are not locally or 'indigenously' made. This has created a form of mutual dependency, if not of reciprocity, and any loss of trade share can come to be seen as deeply threatening to the economic and cultural prospects of a nation state.

Thus in the United States, for example, it was estimated in the early 1990s that the American entertainment industry 'collects more revenue from foreign sales than any other US industry except commercial aircraft' (Kessler, 1995: 1). By contrast, and viewed from the point-of-view of the importing countries, the European Union had an estimated audio-visual trade deficit with the US of $8.2 billion in 2000. And in the sub-sector of cinema the US share in European markets in 2003 ranged from 86 per cent in the United Kingdom to 53 per cent in France (Iosifidis et al., 2005: 133; European Audio-Visual Observatory, 2004: 41). A more global snapshot attempted in 1992 indicated that the percentage of nationally-produced television programming in peak time varied from a share of 34 per cent in Lebanon and 46 per cent in Mexico, to 72 per cent in Brazil and 92 per cent in Japan (Straubhaar, 2001: 146).

World trade talks have been used by the big players to protect and if possible to extend their market share while small or aspirant players have sought to enter markets where they were previously absent. But in all these trade negotiations there has been little space for reflecting upon the importance of film and television as distinctive means of human expression and communication, reflecting the values and beliefs of their culture of origin.

It is for this reason that in October 2005 the General Conference of the United Nations Educational, Scientific and Cultural Organisation (UNESCO) adopted a new Convention designed to protect and promote cultural diversity. The official title of the document is the *Convention on the Protection and Promotion of the Diversity of Cultural Expressions* (UNESCO, 2005). Of the 192 member states of UNESCO a significant majority wished to record their views on this issue and to support the aims of the Convention. Thus 148 countries voted in favour, four abstained and two – the United States and Israel – opposed. It is clear that there is world-wide interest in this subject at least among governments and among many cultural producers and policy-makers. Evidence for this is the formation over recent years of over 30 national coalitions for cultural diversity comprising a broad range of creators who have argued for a measure of legal protection and support for such diversity (*Coalition Currents*, 2006:1).

For the Convention to become law, attaining the status of an international legal instrument, it must be ratified by 30 states. This process will take time and smaller and weaker countries may find themselves coming under considerable pressure from the United States which sees the document as potentially threatening to the global interests of its entertainment industries. Some vivid accounts exist of 'arm-twisting' tactics in the context of international trade negotiations, and these make it clear that agreements and treaties may be less the product of rational discussion and more the 'all that is left' after the clash of interests and the differential exercise of power (Jawara and Kwa, 2004: 148–183).

However, the first stage adoption of the Convention by UNESCO's General Council does seem to indicate the emergence of a new global consensus on this issue. A large number of developing countries, including China, Brazil, Malaysia, Senegal and Vietnam expressed their support for the initiative at the annual Ministerial meeting of the International Network on Cultural Policy (INCP, 2004), the European Union has thrown its considerable weight and legal expertise behind it (*Coalition Currents*, 2005), and Canada, a country that had already negotiated a cultural exemption for the North American Free Trade Agreement, was the first to sign in favour of the ratification of the Convention (Grant and Wood, 2004: 362).

What does this Convention say, why is it needed or opposed, and how did it come about?

The longer pre-history of this 2005 document can be traced back to the MacBride Report (*Many Voices, One World*) produced for UNESCO in 1980 and linked at that time to a ferocious debate about the possibilities of constructing a 'New World Information and Communications Order'(NWICO). During the 1970s this NWICO was predominantly advocated by those newly independent states in Africa and Asia whose political leaders wished to limit the power of western-controlled news agencies and media corporations and to insist upon the rights of sovereign states to control the information flows across their borders. In the age of the internet

Chapter 16 • Trading cultural commodities or promoting cultural diversity?

and of widespread satellite and mobile communication it has become difficult to see how nation states either could or should seek to control their information 'borders' in this way. But, at the time, this advocacy of national rights was seen (by its defenders) as one more chapter in the necessary history of decolonisation.

The critics of the proposed 'New Order', principally the multi-national companies that had become dominant in the media and communications sector, predictably opposed the concept of the NWICO and managed to persuade their national governments not only that such polices were a threat to western economic interests but also that they constituted a threat to the democratic principle of free flow of information (Tomlinson, 1991: 15–31). In the fall-out from this clash of interests and of values, the two western nations which at the time were leading the charge of revived neo-liberal values – the United States under the Presidency of Ronald Reagan and Britain under the premiership of Margaret Thatcher – withdrew from UNESCO (in, respectively, 1985 and 1986).

More than a decade was to elapse before Britain rejoined UNESCO in 1997, and it was to be nearly twenty years before the US returned in 2003. During this period communications technologies were developing at a very fast pace and the new instruments established for international trade negotiations were coming under increasing pressure. The World Trade Organisation (WTO) replaced the General Agreement on Tariffs and Trade (GATT) in 1995. But the meetings of the WTO in Seattle in 1999 and then in Cancun, Mexico in 2003 were to attract increasing public scrutiny and criticism, including on occasions the presence of violent counter-demonstrations. As one commentator noted in 2003 regarding the shifting political relations between the countries of the global north and of the global south, 'the South has awakened' (Jawara and Kwa, 2004: ix and 305).

These increased tensions, along with a sharp sense of injustice felt by those poorer nations who saw unequal trade deals as a kind of continuing colonialism, and the private anger of those who thought that their beliefs and values were being treated with contempt, were to have widespread repercussions. The attack on the World Trade Center in New York on 11 September, 2001, can be seen as the terrifying accentuation and embodiment of some of these tensions, though the complexity of the causes of this attack remain as yet not fully examined.

It is notable that in the year prior to the terrible events of '9/11', a European Conference under UNESCO patronage – held at Valencia in Spain and bringing together film and policy-makers from every continent – had asserted the links between 'culture, community and human security' (Valencia Statement, 2000). And it is perhaps something more than a coincidence that shortly after the pitiless attack on the twin towers in September 2001, and just before the opening of the WTO talks at Doha in November, another General Conference of UNESCO gave unanimous approval to a new *Universal Declaration on Cultural Diversity* (UNESCO, 2001). The political significance of a public statement of respect and recognition for the culture of others is especially well explained by the former Minister of Culture of the Republic of Ireland, Michael D. Higgins. In an interview conducted in 2001 he observed that human rights are 'mediated by culture'; we can infer from this that

223

the promotion of cultural diversity – along with economic development and the search for non-violent solutions – can become one of the basic grounds for peaceful co-existence both locally and globally (Higgins, 2004: 8).

The Declaration of 2001 can be seen as a precursor to the Convention and outlines a number of key principles. In an ambitious prefatory statement the Director-General of UNESCO suggested that the document could be a 'tool for development, capable of humanising globalization' and that intercultural dialogue could serve as 'the best guarantee of peace' and an alternative to 'the theory of the inevitable clash of cultures and civilizations' (UNESCO, 2001). Subsequent military actions by member states in Iraq and elsewhere, and widespread human catastrophes and suffering put these fine words in perspective.

Nonetheless the Declaration signals a new way of thinking about the role of culture and cultural diversity because it entails 'a commitment to human rights and fundamental freedoms', while also recognising that the right of all to enjoy 'their own cultural practices' must itself be subject to the principle of respect for human rights (Articles 4 and 5). Cultural expression and support for cultural diversity are thus no longer optional extras for rich societies and can perhaps no longer be contained by existing definitions of art or of entertainment; rather they involve 'an ethical imperative, inseparable from respect for human dignity' (Article 4). A powerful and memorable analogy is proposed with the claim that:

> ...cultural diversity is as necessary for humankind as biodiversity is for nature (Article 1).

This 'Universal Declaration' makes useful statements in support of media pluralism and linguistic diversity and recognises that in so far as cultural goods and services are the carriers of 'identity, values and meaning' they cannot be treated as 'mere commodities or consumer goods' (Articles 6 and 8). However, the very terminology of 'cultural goods and services' makes it difficult to think of these things as anything other than commodities, what Geoffrey Nowell-Smith refers to at the beginning of this volume as 'a trade in property rights'. It is perhaps for this reason that Michael D. Higgins prefers to think of culture as 'about the way of life of the people', considering creativity to be the 'mediated experience' of particular human beings, and believing that 'the cultural space' is wider than 'the economic space' (Higgins, 2004: 6, 2, 4).

The 2001 document recognises that 'market forces alone cannot guarantee the preservation and promotion of cultural diversity', yet it is itself caught up in the language of markets and in the advocacy of new markets and cultural industries especially for 'developing countries and countries in transition' (Articles 10 and 11). All of this is understandable and perhaps inevitable given the imperative that UNESCO must try to represent the interests of all its members. But, by contrast, and perhaps with the freedom that comes from no longer holding Ministerial office, Higgins is more trenchant in his critique of the effects of the entertainment industries and of the market in culture. What he calls 'neo-liberal savagery' is incapable – in his view – of developing a theory of culture, and he rejects the kind of developments that erode public space and transform societies from 'a mosaic of citizens into … a pool of consumers' (Higgins, 2004: 7).

The Declaration formally recognises the link between policies on cultural diversity

Chapter 16 • Trading cultural commodities or promoting cultural diversity?

and the encouragement of citizen inclusion and participation, seeing these activities as key elements in building or maintaining a democratic framework (Article 2). In this regard it is an important if limited statement of principles. But perhaps one of its most important elements is to be found in its forward-looking Action Plan. This includes a commitment to explore 'the advisability of an international legal instrument on cultural diversity' (Action Plan, section 1). Moving with astonishing speed for a membership-based international organisation, this legal instrument was in fact drafted and endorsed by October 2005 – the already mentioned *Convention on the Protection and Promotion of the Diversity of Cultural Expressions*.

The quick passage of the Convention, is in part the consequence of a break-down or at least a slowing down in the multilateral trade negotiations being conducted through the WTO. Des Freedman's chapter earlier in this volume explores the WTO's attempts at reaching agreement on some aspects of audio-visual trade, through the mechanism of the General Agreement on Trade in Services (GATS). But critics and supporters of the WTO alike have recognised the potential for cultural issues to throw off-course major economic initiatives ostensibly designed to remove trade barriers. For in December 1993 one of the most complex and multi-stranded agreements on international trade ever developed was almost destroyed by the arguments for and against a 'cultural exemption' – in brief the view that audio-visual production and services should not be subject to the emerging new norms of international trade (Grantham, 2000). After a long seven years of talks in the 'Uruguay' round of negotiations of the General Agreement on Tariffs and Trade (GATT, the predecessor body to WTO), final agreement was reached in 1993, but only because American negotiators agreed to accept, albeit temporarily, the case for a cultural exemption. When US President Bill Clinton declared 'we agreed to disagree' (Puttnam, 1997: 343) this embodied a reluctant recognition that some countries wished to continue to support their indigenous audio-visual industries whether this took the form of a compulsory licence fee to fund public broadcasting, as in Britain, or a determination to maintain quotas and subsidies for a national film industry, as in France or South Korea.

Since the replacement of GATT by WTO in 1995, and the increasing tensions around the actions of the WTO, there has been a tendency for countries to enter into bi-lateral (one to one) not multi-lateral talks. For smaller countries this has been a difficult process and the Convention has seemed to offer the promise of legal protection for national cultural initiatives that might otherwise be seen to contravene the principles of unrestricted trade. Unlike the 1991 UNESCO Declaration, the Convention – if and when ratified – will enter the pantheon of instruments of international law, as recognised by the American Ambassador to UNESCO in the briefing she gave to journalists immediately after the vote on the Convention (Oliver, 2005: 6). And this law, it is believed, may give greater comfort to nation states wishing to realise the principle of cultural diversity within their borders, to enable the creativity of their citizens and to support various forms of indigenous cultural expression including, for example, support for licence fee funded public service broadcasting.

How might the Convention of 2005 support these aspirations and why has it been opposed? The two key features of the document are *firstly* that it aspires to the status of international law and *secondly* that it offers a definition of cultural content that links content to cultural identity and therefore, potentially, to human rights. Article 4 of the Convention states:

> 'Cultural content' refers to the symbolic meaning, artistic dimension and cultural values that originate from or express cultural identities. (UNESCO, 2005)

Free speech rights in some legal regimes are awarded to corporations and not only to individuals. It is this that supports, among others thing, the rights of 'advertising speech'. However, human rights are awarded to individual human beings, not to corporate actors. The apparently unremarkable definition of cultural content offered in the Convention suggests that both cultural content and cultural diversity are linked to the identities of human beings and therefore to their ways of living. There is therefore something else or something more at stake here than the managing of cultural commodities or intellectual property rights. Thus the preamble to the Convention notes 'the importance of cultural diversity for the full realization of human rights and fundamental freedoms' and recognises what we might call the bi-polar nature of some cultural production. Thus the preamble asserts that:

> … cultural activities, goods and services have both an economic and a cultural nature, because they convey identities, values and meanings, and must therefore not be treated as solely having commercial value.

This is similar wording to that found in the 2001 Declaration, namely that cultural commodities, bought and sold in the market, are the vehicles, carriers or 'vectors' of 'identity, values and meaning' (UNESCO, 2001: Article 8). But the Convention offers a new wording and potentially a new way of thinking by asserting that symbolic meaning *originates from* or *expresses* cultural identity. In so doing it makes a much stronger connection between the acts or artefacts of human expression and the identities and therefore the lives and experiences of particular human beings. In this regard, the Convention may be said to acknowledge the enlarged definition of culture considered as a 'whole way of life' offered many years ago by the Welsh scholar Raymond Williams (1981:11), as well as the observation made by Michael Higgins that creativity is 'mediated experience' and the assertion by Geoffrey Nowell-Smith – made earlier in this volume – that 'culture is not identical with the products which carry cultural signifiers'. And before it is asserted from within the semiotic paradigm that this is nothing but a reassertion of the old experiential fallacy, it must be remembered that social semiotics is as interested in the speakers as it is in the spoken.

The intellectual framework or model proposed by the Convention – that cultural content originates from or expresses cultural identity and is an aspect of human experience – makes it extremely difficult for the cultural diversity debate to be contained within a purely economic frame of reference. This difficulty is also recognised by some free-market economists and is well expressed by two American scholars in their book on the international trade in films and television programmes:

> It is, of course, impossible to estimate, or even to define precisely, the value of cultural preservation to a sovereign nation. For this reason, cultural differences and their importance to national identity cannot be readily incorporated into a framework for analysing barriers to trade in films and programs. (Wildman and Siwek, 1988: 163).

It is because of this incompatibility of the language of cultural value on the one hand and the language of free trade on the other that most work advocating fewer barriers to audio-visual trade avoids the issue of cultural identity as well as the issue of reciprocity in cultural trade. The most famous early theorist of free trade, Adam Smith, writing in 1776 argued:

> If a foreign country can supply us with a commodity cheaper than we ourselves can make it, better buy it off them with some part of the produce of our own industry, employed in a way in which we have some advantage (Smith, 1937: 414).

However, this theory was developed before the full effects of European colonisation could become apparent (denying to most former colonies the exercise of any comparative economic advantage), and before the development of a significant and industrialised trade in cultural production. In respect of these 'cultural industries' the US has, of course, become a prominent player, exercising considerable comparative advantage, partly as a result of continuing and high levels of investment in production, and partly as a result of achieving, in some places, a quasi-monopolistic control of distribution.

As various commentators have pointed out, the audio-visual industries are economically distinctive in that 'first copy' or prototype costs are high whereas the costs of multiple reproduction – especially where this takes the form of broadcasting transmission – are negligible. This both makes the search for larger audiences intense (since, once basic costs are recouped, each additional fee-paying viewer can represent almost pure profit) and gives a special advantage to national players who are able to cover 'first copy' costs in their home market and to export to other countries at low cost, making indigenous production in these countries economically unviable (Grant and Wood, 2004; Graham and Davies, 1997; Garnham, 1990). The economic logic of these commodity characteristics suggests that the universal application of free trade rules in the film and television sector could have the effect of wiping out most national audio-visual industries. Certainly the removal of trade barriers in the countries of Central and Eastern Europe seems to have had the effect of drastically reducing the share of the market previously held by indigenous producers (Lange, 2003).

It is for these reasons that the majority of UNESCO's members felt the need to create an international agreement that recognised both the new opportunities for 'enhanced interaction between cultures' and the risk of 'imbalances between rich and poor countries', while also establishing the right of sovereign states to adopt 'regulatory measures aimed at protecting and promoting diversity of cultural expressions' (UNESCO, 2005: preamble and Article 6).

The second key feature of the Convention is its potential status as an internationally recognised legal instrument. It is here that much of the political controversy is focused. From the point-of-view of the United States there is a concern that the Convention might be used to subvert existing agreements on audio-visual trade or to facilitate the setting up of new trade barriers designed to limit the export of American films and television programmes. In addition, US representatives have sought to make a positive link between the free trade agenda and the human rights agenda, associating individual liberty with the rights of consumers, and suggesting that some governments might use the Convention to 'control the cultural lives of their citizens' by limiting cultural imports (Oliver, 2005: 1).

The belief that state intervention is hostile to individual liberty is deeply rooted in American political culture and directly counter-posed to the view that the democratic state might intervene to ensure free speech rights or to enable the work of indigenous cultural producers. Moreover, this embedded anti-statist view is sufficiently strong to discount event the robust opening statement in the Convention that 'cultural diversity is strengthened by the free flow of ideas' and that 'No one may invoke the provisions of this Convention in order to infringe human rights' (UNESCO, 2005: Preamble and Article 2).

It is difficult to judge how realistic are the US concerns about the proliferation of new trade barriers. Following the 1993 debacle around the GATT agreement and the creation of a general though temporary cultural exemption for the audio-visual sector, it might have been assumed that European countries in particular would take advantage of the exemption to reduce their reliance on imported films and television programmes. However, the opposite seems to have been the case as the import of American television programmes went up and not down, largely as a result of the advent of a large number of new satellite services relying principally on US imports. This had been facilitated by earlier political action. As the journalist John Cole noted the British Prime Minister had intervened, at the behest of the American President Ronald Reagan, to ensure that a European Directive designed to protect the audio-visual market was weakened in key respects. Thus, in the 1989 *Television Without Frontiers* Directive, the quota proposal that a minimum of 51 per cent of screen time should be devoted to EU home-grown programmes was watered down by the introduction of the qualifying phrase 'wherever practicable' (Cole, 1995: 347; Goldberg et al., 1998: 61). New cable and satellite channels in particular have used this loophole to carry mainly US imports. As a consequence, and as already mentioned, one estimate suggests that the European Union's audio-visual trade deficit with the US rose from $4.8 billion in 1995 to $8.2 billion in 2000 (Iosifidis et al., 2005: 134).

Following the large majority vote in favour of the Convention, the United States indicated the strength of its disapproval by voting against the adoption of UNESCO's budget and programme of work. Although it has also recognised that, under the rules of majority voting, it lacks the power to halt this work. Whether or not the reappearance of a deep rift in relationships might lead to a second withdrawal from membership of UNESCO remains to be seen. But this seems unlikely, particularly in view of the fact that many countries have re-iterated their support for the principle of removing barriers to trade (Oliver, 2005: 3).

Moreover the European Union believed that it had created a basis for compromise by supplying some wording for the Convention designed to confer equal status on this and other treaties – including, by implication, the un-named but ever present WTO treaty obligations (European Commission, 2005). Article 20 states that the various treaty obligations should be seen as mutually supportive and declares that 'when interpreting and applying the other treaties… Parties shall take into account the relevant provisions of this Convention' (UNESCO, 2005). Whether this wording is evidence of a deep-rooted attachment to the values of private property and the promotion of an increasingly energetic trade in services, or evidence of a commitment to the principle of state intervention in the public interest in the field of cultural expression also remains to be seen. Perhaps like so many 'agreements' its lack of clarity reflects continuing disagreements. Or perhaps it is an example of what former international banker Jacques Attali has referred to as a necessary 'compromise between the market and democracy' (Hobsbawm, 2006: 29).

Cultural producers as well as smaller, more economically vulnerable countries remain concerned about the extent to which the Convention will protect their cultural aspirations and policies. These anxieties are reflected in a statement produced at a meeting of cultural practitioners from 60 countries affirming 'the sovereign right of countries to determine their own cultural policies without fear of sanction or reprisal under trade agreements' (Madrid Declaration, 2005: 2). And there are bigger picture questions, barely touched upon here, having to do with the apparent *inability* of many commercialised forms of cultural production to capture the complexity of human experience. One American film-maker, Charles Burnett, seeking to explore the realities of inner city black communities, has suggested that the commercial film 'has reduced the world to one dimension' (Burnett, 1989: 224). While in the wider world, where three billion people are now living on less than two dollars a day, the most profitable forms of story-telling seem least able to convey or reflect upon the causes and brutal consequences of such a state of affairs. As an American novelist, responding to the work of an African film-maker, observed: 'What's the fate of a black story in a white world of white stories?' (Wideman: 1993: 57).

References

Burnett, C. (1989) 'Inner City Blues' in J. Pines and P. Willemen (eds) *Questions of Third Cinema*. London: British Film Institute, pp. 223–226.

*Coalition Currents (*2005) 'Round II of UNESCO Talks: An Interesting Proposition from the EU?' Vol. 3, No. 2, February, at URL: http://www.cdc-ccd.org/coalition_currents/February2005 (accessed on 16 December, 2005).

Coalition Currents (2006) 'New Coalitions Launched', Vol. 4, No. 1, January, at URL: http://www.cdc-ccd.org/coalition_currents/Janv06/coalition_currents_en_jan06.html (accessed on 1 February, 2006).

Cole, J. (1995) As *It Seemed to Me: Political Memoirs*. London: Weidenfeld and Nicolson.

European Audio-Visual Observatory (2004) *Yearbook 2004. Film, Television, Video and Multi-media in Europe*. Vol. 3, *Film and Home Video*. Strasbourg: European Audio-Visual Observatory.

European Commission (2005) Press Release 'Cultural diversity: a major step towards the adoption of a UNESCO Convention' at URL: http://europa.eu.int/rapid/pressReleasesAction.do?reference=IP/05/676&format=HTML&aged=0&language=EN&guiLanguage=fr (accessed on 16 December, 2005)

Garnham, N. (1990) *Capitalism and Communication. Global Culture and the Economics of Information*. London: Sage.

Goldberg, D., Prosser, T. and Verhulst, S. (1998) *EC Media Law and Policy*. London: Addison Wesley Longman.

Graham, A. and Davies, G. (1997) *Broadcasting, Society and Policy in the Multimedia Age*. Luton: John Libbey Media.

Grant, P. and Wood, C. (2004) *Blockbusters and Trade Wars. Popular Culture in a Globalized World*. Vancouver: Douglas and McIntyre.

Grantham, B. (2000) '*Some Big Bourgeois Brothel*'. *Contexts for France's Culture Wars with Hollywood*. Luton: University of Luton Press.

Higgins, M. (2004) 'Interview with Michael Higgins, Minister of Arts, Culture and the Gaeltacht between 1993 and 1997' in *La Revue LISA/LISA e-journal*, at URL: http://www.unicaen.fr/mrsh/anglais/lisa/publications/enCours/alexDilys01.pdf (accessed on 16 December, 2005).

Hobsbawm, E. (2006) 'The New Globalisation Guru?', *New Statesman*, 13 March, pp. 28–29.

International Network on Cultural Policy (INCP) (2004) 'Shanghai Statement' at URL: http://incp-ripc.org/meetings/2004/statement -e.shtml (accessed on 16 December, 2005).

Iosifidis, P., Steemers, J., and Wheeler, M. (2005) *European Television Industries*. London: British Film Institute.

Jawara, F. and Kwa, A. (2004) *Behind the Scenes at the WTO: the Real World of International Trade Negotiations*. Updated edition. London and New York: Zed Books.

Kessler, K. (1995) 'Protecting free trade in audiovisual entertainment: a proposal for counteracting the European Union's trade barriers to the US entertainment industry's exports', *Law and Policy in International Business*, 26.2, pp.563–611.

Lange, A. (2003) 'Film Market Trends in the New Member States of the European Union' at URL: http://www.obs.coe.int/oen_publ/market/filmmarket_newstates.pdf.en (accessed on 16 December 2005).

Madrid Declaration (2005) at URL: http://www.coalitionfrancaise.org/actus/doc/madrid0505_eng_.pdf (accessed on 16 December, 2005).

Oliver, L. (2005) 'US Ambassador to UNESCO Louise Oliver with Foreign Journalists' at URL: http://www.state.gov/p/io/rls/rm/56586.htm (accessed on 16 December, 2005).

Puttnam, D. with Watson, N. (1997) *The Undeclared War. The Struggle for Control of the World's Film Industry*. London: HarperCollins Publishers.

Smith, A. (1776/1937) *The Wealth of Nations*, Book 4, Chapter 2. New York: Random House.

Straubhaar, J. (2001) 'Brazil: the Role of the State in World Television. Popularity of Local/National/Indigenous in Television' in N. Morris and S.Waisbord (eds) *Media and Globalization. Why the State Matters*. Lanham: Rowman and Littlefield.

Tomlinson, J. (1991) *Cultural Imperialism. A Critical Introduction*. London: Pinter Publishers.

UNESCO (2001) *Universal Declaration on Cultural Diversity* at URL: http://portal.unesco.org/culture/en/ev.php (accessed on 6 June, 2005).

UNESCO (2005) *Convention on the Protection and Promotion of the Diversity of Cultural Expressions* at URL: http://portal.unesco.org/culture/en/ev.php-URL_ID=11281&URL_DO=DO _PRINTP … (accessed on 16 December, 2005).

Valencia Statement (2000) 'Valencia Statement on Globalisation and Cultural Diversity' at URL: http://www.audiovisualforum.net/manifest/index.htm (accessed on 16 December, 2005).

Wideman, J. (1993) 'Writers' Forum: Language and the Writer' in S. Gadjigo, R. H. Faulkingham, T. Cassirer and R. Sander (eds) *Ousmane Sembène. Dialogues with Critics and Writers*. Amherst, Mass.: University of Massachussetts Press, pp. 56–58.

Wildman, S. and Siwek, E. (1988) *International Trade in Films and Television Programs*. Cambridge, Mass.: American Enterprise Institute/Ballinger Publications.

Williams, R. (1981) *Culture*. Glasgow: William Collins/Fontana Paperbacks.

Index

A
academic film studies 133
Allied Artists 196, 197, 198
Amaral, Tata 96
American culture 16
  American interest in English culture 205
  American market for films 177
  revenue from film and TV exports 221
    foreign films and 191ff
  television 181
  see also Hollywood
Americanisation of culture
  in Arab world 72
  in Europe 14
Anglo-American co-operation, production
  and relations 147ff, 157, 159, 162, 166ff, 178, 180ff
Arab cultural policies 62ff, 71
  US criticism of 63
Arab states, broadcasting and films in 71, 73
  see also Lebanon
Arendt, Hannah 8
art cinema 17, 135, 136
  European 200
  in US 191ff
Arte, (French TV) 97
Asia and the Pacific, region 9, 60
  new markets in 105ff
  see also India
Asian cinema, rising profile of 105
Asian media content, tradability of 106
Astroff, Roberta 123
Atlantic Charter (1941) 4, 7, 48
Attali, Jaques 229
ATV 181–182, 184
audiences, national and international 59
audio-visual industry 22, 27
  and audiovisual services 12, 24ff
  complexities of 22, 23
  costs of production, reproduction and trade 227
  developing countries and 28
  differential benefits of international trade 227
  domination by US 26
  liberalisation of 27–28
  regulatory frameworks 64
  trade 2
  WTO US bilateral free trade agreements 28–29
Austen, Jane, adaptations 206 ff
Australia 28–29, 109, 113, 114, 115
auteurs and auteurist films 97, 139, 143, 167, 191, 193, 194
authorship, questions of 100ff

B
Bardot, Brigitte 193ff
  sex appeal of 195
BBC 12, 52, 54, 55, 49, 181, 207
  historical aspects 51, 52
Bernardet, Jean-Claude 96
Bollywood 60, 77, 85–87, 89–91, 105
  and English literature 204, 214
  and North American market 77, 88
  and other markets 87
Bonassi, Fernando 96
Brazil 26, 28
  and film industry 9, 95ff
  New Brazilian Cinema, (cinema da retomada) 95
  film structure 96–97
Britain: and Celtic fringe 133
  distinction between terms British and United Kingdom 133
British cinema industry 12
  devolution in 133, 180
  see also Scottish cinema, television UK
British Film Producers' Association 179
British TV programmes in US 175, 183
  Co-productions with US 183ff
broadcasting and film products, developing countries and 28
  policy 49
broadcasting, regional 12
  research into 105
  local and global content 105–106
  Syria 71
  see also Lebanon, television
'Building a Global Audience: British Television in Overseas Markets' (BAGA) 37–42
Burnett, Charles 229

231

C

Cancun WTO ministerial meeting (September 2003)	28
capitalism	3
and films	3
global	215
international	79, 92
modern	14
Casa de Cinema de Porto Alegre	101
CBS	181
News	89
Celador	109, 110, 113
censorship	2–3, 191
Césaire, Aimé	2, 3
Chen Kaige	18
China Central Television (CCTV)	110
China in the world market	17–18, 22, 108, 110, 111
Cinema:	
aesthetics	96
Arab world	59
Asian	105ff
Brazilian	60, 95ff
counter culture	146
Cinema Novo (Brazil)	99
cinematography	1
CITF Inquiry Report,	41
Clinton, Bill	225
Cold War and culture	5
Columbia Pictures	17, 90, 165, 166, 193ff, 198, 200
Commodification:	
of all aspects of life	135
and capitalism	18
content genealogy	107
of cultural signifiers	11, 18
Convention on the Protection and Promotion of the Diversity of Cultural Expression (UNESCO)	8, 222, 225, 226, 227–228, 229
copyright	22
corporations active in the cultural field	9
costume/period drama	176–177, 179, 180ff, 187, 204, 205, 208, 210
counter-culture	192
creative industries and export markets	33–34
Creative Industries Export Promotion Advisory Group (CIEPAG)	34
'Creative Industries Mapping Document'	34–37
Creative Industries Task Force (CITF)	34
cultural:	
content	225–226
foreign	2
debate	9
discount	203
diversity	5, 25, 204, 216, 224
exchange	11, 151–152
expression	3–4, 224
goods	22–23, 25, 49
markets in	49
hybridisation	203
identity	214
imperialism	79, 175, 176, 187
American	187
imports	228
integrity	204
invasion	2
myths	2
policies	229
production	3
representations	203
trade routes	106ff
transactions	145
values	227
'cultural brokers'	123
cultural commodities, goods and services	4, 5, 11, 22, 49, 147, 221
cultural communities, need to protect local	3–4
'cultural continents' (concept)	105, 106
'cultural distance' vs. 'cultural proximity'	72, 73
cultural politics of globalization cultural and political implications of the trade in	9
cultural signifiers permutability of	18
possibility of trading, culture globally	1
culture:	
as a commodity	1, 2
as a concept	1
describing forms	3
homogenisation	162
indigenous culture	47ff
and market trends	18
national	48
opposition between English and American	156
possibilities of trade in	1, 4
in post-colonial period	2
protecting local culture	63, 64–65
state support for	62
not traded	13
regionalism	47
Culture-goods	13
American	16
internet and	14
trade in	14, 16, 213

D

Department for Culture, Media and Sport (DCMS) UK	33, 39, 43
see also BAGA study	
Department of National Heritage (DNH)	37
dialogue between cultures	7
discrimination against goods	15
from US	15

E

East Asia, marketing of media	108–109
mediascape	109
Edinburgh Film Festival	136
entrepreneurial capital	81
ESPN	125
European culture	15
and Americanisation	15
European filmmaking	177
imperialism	50
position	15
European films in US, lack of	14
'European' signifiers.	17

Index

European Union 8, 14, 15, 22, 27, 30, 70, 228
  policies 17, 228
  audiovisual policy 27
  'Europudding' 17
EuroMed Partnership 67
exception culturelle 14
exchangeable commodities, as embodying culture 13

F

Federal Communications Commission 183
Federation of Indian Chambers of Commerce and Industry 81
Fifth Generation films 18, 136
Fiji 113
films:
  in Arab world, origin of 72–73
  in Europe, American origin of 69–70
  festivals 136–139, 140, 141
  international 5
film studios, American, takeover of 16–17
film and television industry 2, 6
  costs of 5–6
  as commodities 221
  economic characteristics of 7
  European 2, 199
  exemption from free trade rules 6–7
  exports 12
    perceived social significance of 5
  independents 136
  US 2
  indigenous 12, 15
  UK 12
    content, control of 3, 4
Format Registration and Protection Association (FRAPA) 108
Fox 17
free speech 5
French cinema 69, 102–103, 195
Furtado, Jorge 101
fusion culture 16

G

game shows 109–111
garbage aesthetics 102
Gavin, Rupert 40
gender relations 159–160
General Agreement on Tariffs and Trade (GATT) 4, 11, 15, 23, 223 225, 228
  and audiovisual sector 6
  see also Uruguay Round
General Agreement on Trade in Services (GATS) 21, 23–30, 63, 62, 71, 74
  and liberalising 'culture' 62
  slow pace of audiovisual negotiations 28ff
geo-linguistic regions (concept) 105
Ghai, Subhash 86
global:
  capitalism 215
  global free trade 49
  homogenisation 216
  market in culture 1
  media practices, changes in 115

'global narrowcasting' 122
globalisation 16, 31, 92, 95, 119, 215
  and cinema 84, 97
  homogenizing effects of on culture 7, 99
  Indian film and television and globalisation 91
  and TV 108–109
globalised societies 97
'golden exiles' 121
Granada Television 55
Grant, Peter 6
'Growing the Creative Industries – Issues for Consideration' 34

H

Hammer Film Productions 166, 167, 180
Higgins, Michael D. 223, 224, 226
Hispanics, US, redefinition as Latino/a 119
Hispanic culture in US 123ff
Hollywood 13–14, 74, 135, 142, 161ff, 177, 192ff, 199, 206, 216
  and Americans used in British films 169–170
  and art films 191–192, 194
  and Bollywood 77, 84, 89, 90
  British companies establishing links with Hollywood 165
  and costs of overseas production 179
  European connection 15, 161–162, 163, 170, 179
  and imports 192ff
  independents 162, 165, 178, 200
  majors 89, 90, 162, 165, 166, 167, 192, 195
  Hollywood majors and Indian market 88ff
  marketing European films 14
  overseas production 163–164
  'runway' productions 162, 164, 179, 180, 184, 185n, 187, 188n
  and subsidiaries 163, 195
  UK connection 145, 157, 161, 163, 179
  UK collaboration 165ff
  see also costume/period drama
Hong Kong 112
  as film centre 18
  film industry 105
human communities 1–2
hybridity 49

I

identities, blurring of 16
IMF 28
immaterials, trade in 16
imperialism 2, 9
  European 50
  and identity 187–188
  marginal imperialism 73
  media imperialism 71–72
independence and inter-dependence in cultural matters 9
India: 9, 77ff, 112
  censorship 90
  cinema and classes 84–85, 91
  cinema and shopping malls 84
  cinema theaters 84
  criminal involvement in film industry 81–82

233

cultural history 78
exports to North American Market 77ff, 87, 88
film and television industry 60, 77, 80ff, 88
foreign investment 91
growth of entertainments industry 80–81
growth of Indian markets abroad 85ff
growth of niche market films 85
imported films 90
Indian capitalists and film industry 92
masala film 83
and Rupert Murdoch 79–80
masses and cinema 91ff
tent cinema 83, 213
TV programs and channels abroad 88–89
indigenous (to a region) groups contrasted with incomers 49–50
exporting indigenous culture to US 203ff, 212, 216
indigeneity and exportability 213
NAFTA and 6–7
transformations of indigenous stories on export 203
Indonesia 112
information borders 223
intellectual property 5, 11, 108
international film festivals 135, 136, 139–140
International Instrument on Cultural Diversity 8
international media flows, multi-dimensional structure to 26
International Network on Cultural Diversity (INCD) 7
International Network on Cultural Policy (INCP) 7–8
internet 16
and de-materialisation of trade in goods 14
Irish Film Board 138
Irish Cinema 141–142
ITV 50, 55ff, 175, 181ff
historical development of 181–182
American involvement with 182–183

J

Japanese television industries 108
animé 14
reality shows 111
José, Paulo 102

K

Korda, Alexander 153–154, 164, 178

L

Latin America
cable television in 125
and television 119ff
Latin Americans in US 119ff
diaspora 120ff
television audience 121ff
Lebanon, audio visual sector 9, 59, 61ff
breakdown of TV output 64–66
film production in 66–68, 70
origin of imported films 73ff
and WTO 70–71, 74

liberalization 92

M

'Many Voices, One World' (UNESCO) 62
Mayer, Louis B. 164
McBride report, Many Voices, One World 62, 222
McCarthy and McCarthyism 176, 186
Media: and change 91
and communications, bilateral, multilateral and free trade agreements in 30
industries 106
media imperialism 71–72
Mexican programs 123
MGM 17, 151, 161, 164, 165, 166, 170, 180, 184
Miami as a Spanish cultural centre 125, 126, 128
migrants, culture and experience of 48
Miramax 17, 206, 212
modernity 86
Motion Picture Association of America (MPAA) 5, 178n, 193
Motion Picture Export Association of America (MPEAA) 89, 178n
multi channelling and adaptation 108, 115
Murdoch, Rupert 17, 78–80, 91
music, non-European 14

N

narratives and content 107
nation state: 3, 9
capacity to control information flow 106
challenges to 48
role of 49
national
cinema and movements 136, 137
culture 145
identity 3, 187
and different perspectives 215–216
businesses and absence of national identity 3
interests and imagery 59
National Telefilm Associates 183, 185–186
native cinema 95
neo-liberalism, India 79, 91
New Brazilian Cinema, (cinema da retomada) 95
'New Labour' 12, 32ff
and commercial policies 42ff
Communications White Paper 42
policies, UK 12
New World Information and Communications Order (NWICO) 222–223
New Zealand 109, 113, 114, 115
as an incubator of programs 115
Niven, David 155
North American film distribution system 83–84
North American Free Trade Agreement (NAFTA) 7, 22, 222
Noticiero Telemundo 125
nouvelle vague, French 101, 136, 196, 197

O

Oceania 113ff
and English language programming 114

Index

and global English geo-linguistic
    configuration 113–114
OFCOM 56
Official Films 184
Oliveira, Manoel de 97
open borders 4–5
Organisation for Economic Co-operation
    and Development (OECD) 25

P

Pacific Rim 113
pan-Hispanic 'Latinidad' 123
Papua New Guinea 113
Paramount decision 178
patenting, copyrighting, registering and trade
    marking of concepts 16
    of nature 16
patriarchy 86, 159–160
Payne, Alexander 100
Philippines 112, 113
political supremacism 49
politique des auteurs 101
    auteurist trail 102
    see also auteurs and auterist films
postmodernity 86, 102
price fixing in film and TV industries 5
privatization 92
property rights, trade in 11
provincial, contrasted with culture of capital 50
Public Citizen 23
publicly owned channels (PSB) 63
PVR Cinemas 84, 91

Q

quiz shows, winner take all format 110, 113
quotas 12, 15

R

Rank, J. Arthur 178, 197
Reagan, Ronald 223, 228
realism 97
reality TV programs 105, 106, 111–112, 114–115
regional culture and attributes 50
    UK 52ff
    see also Scottish Cinema
Reith, John 53
Richardson, Bonnie 5
Right Product Group 40–44
Rocha, Glauber 99

S

Salles, Walter 98, 100
Sands, Philippe 4, 5
Sapphire Films 185, 186, 187
Sassen, Saskia 48
Scotland 59, 60
    in Europe 137, 139–141
    film initiatives 139
    Hollywood and 179
    'Scottish Cinema' 9, 180
    and Scottish origin films 133ff
Scottish Media Group 139
Scottish Screen 139
Sembene, Ousmane 1
sex, films and marketing 193ff, 208, 211, 212
Shah, Bharat 82
Shen Bing 111
Show de Cristina 122
SICC/SIN 121–124
signifiers, presence and absence of 3
Singapore 113
Sivan, Santosh 8
Smith, Adam 227
Society of Independent Motion Picture
    Producers (SIMPP) 178n
Sony Entertainment 88
South Asia and multi-racial format 112ff
    diaspora 89
South Korea 105
'sovereignty, the collapse of' 48
Spanglish 128
Spanish International Communication
    Corporation (SICC) 121
Spanish International Network (SIN), Mexico 121
Spanish language television, in US 119ff
    print and radio 99, 121
    ratings system 125–126
Steemers, Jeanette 6
Stockholm conference 7
subsidies 12
    for film production 179
Sundance Institute (founded by Robert Redford),
    role in Brazil 96, 97, 98, 100, 136
survivor type shows 110–112

T

Taiwan 105
Tele-Liban 64
Telemundo 123, 125, 126, 127, 130
telenovelas 14, 26, 28, 73, 124, 126
Televisa, Mexico 121
television industry 2
Television Programs of America 183
television 1
    Canadian 6
    copycat 105ff
    developments in 107
    differentiated abundance of 107
    dynamics of 107
    and exchange control 106
    landscapes of 107
    and the masses 80
    perceived social significance of 5
    US 39, 121ff
television, UK 33, 35 ff, 180ff
    and American market 175, 180ff
    American production on UK TV 181ff
    and overseas markets 33, 41 44
    UK exports 35ff, 40, 180
    'wrong type of television' 37–39
    arguments against 'wrong model' 39, 42–43
    see also BBC, Building a Global Audience:
    British Television in Overseas Markets
Television Without Frontiers EU Directive 228

235

textual analysis tradition	3
Thatcher, Margaret	223
trade in culture	4, 8, 11,13, 14
in cultural commodities	11
antithesis	13
in immaterials	14, 16
liberalization	21
trade winds of culture	9
transatlantic co-operation and themes	147ff
transnational world	47–48
monotony of	99
TRIPS agreement on intellectual property rights	22
Truffaut, François	101
TV Arte	98
TV channels, Latin America	126, 127, 128, 130
Twentieth Century Fox	88, 164, 167, 180

U

Ullswater Committee	53–54
Un-Americanism	161, 175, 176, 186, 188
UNESCO	3, 7, 8, 30, 61, 62, 222, 223, 224, 227, 228
see also Convention on the Protection and Promotion of the Diversity of Cultural Expression, Universal Declaration on Cultural Diversity	
United Artists	150, 195, 196, 197–198, 200
United Kingdom	49
and American involvement	49ff, 213
and American market	188,196, 203ff
blacklisted US writers working in cinema in	186 50, 203ff
film trade in representations of	216
heritage cinema	205 ff
indigenous culture	203
national and regional broadcasting	47, 51ff
TV exports	33ff
see also Scottish film, television, UK	
United Nations (UN)	3, 4, 47–48
United States film industry	89
and imports	196
film production in Britain	145, 161ff
background	161
United States	7, 9, 14, 25
US administration and European cultural separatism	15
art film	191ff
and audiovisual industry	25, 27
consideration of European subsidies	2–3
and cultural diversity	26
and domination of markets	2
and English culture and heritage	203ff
film imports	191 ff
and GATS	24
growth of cable networks	125

and Hispanic culture	119ff
and Latin America	119ff
and Latin American culture	129
sex and foreign imports	194
Spanish language television in	60, 119ff
advertising and Spanish TV	130, 126, 119ff
and trade barriers	228
trends in post WWII films	191ff
and UNESCO	227, 228
US cultural hegemony: films	2
see also Hollywood, television	
Universal Declaration on Cultural Diversity, UNESCO	7, 29, 61, 223, 224–225
Universal	17, 80, 196, 197, 198, 199
Univisión	122, 123, 124, 126, 127, 129, 130
Uruguay Round of GATT	11, 14, 15, 22, 23
and liberalising services	61ff
US–UK special relationship	145, 148ff

V

Valdez, Luis	119
Variety (magazine)	77, 88, 150, 154, 162, 163, 191, 192, 193, 195
Videofilmes	100

W

Walt Disney Corporation	17, 18, 80, 88, 91, 164, 165, 178n, 179, 185
Warner Bros.	17, 80, 161, 165, 185
Western markets and attitude towards Bollywood	77ff
Williams, Raymond	226
world cinema – independent sector	95
growth of regional	95
World Development Movement (WDM)	23, 27
World Intellectual Property Organisation (WIPO)	22
World Trade Organisation. (WTO) (former GATT)	7, 11, 12, 16, 21, 22, 28, 29, 61, 62, 70, 71, 74, 223, 225
agreement on telecommunications	22
and reaction to GATS	23ff
and audiovisual services	24ff
see also General Agreement on Tariffs and Trade, General Agreement on Trade in Services, Uruguay Round	
world trade talks and media	21, 221–222

Y

Yash Raj Films	87

Z

Zee TV (India) and global market	89
Zhang Yimou	18